Between Two Ages

Between Two Ages

The 21st Century
and the Crisis of Meaning

&

WILLIAM VAN DUSEN WISHARD

6167-WISH

Dedication

To Anne,

whose love, generosity and understanding

for over four decades

have not only brought this book into existence,

but have given me my greatest adventure in life.

ACKNOWLEDGMENTS

"To assimilate the world, and to articulate it," said Goethe to Eckermann, his private secretary. Thus every book is, to some degree, an assimilation and articulation of many minds. Certainly that is true of this work. Whatever truth this book may hold is drawn from more sources than I can possibly remember.

But to those I can remember, I take very great pleasure in acknowledging my debt and thanking them for their generosity.

To Graham T.T. Molitor, whose invitation to join him in presenting a seminar at the World Future Society annual conference provided the opportunity to develop some of the basic themes of this book. To Frank McGee, whose unerring editorial instinct took garbled verbiage and turned it into understandable prose in such a manner as always to enhance the underlying meaning. To Mitchell B. Reiss whose extensive experience in government and international affairs enabled him to prod me to insights and conclusions I would not otherwise have reached. To Dr. James Moncure, whose knowledge of the American century was a generous source of insight. To B. Robert Okun, Frances Steven, Susan Poston, Josh Stevens, Alice Chaffee and Dianne Cordic, who reviewed portions of the manuscript and offered needed corrections and suggestions.

I owe an enormous debt of gratitude to the late Dr. Edward F. Edinger, who not only reviewed portions of the manuscript and offered helpful revisions and advice, but whose understanding of the human personality and its relationship to the course of world events has informed much of this book.

Human life is reduced to real suffering, to hell,
only when two ages, two cultures and religions
overlap. There are times when a whole generation
is caught in this way between two ages, two modes
of life, with the consequence that it loses all power to
understand itself and has no standard, no security,
no simple acquiescence.

Herman Hesse

Truth is eternal, but her effluence, with endless change,
is fitted to the hour; her mirror is turned forward to
reflect the promise of the future, not the past.

James Russell Lowell

Contents

FOREWORD

Dr. Mitchell B. Reiss
Dean of International Affairs
College of William & Mary

Standing at the threshold of the twenty-first century, we should be humbled by all we survey. The United States is at peace, the Cold War is history and no challengers to our unipolar moment are in evidence. We have been serenaded by the "irrational exuberance" of the greatest sustained bull market in economic history; as the new national pastime, families daily plot the growth of their investment portfolios. Space-based telescopes plumb the outermost reaches of the universe, while scientists look inward and map the human genome. The momentum of technological innovation promises ever-greater marvels. In Tom Wolfe's memorable phrase, each of us is a "master of the universe." Or, if not quite a master, at least able to act like one by playing with the latest Palm Pilot while watching our flat-screen TV and sipping $3 frappacinos. Truly, our bounty is unprecedented, our horizons unlimited.

And yet something is terribly wrong with this picture. From time immemorial, the sages knew that mere acquisitiveness has never been an end in itself. Man has always needed a spiritual component to provide a larger meaning to life. For some, this meaning has been provided by organized religion. For others, meaning has been constructed through service to family, friends, or country.

Today, this goal seems more elusive than ever. The dizzying pace of our lives, the increasing demands of the workplace, the nomadic career paths that conspire against our becoming rooted in a single neighborhood for more than a few years, and the new technologies that ensure we are never, ever out of touch for even a moment – all these developments are gradually turning us into T.S. Eliot's "hollow men." The result is that we possess all the superficial accoutrements of success, but have no interior life that can connect us to something larger than ourselves. In short we have inherited the world, yet have lost our souls.

How has this disturbing state of affairs come to pass? And how can we find our way and restore meaning to our lives? These penetrating questions lie at the heart of William Van Dusen Wishard's *Between Two Ages: The 21st Century and the Crisis of Meaning*.

Few people are more qualified than Van Wishard to ask and answer these questions. For over thirty years, he has traveled the world, thinking, writing and lecturing about these issues. In *Between Two Ages*, Van Wishard has provided us with a masterful synthesis of the main currents of history, ranging over the centuries with an expert's eye to identify the key trends in economics, technology and culture that have led us to this place in time.

By itself, this would be an important contribution to our understanding. But the true significance of *Between Two Ages* lies in his placing this analysis within a profoundly moral and ethical framework. Van Wishard has not simply diagnosed the reasons for our spiritual malaise. He has also suggested how each of us can overcome this malaise and find a larger purpose or meaning to our lives.

As we stand between two ages, with all the attendant complexities and chaos, Van Wishard has performed a rare public service. He has offered us a profoundly optimistic message for the future by recognizing that man's search for meaning is not only timeless, but also attainable. *Between Two Ages* appears not a minute too soon.

INTRODUCTION

There are times of chaos in the life of nations when simply creating understanding is the highest service.

Thomas Carlyle

In the winter of 1962 I found myself in Palm Springs, California, discussing the future of America with President Eisenhower. Ike had not yet moved to his Gettysburg farm, so he was staying in one of Palm Springs' more comfortable hotels. I had recently returned from working with a public information and education program in South America, and Eisenhower was particularly interested in knowing of developments in Brazil, Peru and Chile.

After a discussion of the militant dock workers in Rio de Janeiro, of the San Marcos University students in Lima who had rioted against Vice President Nixon, and especially of Chile's Eudocio Ravines, the Communist revolutionary who had written a classic textbook for Communist infiltration and insurrection in South America and a man I had come to know, the conversation turned to the United States.

Eisenhower was deeply troubled. Not by political events, but by what he felt was the weakening moral fiber of the country. America was, after all, being introduced to *Playboy*, Marilyn Monroe, and the erupting reality of *Peyton Place*, all of which, for many Americans, represented a whiff of decadence.

Finally, Ike stood up, strode across the spacious living room, waved his clenched fist through the air, and decried with all the force of an Old Testament prophet, "We are living through the final stages of the Roman Empire, we're living through the final stages of the Roman Empire!"

Eisenhower's remarks struck a resonate chord in me, for I had asked myself "Is America in decline?" six years before meeting Ike, when I was working in South Africa. I had been in South Africa as part of an international task force asked to help develop some basis of unity that could transcend not only the divisions between black and white, but also between the English and Afrikaans, as well as between the Africans and the Colored (mixed blood).

While in South Africa, I began reading de Tocqueville's *Democracy in America*. Reading de Tocqueville, and seeing America from the perspective of Africa, gave me a fresh assessment of the country for which, only four years earlier, I had been wounded in Korea.

For the next 25 years, long after I had returned home and was working for the U.S. Department of Commerce, I chewed on that question, "Is America in decline?" Finally, I cannot remember exactly when, I came to a conclusion. *I was asking the wrong question!* A more relevant question was, What is happening to America and the world that is turning our life so upside down? The question "Is America in decline?" is a closed question; it forces one of two answers. The question "What is happening to America?" is an open question; it invites multiple insights and perceptions.

In a nutshell, my conclusion is this: America–and indeed, the world– has entered a zone of possibility and uncertainty that has no parallel in history. If one were forced to seek the closest historical similarity, it would have to be what happened when the ancient world was transformed into the early beginnings of modern Europe. That was a process that took place in a limited portion of the earth over centuries of time. What's happening today is taking place worldwide, and it's measured in decades, even years and months.

No one expressed America's current circumstance more clearly than Adlai Stevenson, Eisenhower's opponent for the presidency in 1952 and 1956. Stevenson shared Eisenhower's perspective on the American condition, but he expressed it somewhat differently. "Are America's problems," asked Stevenson in 1954, "but surface symptoms of something even deeper, of a moral and human crisis in the Western world which might even be compared to the fourth, fifth, and sixth-century crisis where the Roman Empire was transformed into feudalism and primitive Christianity? Are Americans," Stevenson queried, "passing though one of the great crises of history when man must make another mighty choice?"

The Most Decisive 30-year Period in the History of Mankind

Despite the stratospheric heights of the Dow in recent years, the allure of prosperity and the astounding possibilities opening up for human fulfillment, the next three decades may be the most decisive 30-year period in the history of mankind. Thus you and I are living in the midst of perhaps the most uncertain period America has ever known–more difficult than World War II, the Depression or even the Civil War. With these earlier crises, an immediately identifiable, focused emergency existed, an emergency people could see and mobilize to combat.

But the crisis today is of a different character and order. For America is at the vortex of a global cyclone of change so vast and deep that it is uprooting established institutions, altering centuries-old relationships, changing underlying mores and attitudes, and now, so the experts tell us, even threatening the continued existence of the human species. It is not simply change at the margins; it is change at the very core of life. Culture-smashing change. Identity-shattering change. Soul-crushing change.

In earlier periods of great change, people tried to understand its effects, adjust to its demands, and capitalize on its promise just as we do today. But there was one major difference. Prior generations faced change within a context of established institutions. Earlier generations had a more stable–if less comfortable–framework and clearly defined reference points. Our era doesn't have such guides, for all of America's institutions, from government to family, from business to religion, are in upheaval. The past century saw civilized life increasingly ripped from its moorings. The immutable certainties that anchored our ancestors no longer seem to hold in a world where the tectonic plates of life are clashing, where human antagonisms obliterate tens of thousands of people in Africa, Bosnia or Chechnya in a matter of a few days or weeks, where a stray bullet ends the life of an elderly lady quietly walking home from church in Washington, D.C. In so many ways, a life that has lost its essential meaning has cut giant swaths across humanity. What does all the confusion and carnage add up to? Is this the end? Or, in some unknown way, could it be the opening of an era of even greater awareness and possibility?

Standing at a Great Divide

In Peter Drucker's view, "No one born after the turn of the [20th] century has ever known anything but a world uprooting its foundations, overturning its values and toppling its idols." Clearly, we have been standing at a unique historical dividing line–the end of the modern era, as well as the Industrial Age, the end of the colonial period, the end of the Atlantic-based economic, political and military global hegemony, the end of America's culture being drawn primarily from European sources, the end of the masculine patriarchal/hierarchical epoch, and, as Joseph Campbell suggests, the end of the Christian eon. Obviously, one era doesn't stop and a new one start in a week. Years–even decades or generations–of overlap sometimes take place.

The sense of an age ending and something new emerging was evident during the earliest years of the 20th century. In 1913, George Santayana, one of the America's leading philosophers, noted: "The civilization characteristic of Christendom has not yet disappeared, yet another civilization has begun to take its place." By 1929, Walter Lippmann saw Americans "living in the midst of that vast dissolution of ancient habits which the emancipators believed would restore our birthright of happiness." Five decades later, Lippmann's concerns were echoed by *The Wall Street Journal*, noting "our century is a time of flux, an interstice between eras. Old beliefs have decayed and the new beliefs have not sprung forward to replace them."

The truth is that all the vast changes we are bringing–instant global communication, control of plant, animal and human characteristics through genetic engineering, our ability to build new structures atom by atom, the doubling and even tripling of the human life span thus creating social pressures never before experienced–these and countless more developments point to one underlying reality: We are in the midst of redefining the human experiment with Life. We are asking ourselves questions no generation before has had to ask: "As technology takes over ever more of our work, what are humans for? What does it mean to be a human being in a world of total technical possibility? Are the warnings of technological extinction credible, and if so, what do we do about them? In an age when information overwhelms us and power is unlimited, what gives purpose and restraint to such power?"

A New Civilization or an "Interregnum"?

Certainly new human capacities, scientific insights, forms of wealth, modes of production and organization, and patterns of social relationship, as well as expressions of individual and collective belief, are taking the place of an earlier America. But just what kind of "civilization" is emerging is open to question.

The cultural concept of civilization has always been based on more than just progress beyond "primitive" ways and attitudes, more than just economic and technical betterment. Civilization implies stable institutions–above all, a cohesive family unit that trains the young for adult social responsibility. Civilization represents a people's view of the meaning of their collective association. Civilization manifests those attitudes, beliefs, ethical standards and restraints a people hold in common. At the core of every great civilization has been some cohesive spiritual conviction. What was once known as "Christendom" was just such a spiritual impulse for America and the West.

But the Judeo-Christian impulse is no longer the inner dynamic of Western culture or social life, it no longer interprets our *collective belief*–especially among the "creative minority." While Americans pay lip service to the convictions underlying the Declaration of Independence and the Constitution, the reality of our daily functional belief is more apt to be expressed in the secular faith of materialism as defined by science and technology, as well as in the civic religion of "freedom" as characterized by absence of restraint.

In sum, despite the mind-boggling technology developed over the past ten decades, despite the expansion of human awareness and capability, despite the thousand-fold increase of wealth, we have not yet achieved the central hallmark of a civilized society–a core conviction about the meaning of the human journey, a set of common purposes, convictions and meanings fused into one framework of value and perception–a framework with its own distinct character and worldview, with its unique spiritual underpinning.

Broadly speaking, we are in the midst of what could be termed a "crisis of meaning." Even as I write these words, today's *Washington Post* carries an article that begins, "Everywhere you look, people are searching for meaning in life." Nor is this crisis limited to America. John Pomfret writes in the *International Herald Tribune* from China, "Across China people are struggling to redefine notions of success and failure, right and wrong. The quest for something to believe in is one of the unifying characteristics of China today." The crisis of meaning is universal.

Until a new order of value and perception is achieved, we shall be between two expressions of social organization, cultural definition and spiritual experience–between two ages. We shall be in what I choose to term an "Interregnum," which Webster defines as "an interval; a break in a series or in a continuity." How long this Interregnum will last is anyone's guess. But it is the exploration of the Interregnum, this "in between" period, as it has existed for the past one hundred years–and continues to shape our life today–that is the subject of this book.

Between Two Ages

These pages offer perspective on the meaning of our times. Even more, they offer a few core thoughts on how one can make sense out of the senseless, find stability in the midst of upheaval, and find direction in the midst of uncertainty.

In sketching the Interregnum, I should note that this book is *not* intended to be a history of our times; rather, it is an assessment of some of the highlights, trends and events that have been and are shaping the Interregnum. Nor is this book intended as a forecast of tomorrow.

I have sought to find meaning in what has already happened, to understand how science, psychology, technology and culture are reshaping our daily activity, the content of our inner being, as well as the global context in which all nations live. I have sought to trace some of the events of the twentieth century in order to comprehend the origins of the twenty-first century crisis of meaning.

As this narrative encompasses a century of the Interregnum, much is omitted that I wish might have been included; many issues need a more complete treatment. For example, as I believe the two major forces shaping the last hundred years have been the development of technology and a spiritual/psychological reorientation as expressed in our culture, these trends are emphasized more than political events, which have been so thoroughly treated elsewhere.

The first half of the book covers 1900 to 1950, while the second half addresses the subsequent 50 years. While the period from 1900 to 1950 is clearly a formative period of the Interregnum, the first half of the century may not be of as much interest to some readers as are the events since 1950. If that's the case, you're encouraged to skip the first half and go directly to "The Context," the chapter offering a standpoint from which to view the restructuring of today's global landscape. Indeed, some readers may wish to begin with the final chapter, "The 21st Century and the Crisis of Meaning," which may offer a deeper understanding of the rest of the book.

However you choose to approach this book, I am intensely interested in how *you* see today's America, what you see as the promise and the danger of the American future. To that end, you are invited to send your thoughts, either by fax, e-mail or letter, to the following address:

Van Wishard
WorldTrends Research
1805 Wainwright Drive
Reston, VA 20190
Tel./Fax: 703.437.9261
E-mail: vwishard@worldnet.att.net

Chapter One

At the Core of the Interregnum

SUMMARY: Henry Adams's view of America in 1900. The accretion of mechanical power. The Outer Discovery–an expanding universe. Einstein fudges his seminal discovery. Technological advances of the century's first decade. Hubble proves existence of other galaxies. Making contact with the beginnings of time, space and matter. From knowledge to power–a shift in the purpose of science. The Inner Discovery– Freud and the unconscious.

The central dynamic of this Interregnum period, this shift from one age to another, is growth in technical power. In 1900, no one understood this better or chronicled its significance more clearly than Henry Adams. Adams stood virtually alone among the thinkers of his generation in understanding the potential consequences of the new forces of science and technology. Indeed, he predicted the atom bomb a generation before its invention.

It's impossible for us today to realize how radically life was being changed in 1900, how fundamentally space, time, tradition and belief were being reordered by the expanding forces of science and technology. Since Adams clearly saw the challenge these and other developments would pose not only to the Americans of his day, but also to the Americans of 2000, it's worth getting to know the man.

Henry Adams was born in Boston in 1838 into what arguably stands as America's greatest family. For perhaps no other American family has combined a distinguished role in history with an astonishingly high level, generation after generation, of intellectual competence and achievement. Henry's great-grandfather, John Adams, was one of the four drafters of the Declaration of Independence, and he was the first vice president and second president of the United States. Henry's grandfather, John Quincy Adams, was not only senator from Massachusetts, secretary of state, and sixth president of the U.S., but he is the only American president to be elected to Congress *after* having served as president.

For eight years following 1860, Henry Adams served as private secretary to his father, Charles Francis Adams, who was then U.S. Minister to Great Britain. It was in this position that the wisdom and dignity of Henry's father was credited with preventing British recognition of the Confederacy during America's Civil War. The elder Adams's achievement stands as one of the great unrecognized accomplishments of American diplomacy, for English intervention might well have saved the Confederacy.

Between 1869 and 1876, Henry Adams was assistant professor of history at Harvard University, where he introduced the seminar system of instruction. Like his two brothers, Henry was a prolific writer, and aside from his nine-volume *The History of the United States,* his two best-known books are *The Education of Henry Adams,* an autobiography for which he posthumously received the Pulitzer Prize in 1919, and *Mont-Saint Michel and Chartres,* a penetrating discussion of medieval life and culture.

As a historian, Adams was absorbed with the question of the shift from the "unity" of life as represented by Chartres Cathedral and Thomas Aquinas's synthesis of Aristotle's naturalistic philosophy and Christian theology (Aquinas's *Summa Theologica),* to the "multiplicity" of life as shaped by the on-rushing age of electrical and mechanical power. The starting point for his concerns was the belief that, "measured by any standard . . . the tension and vibration and volume and so-called progression of society were fully a thousand times greater in 1900 than in 1800;–the force had doubled ten times over." It would seem the Interregnum was at least visible by mid-19th century.

Adams forecast the likely result of this increase in "progression" in a 1904 letter to the historian Henry Osborn Taylor: "The assumption of unity, which was the mark of human thought in the Middle Ages, has yielded very slowly to the proofs of complexity ... [I]t is quite sure ... that at the accelerated rate of progression since 1600, it will not need another century or half century [1950-2000] to turn thought upside down. Law, in that case, would disappear as theory or *a priori* principle and give place to force. Morality would become police. Explosives would reach cosmic violence. *Disintegration would overcome integration.*" [Emphasis added]

In 1905, Adams wrote *The Education of Henry Adams*, an autobiography written in the third person and written for a select Boston readership rather than for the general public. In his autobiography Adams expressed concern that proliferating scientific knowledge was extending the horizons of man's technical power more rapidly than the pace of man's ethics. In Adams's view, cosmic power coupled with moral nihilism led inevitably to disintegration. Thus he sensed that the world in which he spent his life was in such flux as to make the remarkable education he had received obsolete. Almost each day, he wrote, he awoke in an altered world.

In a concluding chapter titled "A Law of Acceleration", Adams wrote:

> Power seemed to have outgrown its servitude and to
> have asserted its freedom ... the next great influx of new
> forces seemed near at hand, and its style of education
> promised to be violently coercive. [Holocaust and
> Hiroshima] The movement from unity to multiplicity,
> between 1200 and 1900, was unbroken in sequence and
> rapid in acceleration. Prolonged one generation longer, it
> would require *a new social mind* [emphasis added]
> At the rate of progress since 1800, every American who
> lived into the year 2000 would know how to control
> unlimited power. He would think in complexities

unimaginable to an earlier mind. He would deal with
problems altogether beyond the range of earlier society.

Henry Adams's concern about the expanded degrees of power
being placed in humanity's hands was expressed just at the moment in
history when science was uncovering the formulae for the greatest
expansion of power ever achieved. Just consider: In 1900, Max Planck
announced the first steps toward the formulation of quantum theory,
which is the basis for today's information technologies. In 1903, the
Wright brothers inaugurated the age of flight.

In 1905, the year Adams wrote *The Education of Henry Adams*,
Albert Einstein published the Special Theory of Relativity, which determined that space and time are relative, rather than absolute, in terms of
measurement. There is no universal time. Time and space are relative to
each of us, that is, to our place and speed. This was vastly different
from Newton's view of time and space as forming an absolute framework. The Special Theory went on to establish the law of mass-energy
equivalence, eventually seen as the theoretical starting point for development of the atom bomb. As if that weren't enough for one year,
Einstein also published the Browian theory of motion and the photon
theory of light. In one year, Einstein established relativity as the understanding of the world not as events but as relations.

Planck and Einstein represented the Himalayan heights of scientific discovery. But during the first decade of the 20th century, new
scientific and technological developments were exploded in every field
of research. Rutherford's theory of the atom, the submarine, the helicopter, the transatlantic telegraphic radio transmission, the arc genera-
tor, radiation pressure of light, high-voltage ignition for internal com-
bustion engines, the electric locomotive, the ultra-microscope, the diri-
gible, the gyroscopic compass, the Geiger counter, the first practical
photoelectric cell, the vacuum tube, artificial insemination, stainless steel,
the directional radio antenna, the first artificial human joint, the ultra-
violet lamp, superconductivity in mercury, the first telegraphic transmission of photographs, color photography, the technique for rejoining
severed blood vessels, the electrocardiograph, the first railroad tunnel

under the Hudson River–these developments and many more were placing in human hands scientific powers that would make changes in man's internal and external worlds never before envisioned even by the greatest minds of earlier centuries.

A fundamental change in the character and meaning of human existence was taking place. Science was no longer simply interested in knowledge for the sake of knowledge; it now sought knowledge for the sake of power. As the great British art critic Kenneth Clark wrote, "From the time of Einstein, Niels Bohr and the Cavendish Laboratory, science no longer existed to serve human needs, but in its own right." What earlier eras had considered to be "God-like" powers were now being placed in human hands. Prometheus and Faust, the giant shadow figures of Western history, now walked the Earth. This new attitude had been foreshadowed in Christopher Marlowe's *Faust* (c. 1588):

> O what a world of profit and delight,
> Of power, of honor, and omnipotence
> Is promised to the studious artisan!
> All things that move between the quiet poles
> Shall be at my command.

With the onset of the 20th century, knowledge and power were expanding faster than were the moral capacities needed to control their consequences. This trend was to become the central theme and contradiction of the 20th century. What seemed dimly apparent to only a few was the reality that knowing more about the laws of nature, an increase in power over nature, demands a corresponding increase in integrity and wisdom. The heart of wisdom is self-knowledge, insight into one's own nature with all its good and evil. Thus the more man learns about the laws of nature, the more he must become aware of *his own nature* if he is to survive the destructive potential of his new powers. Henry Adams wrote that it would take a "new social mind" to cope with such enlarged degrees of power. Einstein echoed Adams when he wrote: "The significant problems we face cannot be solved at the same level of thinking we were at when we created them." Adams and Einstein seemed to be calling for awareness commensurate with the new powers being placed in man's hands in the 20th century. And who should know better than Albert Einstein?

Discovering the Universe

Just as early 20th century physics was yielding nature's secrets of the micro, so also did nature reveal new mysteries of the macro.

From 3500 BC–when the Mesopotamians first developed elementary astronomy–up through the Greeks and Aristotle, on through Copernicus in the 16th century and Newton in the 17th century, right up until 1914, everyone thought we lived in a closed universe. The dimensions of the universe were seen as fixed and static. Not only that, the Milky Way was thought to be the only galaxy in existence.

Then, in 1914, an extraordinary episode took place which Brian Swimme describes in his book, *The Hidden Heart of the Cosmos.*

In 1914, as the clouds of World War I were gathering over Europe, Albert Einstein was the director of theoretical physics at the Kaiser Wilhelm Institute in Berlin. Three months after war broke out, Einstein did something which, in the longer sweep of history, had a greater effect on humanity than did the war. He articulated the gravitational dynamics of the universe in the form of his field equations. After four years of research, he created his General Theory of Relativity.

To the layperson, those last two sentences don't mean much. But their actual significance is that, in developing the General Theory, Einstein's equations not only showed gravitation as a determinator of the curvature of the space-time continuum, but the equations also refuted four thousand years of accepted belief about the nature of the universe. His field equations were telling him that the universe is expanding in all directions. An expanding universe! A completely new scientific insight. Aristotle hadn't known it. Nor had Copernicus, Galileo or Newton. Einstein himself had lived his whole life believing the universe to be an unchanging space, a closed system, a vast and fixed place. Yet here he was writing down equations that were telling him that Copernicus, Galileo and Newton, the greatest scientific minds in history, had accepted an interpretation of the universe that was false. His equations were telling him that space was expanding in all directions, that it is infinite!

Einstein's field equations stood conventional scientific belief on its head. If Einstein's equations were proved accurate–and he insisted on verifying his equations by three tests which he devised, and which were completed by 1923–it would smash the conclusions of history's greatest minds. It would be a change in the human view of ourselves and our place in the universe that was at least as great, if not greater, than when Copernicus told us in 1543, "Sorry, folks, the sun doesn't circle the earth. It's the other way around."

To stand against the revered knowledge of the greatest minds of history required extraordinary courage, even for Einstein. Remember, in 1914 he had not yet been accepted as one of the great scientific geniuses of history. He was only 35 years old and still seeking his place in a competitive scientific community.

And so it was that Albert Einstein, having made one of the seminal discoveries of history, doctored his findings. He could not bring himself to announce to the world the full significance of his discovery. He included in his field equations something known as the "cosmological constant," which left intact the effects of gravity on space-time, but which hid the deeper truth of his findings and preserved the concept of a static universe.

Other scientists, however, were hard at work on the same questions that so absorbed Einstein. In 1917, while Harlow Shapley estimated the size of the Milky Way, a Dutch astronomer discovered that it takes 250 million years for our solar system to travel once around the circumference of the Milky Way.

In 1924, Edwin Hubble proved the existence of other galaxies. For the whole history of the human race–Hammurabi, Plato, Alexander the Great, Caesar, Charlemagne, Genghis Khan, Dante, Leonardo da Vinci, Martin Luther, Napoleon, Washington, Lincoln, Marx, Edison–not one of them knew what we know today; no one knew until 1924 that galaxies other than our Milky Way were in existence. (Even as late as 1950, we could identify only two galaxies. We now know there are trillions.) Hubble finally brought Einstein to the giant Mount Palomar telescope in California to view the cosmos for himself. It was then that Einstein knew: Yes, his field equations of a decade earlier had been correct. The universe is, in fact, a dynamic, expanding phenomenon.

To visualize the universe Einstein, Hubble and others had discovered, picture yourself blowing up a black balloon that is covered with many small white dots. The larger the balloon expands, the further apart become the dots. That is what is happening to our universe.

The discoveries made by Einstein, Hubble and a host of other scientists in the first half of the 20th century were enlarged and confirmed in succeeding decades. Hubble's confirmation of an expanding universe answered the question people have had since earliest history about how the universe began, a question which is at the heart of every religion. Hubble's theory became the basis of the view that the universe was created by a huge explosion, and that the galaxies are the debris flying in all directions. This hypothesis was supported in 1927 by Georges Lemaitre, a Belgian who proposed that the universe had started by the explosion of a "primeval atom"–the concentration of all the mass of the universe in an extremely small space. This explosion eventually became known as the Big Bang.

The strongest confirmation of the Big Bang theory came in late 1965. Two Bell Telephone physicists, Arno H. Pensias and Robert W. Wilson, discovered cosmic background radiation. As Brian Swimme writes, "Here was the dim glow left over from the eruption of the universe at the beginning of time. Penzias and Wilson captured the photons–the particles of light–that had been set in motion fifteen billion years ago when the universe erupted into existence."

"When the universe erupted into existence." In other words, in the 20th century, the human race appears to have made contact with the beginnings of time, space and matter.

Make contact with the beginnings of time space and matter. That is a thought that is almost beyond comprehension, and we will be decades in absorbing its significance. For it raises the question of what was there before time. In what environment (if any) did space emerge? What was the nature of the Nothingness out of which time, space and matter exploded?

We have arrived at the outer edge of human understanding.

The Inner Discovery

While Einstein and others were probing the essence of matter and the universe, Sigmund Freud was probing the core of the human mind. Freud's publication of *The Interpretation of Dreams* in 1900 (the first edition sold only 351 copies) represents the discovery of the unconscious mind as an empirical reality. Freud postulated that the phenomenology of the psyche contains more than simply the measurable facts of the natural sciences; it embraces the mystery of the mind. He moved this investigation from an earlier "suggestion theory" (hypnosis, etc.), to the demand that the cause of emotional disturbance be made conscious, a practice which became the basis of most forms of psychotherapy.

Today, however, Freud is primarily remembered for his theory of sexual repression as the sole cause of neurosis, a theory which has been discarded even by Freud's own adherents. Freud's contemporary importance would seem to be indicated by a 1997 *Harvard Magazine* article reporting that a computer search of Harvard University's course catalogs for classes mentioning either Freud or psychoanalysis turned up nothing in the psychology department, but did turn up courses in literature (Freud is considered one of the 20th century's greatest writers of German prose). Freud's long-term impact on Western civilization may actually have been more in the realm of affecting established bonds of morality and religious belief than in developing psychological health.

But Freud represented something quite deep taking place in the inner life of Western man. Ever since Descartes in the mid-1600s depreciated man's subjective life as irrelevant to external reality, the Western emphasis (with exceptions) has been on man's external estate—on the structure and laws of nature and society. From the Enlightenment to Hegel to Marx and Weber, the primary question asked was: "How do we discern and control the laws of nature, and apply what is learned to the shaping of society for the betterment of man?" Freud, on the other hand, represented a turning inward. With a growing inward orientation, America and the West once again faced the age-old subjective questions of human existence–individual meaning and purpose and their relation to freedom.

"A Spool on Which to Wind the Thread of History"

This, then, is the backdrop against which the Interregnum unfolded in the early decades of the 20th century. An infinite increase in automated power which has introduced technical possibilities only dreamed of in earlier ages; a new cosmological orientation that is affecting our ideas of who we are, where we came from and what our destiny might be; and an understanding of the deepest reaches of man's inner world that sheds fresh perspective on all the world's myths and religions.

Historians are prone to seek *the* single cause of historical development. Some would say it's geography. Some say it's chance. Others say it's the Great Man theory. Darwin said it is biological evolution; Marx thought it to be dialectical materialism, the class struggle and economic causation. For Toynbee it was "challenge and response."

There is, of course, no "single cause" of historical development. History is a tapestry, woven with many threads. And no one knew this better than Henry Adams. Nevertheless, Adams reached for some context within which to assess historical development. As he wrote, "One sought no absolute truth. One sought only a spool on which to wind the thread of history without breaking it." For Adams, that spool was the "accretion of new forces, chemical and mechanical . . ." He wrote of how the compass, gunpowder, telescope, printing press, and microscope had caused the accumulation of new forces to grow in volume "until they acquired sufficient mass to take the place of the old religious science, substituting their attraction for the attraction of the *Civitas Dei* . . ." In more contemporary parlance, Adams might say that the vision of Bill Gates has replaced the vision of St. Augustine.

But the "accretion of new forces" only partially serves the function of a "spool on which to wind the thread of history." For the dynamic that lies behind the accretion of new forces is the never-ending pursuit of an *increase in knowledge*. It is the expansion of knowledge, whether by accident or design, that has propelled the development of mechanical power at ever-increasing orders of magnitude.

This expansion of knowledge is first and foremost the product of man's curiosity, man's insatiable desire to know and to understand. The source of this desire to know is, in part, a reflection of his quest for the infinite in life. There is something about man that constantly reaches out for wider dimensions of knowing and being, and the story of the Interregnum is the chronicle of how that pursuit has evolved in all its wonder, in all its terror.

Chapter Two

Life in 1900

SUMMARY: 1900–the end of national histories and the
emergence of a world process. The global picture–Boer War,
Boxer Rebellion, U.S. troops in the Philippines, European
nations expand holdings in Africa, the Kaiser announces
expansion of German navy. Picture of an optimistic America still
expanding. The shift from an agricultural to an industrial
America. Sports, entertainment and culture. The virtues and
discontents of capitalism. Revolt of the American conscience
creates new laws on food and drugs, safety standards, workmen's
compensation, child labor law. Samuel Gompers of AFL and
rejection of Marxism sets tone for American labor.

Against the background of the expansion of knowledge and
power leading up to the Interregnum, let's, look at what life
was like in 1900, a year which was somewhat of a dividing point. For
with 1900, a new tempo in world affairs begins in which contemporary
history becomes world history. The first decade of the 20th century
brings to a close distinctive national histories, and it begins to merge
major scientific and political events into a worldwide process. As German physicist Ernst Macks wrote in *The History of Mechanics* in 1903,
"The world . . . is more than ever before one great unit in which every-

thing interacts and affects everything else, but in which also everything collides and clashes."

In 1900, there were fewer than 50 sovereign nations in the world (now there are close to 190, many having populations smaller than Dallas or Boston). Two thousand four-hundred U.S. forces helped relieve Beijing during China's Boxer Rebellion; American sentiment strongly supported the Boers in South Africa's Boer War (in which the British interned some 120,000 women and children in concentration camps); The U.S. had 60,000 troops in the Philippines as a result of the Spanish-American War; Germany, Belgium, France and Great Britain all expanded their holdings in Africa; the Trans-Siberian Railway opened between Moscow and Irkutsk; the Kaiser announced expansion of the German navy so that "the German Empire may also be in a position to win the place which it has not yet attained"; V.I. Lenin returned to Moscow after three years' exile in Siberia; and the Commonwealth of Australia was created.

Looking back at 1900 from the vantage point of over half a century, Herman Kahn wrote in 1967, "The Parliamentary ideal was widely accepted, and Christianity was almost everywhere triumphant or on the rise . . . National self-satisfaction, optimism, and faith in the future of most Western or Westernized people are, to modern eyes, perhaps the most striking characteristics of the year 1900 . . ."

The average American in Topeka or Tulsa, however, was too busy simply completing the building of a nation to be aware of any Interregnum or broader historical currents affecting America. In 1900, the Census Bureau determined the center of the U.S. population was in Columbus, Indiana; only the Eastern seaboard had really established itself in permanence. The rest of the country was still a frontier, with people on the move; some 2 million mustangs (wild horses) roamed the U.S. prairie, but the nation had fewer than 30 head of bison, down from 1,090 in 1893; the federal government was still settling the "territories" such as Oklahoma by giving land to settlers; Cody, Wyoming, was founded by "Buffalo Bill" Cody in order to have a railway run transportation to large tracts of land he had acquired near the Shoshone River; the Grand Army of the Republic (veterans of the North in the Civil War) was still a substantial organization of influence; Hawaii was made a territory; Woodrow Wilson was the president of Princeton University, Herbert Hoover was a construction engineer in China, Teddy Roosevelt was governor of New York, and Calvin Coolidge was an obscure lawyer in New England.

In New York, the lead editorial of the January 1, 1900, *New York Times* set an optimistic tone for the new century: "It would be easy to speak of the twelve months just passed as the banner year [in business and economics] were we not already confident that the distinction of highest records must presently pass to the year 1900 . . . The outlook on the threshold of a new year is extremely bright."

Such sentiments reflected the consensus of America's best journals, which were not overly concerned with the fact that the average person earned about $500 a year (nominal dollars) and most of the 448,572 immigrants who arrived on our shores in 1900 scrounged for far less. Ten million lived in what was then considered poverty, and four million of those were described as "public paupers." However, sugar sold at 4 cents a pound, eggs at 14 cents a dozen, butter 24 cents a pound. Boarding houses offered turkey dinners at 20 cents and breakfast and supper for 15 cents. The hamburger was first sold in New Haven, Connecticut, where Louis Lassen ground 7 cents worth of lean beef, broiled it, and served it between two slices of toast (no catsup or relish) to customers at his three-seat lunch counter. A male stenographer earned $10 per week and an unskilled girl $2.50. At the other end of the scale, Andrew Carnegie's personal income that year was over $23 million, on which he paid no income tax.

But that was only one aspect of the America of 1900. Every decade since then, America's living standard has advanced by more than 20 percent. (In 1985 dollars, the per capita personal consumption expenditure in 1915 was $3,520; in 1985 it was $10,811.)

In 1900, only 13,842 automobiles were registered in the whole country. There were less than 144 miles of hard-surfaced roads. Some 30,000 trolley cars provided transportation in every major U.S. city. The first auto show ever held was in 1900 in Madison Square Garden, where one-third of the cars exhibited were electric. New York State passed a law limiting automobile speed to 10 mph in the built-up areas and 20 mph in less crowded districts. The first coast-to-coast automobile drive took 65 days. Horses were still the main power of transportation. Boston boasted the only completed subway, while New York was electrifying its steam-run elevated railway, even as it completed its first subway. Communities were widely separated from each other, and a town that was not situated on a railroad line was virtually isolated. Thus each town or farm was far more dependent on its own resources than today. A trip to see friends 10 or 12 miles away was virtually an all-day expedition.

Total U.S. population came to 76 million people, of whom 9 million were African-American and 237,000 were Native American. Los Angeles boasted 102,489 people, while Houston bulged with 44,633. Thirty-five percent of all Americans lived on a farm. Life expectancy stood at 49 years, and the infant mortality rate was 122 per 1,000 live births. Sixty percent of all men over 65 years of age were still working. Immigrants were pouring into America–448,572 in 1900, 1,285,349 in 1907 (peak year), and a total of 14,531,197 in the first two decades of the century. Of the immigrants who arrived in 1920, 87 percent came from Europe, 4 percent from Latin America and 1 percent from Asia. (In 1996, of the immigrants arriving in America, 17 percent came from Europe, 50 percent from Latin America and 27 percent from Asia.)

The tallest building in the country was all of 29 stories which towered skyward a vertigo-inducing 382 feet. There was little electric street-lighting, and the city lamplighter turning on the gas street light was a common sight.

The first sluice gates on the Colorado River were opened to bring water from Arizona to California's Imperial Valley. Steam tractors appeared on the wheat fields of the Pacific Northwest, but their main use was to move portable threshing machines, many of which were still pulled by 40 horses driven abreast. Hills Bros. of San Francisco began packing roast ground coffee in vacuum tins, which began a new era in coffee marketing. Battle Creek, Michigan, boasted 42 breakfast cereal plants, Wesson Oil was first put on the market, and Honeydew melons were introduced to U.S. buyers.

Despite more than a million miles of telephone lines in the U.S., communication was slow, as America had only 1.3 million telephones (one phone for every 13 homes), and most of these were in businesses and homes of the wealthy. The telephone had been developed to the extent which permitted one person to talk with another over a distance of 1,400 miles, from New York to Omaha. Radio had yet to be invented, and what motion pictures existed were crude affairs generally seen at vaudeville theaters. The first movie to tell a story, *The Great Train Robbery*, was still three years away.

In literature, in 1900 L. Frank Baum published *The Wizard of Oz*, Jack London published *The Son of the Wolf*, a collection of short stories, and Theodore Dreiser wrote the novel *Sister Carrie*. During the same year in Europe, Beatrix Potter created *The Tale of Peter Rabbit*, and Joseph Conrad published *Lord Jim*. Magazines such as *The Saturday Evening Post* and *The Ladies' Home Journal* existed, but none had a circulation of over a million readers (Fifty years later, there were 38 such magazines).

Even though the American frontier had been declared "closed" in 1890, in 1900 Alaska, Arizona, Hawaii, New Mexico and Oklahoma were not yet part of the United States. The budget of the U.S. government was roughly $500 million, which was less than the budget of the state of New York 50 years later. The national debt was $1 billion. The White House staff numbered less than 20 people. President McKinley campaigned for re-election with "the full dinner pail" slogan symbolizing Republican prosperity. He received a plurality of nearly one million popular votes, defeating the Democratic candidate William Jennings Bryan. Thousands of urban workers cast their vote for the Socialist party candidate Eugene V. Debs.

The national divorce rate in 1900 was 1 in 12.7 marriages. Just over 20 percent of the female population was in the work force, with some, such as "servant girls," receiving $6-$8 per week. Annual production of consumer products was at a rate unrecognizable in today's America–155,000 pairs of silk stockings, four billion cigarettes. The illiteracy rate was less than 11 percent, contrasted with today's approximate 25 percent functional illiteracy. Only three universities in the world had an enrollment over 5,000 students, and none of them were in America. Carnegie Institute of Technology was founded in Pittsburgh with a gift from Andrew Carnegie. The College Entrance Board Examination was founded and initiated SAT tests.

There was minimum opportunity for recreation, with virtually no tennis, golf or basketball for most people. Football was played primarily at the universities, but it was a bone-breaking sport with no forward pass. In 1900, the All-American team consisted of players drawn solely from Yale, Harvard, Cornell, Columbia, Lafayette and the University of Pennsylvania. Christy Mathewson left Bucknell University to pitch for the New York Giants, winning 20 games in 1903. The first Davis Cup tennis matches opened in Brookline, Mass., the U.S. team defeating the British to gain possession of an $800 silver cup donated by Harvard senior Dwight Filley Davis, who had commissioned a Boston jeweler to design and produce the challenge cup.

There were no gyms and nothing approaching physical education in the schools. There was no YMCA, no Boy Scouts, no 4-H clubs. Most men and boys were expected to get their active amusement out in the open countryside in hunting, fishing, swimming and riding. As for young women, it was not considered "proper" for them to engage in such strenuous activities. Any daughter who would venture out for an evening's entertainment would be accompanied by a chaperone. Indeed, it was a time when a woman in New York was arrested for smoking a cigarette in public.

Capitalism was a system whereby businesses were run by their owners. As one historian noted, it would have seemed "wildly irrational that a man should manage the destinies of a corporation while owning only a minute fraction of its stock." While in Britain, Germany, France and Japan, the great fortunes of the early 20th century belonged to landowners, bankers, merchants and other members of long-established wealth-controlling upper classes, in America the great fortunes belonged to the captains of industry who were "self-made" men. John D. Rockefeller had started his career as a $4-a-week clerk; Andrew Carnegie began as a $1.20-a-week bobbin boy in a Pittsburgh cotton mill; Edward H. Harriman started work at $5 a week in a broker's office. None of the eight most powerful corporate magnates in 1900 possessed a college degree, and all thought the study of economics to be absurdly impractical. These were men who held a certain pattern of attitudes such as independence of decision, curiosity, the search for "useful" and "practical" knowledge and ideas, fascination with machines, the desire to make a buck and be somebody, the desire to apply knowledge, machines and systems to the production of marketable goods or services. These were the attitudes that had driven the late 19th-century Americans, and had made American production the envy of the world. A British report summed it up: "The Americans display an amount of ingenuity combined with undaunted energy, which as a nation we would do well to imitate if we mean to hold our present position in the great market of the world."

No corporation in the country counted over 60,000 stockholders; AT&T claimed only 7,535 (50 years later, it had more than one million). Firestone Tire & Rubber was founded by Harvey S. Firestone, who had developed a new method for attaching tires to wheel rims. General Electric established a research laboratory in Schenectady, New York, and Andrew Carnegie created the United States Steel Company, which, with its command of over 800 major plants, controlled 60 percent of the steel-producing capacity of America. Between 1897 and 1903, 276 big-business combinations—corporations that were holding companies owning and controlling other corporation—were created in America. The use of advertising, essential to the free market system, was growing at a rapid pace. In 1880, about $200 million was spent on advertising by American business. By 1904, the figure had reached $800 million—approximately 4 percent of the gross national product. Advertising costs remained about 4 percent of the GNP throughout the 20th century.

The average working day was ten hours, six days a week. Twenty-six percent of America's boys between the ages of 10 and 15 were "gainfully employed"; 10 percent of the girls. Most of these young people were engaged in farm work, but 284,000 labored in mills and factories. In Boston, unskilled workers earned $9-$12 a week, while skilled workers made $13-$20. Safety standards were at a minimum. In the railroad industry in 1900, 1 employee in every 400 was killed, while 1 in every 26 was injured.

Only 868,500 workers, 3.5 percent of the work force, were unionized, and employers were free to hire and fire employees at will. The American Federation of Labor (AFL) counted 548,321 members (up to 20 million by 1920). The International Ladies' Garment Workers Union (ILGWU) was founded representing 2,310 workers–working 70 hours a week–in New York and other east coast cities. Union-busting by employers was common, frequently using hired thugs and employers' "scabs" in violent, bloody conflicts. It had only been two years since the United Mine Workers won their first important strike, when a group of them in Virden, Illionis, armed with shotguns, revolvers and rifles, "vanquished a trainload of similarly accoutered strikebreakers and company guards, with great loss of life on both sides," according to Herbert Harris's *History of American Labor.* Workers' rights were won in America at a cost unimaginable to today's work force.

The increasing concentration of capital in holding companies, along with the deplorable working conditions, finally generated a revolt of the American conscience. In 1902, President Theodore Roosevelt's attorney general brought suit for the dissolution of the Northern Securities Company, which just happened to be the holding company set up by J. Pierpont Morgan and Edward H. Harriman, two of the most powerful businessmen in America. In November of the same year, Ida Tarbell's expose of the Standard Oil Company began appearing in *McClure's,* a national magazine. A decade later the U.S. government broke up the Standard Oil Trust into fourteen companies, each of which soon became larger than the original parent company. In 1902, *McClure's* carried Lincoln Steffens' first article on municipal corruption, "Tweed Days in St. Louis." Tarbell and Steffans were two of the journalists who started a new trend in American journalism, a searching, factual reporting of what was actually going on in American business and politics.

This revolt of the American conscience would generate vast changes in America in the following years. New legislation would bring food and drug laws, collective bargaining, woman's suffrage, minimum safety standards, workmen's compensation laws, child labor laws, popular initiative and referendum, the graduated income tax, and social service as a respected profession. In 1935, the National Labor Relations Board (NLRB) was established with powers to determine the machinery for forming unions, thus preventing certain employer practices aimed at frustrating unionization. The same year the Committee for Industrial Organization (CIO) was established as part of the AFL to unionize workers by industry rather than by individual company. In 1937, the CIO split, changing its name to Congress of Industrial Organizations. When the AFL and the CIO reunited in 1955, their combined membership reached some 16 million in the U.S. and Canada.

In government, new laws would establish the Federal Reserve system, the Federal Trade Commission, the Department of Labor, direct election of senators, and a national incomes account.

These changes would have far-reaching importance. In Europe, Marxism had taken root, due in part to the excesses and sometimes crass insensitivities of capitalists. It's a fact we sometimes forget, but Marxism and Communism were reactions to the injustices and inequalities of capitalism. For the better part of a century, Europe chose the path of class war.

As capitalism expanded in America and its dark side left human misery and wreckage in its wake, the inevitable question arose as to how America would respond. Would class war take root in America as it had in Europe? In 1912 and 1913, there were bitter and savage strikes by the International Workers of the World (I.W.W.), established by Eugene Debs in 1905. The I.W.W. declared itself "founded on the class struggle . . . and the irrepressible conflict between the capitalist class and the working class," adding that it would go on "until the workers of the world . . . take possession of the earth, and the machinery of production, and abolish the wages system." A majority of American workers, however, favored the wage system, which gave them, at least by world standards, decent wages.

It was during these years that the Socialist party, whose platform advocated a total change in America's economic system, ran Eugene Debs as its candidate in the 1912 presidential election. Debs won only 890,000 votes.

A different approach was advocated by Samuel Gompers, founder and president of the AFL (1882-1924), who had studied Marx and concluded American unions were weakened by the impracticality of revolutionary theorists, as well as by the hatred their theories generated both with the workers and the public at large. Thus Gompers eschewed class war and steered the AFL toward collective bargaining.

So class warfare was resisted as an American democratic ideal. America would be a place where people of every background and condition worked together for the benefit of all. It was clear that if everyone had a chance for a good education and a decent job, then everyone would benefit. Class war was rejected, and cooperative, experimental change became the overriding attitude. Such change did not happen overnight, and America's working men and women would fight many a battle before there was anything approaching what might be considered labor-management cooperation as it's been known over the past three decades. But a basic pattern had been set, which helps explain why Socialism and Communism had so little appeal to the broad mass of Americans during the Great Depression.

This was the America of 1900. It was an America that was changing from a nation of isolated farms and villages to a land of crowded cities and roaring towns. It was an America shifting from a base of agriculture to an industrial base of steel, electricity and chemicals. It was an America where the sense of what is stable and what life means was beginning to change, where the certainty of moral values and the inevitability of progress were not as clearly anchored in the national imagination as in earlier times. It was an America unknowingly moving more deeply into the Interregnum.

Chapter Three

The Great Expansion

SUMMARY: Introduction of mass production. Economic and social effects of Ford and the automobile. Edison lights up America. First radio station goes on air in 1920, and radio boom takes off. Emergence of the middle class. National credit system instituted to support continental economy. Economic advances based on inventions of last third of 19th century.

Exploration of mass and energy, of space-time, and of quantum physics became the most significant determinants of the Interregnum, and they were radically altering the atmosphere of scientific and intellectual America. But such esoteric subjects had little effect on the day-to-day living of most people. What altered life for most was the on going creation of a consumer society which had three basic supports–mass-marketing of the automobile, widespread availability of electricity, and completion of a continental economy.

It was in 1885 that Daimler and Benz devised the type of automobile engine found in most cars today. In 1896, Henry Ford built his first car, and in 1903 he formed the Ford Motor Company. Ford took the American system of manufacturing, which was based on the assembly of interchangeable parts (Samuel Colt's 1850s manufacture of revolvers), and transformed the system into a moving assembly line which, in 1914, introduced modern mass-production (and caused the demise of such custom-made cars as the Dusenberg Model J). Mass production is one of the most consequential inventions of the 20th century. It was a new system of organizing people to work together. In earlier centuries, hardly anyone worked for anything resembling an institution, unless they worked for the Church or an army. But by the 1950s, mass production had created a situation where most people worked in organizations. If these organizations were not completely driven by mass production, they were at least structured along mass-production lines.

Ford wanted to provide every American who wanted one with a car. So he reduced his prices. In 1910, Ford's Model T roadster sold for $680. By 1914, the car had been reduced to $440, a price no comparable car in the world could match. Ford also decided that any of his employees who wanted a car ought to be paid enough so that they could afford one. So the company reduced its work day to eight hours and raised all wages to a minimum of $5 per day, an unprecedented act in its time. Sales of the Model T more than doubled in two years. In 1900, there were only 13,000 automobiles registered in America, but by 1930, there were 26.5 million registered. By 1992, Americans possessed over 144 million vehicles. In 1900, an automobile was considered a plaything of the wealthy. Today, over 90 percent of America's 93 million households have access to at least one vehicle.

It's hard for us to imagine the changes the automobile brought to America in just a few years. The growth of paved roads tells the story. In 1900, there were virtually no paved roads outside the larger cities. By 1991, America had 3.5 million miles of surfaced roads. Quite possibly, the automobile fostered more changes and new industries than any other single invention. Just consider the advent of automatic traffic lights, gasoline stations, officially numbered highways, tourist homes, roadside diners, used car lots, one-way streets, new companies to make automobile parts from tires to spark plugs, and the downtown parking garage. These new businesses and industries meant new jobs, greater consumer spending, increased tax revenues and the continuing expansion of the American economy.

There were social effects brought by the automobile as well: suburbs accessible by car rather than just by train; businesses which no longer had to plan their location according to train transport; a decline in railroad passenger travel as more people drove to their destination; the decline of the huge summer hotels as cars now took people to out-of-the-way places or wherever they wanted to go; the end of the isolation of the farmer, who no longer required an entire day to make a trip to town; a weakening of family cohesion as sons and daughters had easy transport to other venues; a general broadening of people's geographic horizons; and, regrettably, a new form of sudden death (by the end of the century, more Americans would be killed annually in car accidents than were killed in the Vietnam War).

In sum, the advent of an affordable automobile gave the average family unprecedented mobility, expanded their personal horizons, offered access to new markets, jobs shopping, vacations and financial growth, and gave millions the chance to reach for a better life not possible just a decade earlier.

No technology has changed America as much as has the automobile—unless it is electricity.

In 1889, less than 2 percent of the power used in industry had been electric; 20 years later, it was over 30 percent. In 1901, there was only one generating station producing over 5,000 horsepower of electricity. By 1925, there were 50 generating stations, each exceeding 100,000 horsepower of electricity. New industries were created to bring us home lighting, street lights, trolley cars, movies, air conditioning, and home appliances such as refrigerators, washing machines and radios, to name only a few items. It was the availability of these home appliances that made America a consumer society in the 1920s.

The single individual most responsible for the introduction of electricity into all areas of American life—indeed, the life of the world—was Thomas A. Edison. With only three months of formal schooling, Edison held over a thousand patents for new inventions, including the carbon microphone, the record player (1878), and the kinetoscope for motion pictures.

Edison's most significant contributions, however, were the development of the first commercially practical incandescent lamp (1879) and his design for a complete electrical distribution system for lighting and power, a system culminating in the world's first central electric light power plant in New York. Edison's New Jersey workshop was the forerunner of 20th century research labs, in which teams of researchers, rather than a lone inventor, systematically searched the outer realms of science for solutions. As Henry Ford said to Edison, "You built an assembly line which brought together the genius of invention, science and industry." It's no exaggeration to suggest that Thomas Edison changed the way the world lives more fundamentally than did any other 20th century American.

Given the practical application of electricity to both sight and sound, it was during the 1920s that America moved into the Information Age. In 1920, the year the Boston Red Sox sold Babe Ruth to the New York Yankees for $125,000, the Westinghouse Company launched the first radio station in America, KDKA in Pittsburgh. Spurred by the increasing availability of electricity and by mass production, a radio boom took off, and sales jumped from $60 million in 1922 to $750 million eight years later. By the 1930s, radio networks made national advertising possible, and consumer advertising became the first industry to transmit massive amounts of information to the public.

The automobile and electricity, as powerful transformers as they were, needed a third element to create a consumer economy. That element was a continental economy supported by a national credit system. In 1863 a national banking system had been established; in 1896 the transcontinental railroad was completed; and the passage of the Federal Reserve Act in 1914, bringing the banking system under public control, concluded the making of a truly continental economy.

America had entered a new epoch in which the amenities and possibilities of life which had been the possession of the wealthy few became available to a growing and more prosperous middle class. As historian Charles Beard put it, America was "moving from one technological triumph to another, overcoming the exhaustion of crude natural resources and energies, effecting an ever-widening distribution of the blessings of civilization. . . ." The growth industries of this new consumer epoch were all based on the experience-based (as opposed to knowledge-based) inventions of the last third of the 19th century.

And with the new wealth and strength came a wider role and responsibility. America had become *a* world power by the time of the Spanish American War in 1898. But it was the First World War that led America into becoming *the* world power.

Chapter Four

World War I

SUMMARY: After 300 years, flow across the Atlantic reverses and America returns to the "Old World." End of laissez faire economics in America as government becomes involved in the functioning of the economy. The end of three imperial European monarchies and of Victorian Europe. Entire European generation lost. The exhaustion of Britain creates a global vacuum enabling the rise of communism, fascism, the Great Depression and, eventually, World War II.

In 1917, America went through a major transformation when it entered World War I. For the previous 300 years, the movement across the Atlantic had been from Europe to North America. In 1917, this flow was reversed and America returned to the Old World.

Historian John Lukacs writes that in 1914, "not one American in a thousand thought the United States would, or should, intervene in the great European war." War raged in Europe for two and a half years before America abandoned a policy of neutrality and entered the war on the side of Britain and France.

American business, however, had been involved in the war from the start. Arms, munitions, grains, cotton and manufactured goods were sold to the Allies. The J.P. Morgan bank became the Allied governments' purchasing agent and the chief Allied loan agent of the U.S.

Between 1914 and 1918, $2.5 billion of loans were floated for Allied governments. Such massive financial activity helped the United States to become a creditor nation by 1918. By the end of the war, the center of world money markets had shifted from London to New York.

During the war, the U.S. government became deeply involved in the functioning of economic activity, which was a radical break with pre-war laisse-faire economics. President Wilson established the War Labor Policies Board, the War Industries Board, the Food and Fuel Administration (headed by Herbert Hoover), as well as many other boards and commissions on which numerous businessmen served without financial remuneration. In fact, it's been argued that modern government had its origins with World War I. While the Allied military bureaucracy was viewed as a failure as a result of its performance, the civilian bureaucracy was seen as such a success that from that moment on, the conviction grew that government could and should extend its powers into virtually every domain of domestic activity.

Yet it is odd that government planning should expand just at the precise moment when, in Peter Drucker's words, socialism had "ceased to be an alternative economic system to capitalism," becoming instead "a mere opposition within capitalism." This had happened, Drucker noted, because the solidarity of interests between labor and capital in each country during the war was far stronger than "the international solidarity of the working class."

It is virtually impossible to understand today the prevailing Allied atmosphere when the war commenced. This was not just one more war. It was The Great War for Civilization. As H.G. Wells wrote, "This is the greatest of all wars . . . it is the last war!" C.E. Montague wrote that "All the air was ringing with rousing assurances." George Panichas tells us that it is "on transcendent levels of the abstract, the ideal, and the romantic that we first view the waging of this war." Comradeship, glory, nobility and honor were still held as values vital to a humane civilization. This was the tone of 1914.

But the high tide of enthusiasm receded, and the idealistic world of 1914 disappeared in the carnage of a war that reflected the character of a civilization that was becoming increasingly industrialized, mechanized and urbanized. Those who had been raised in the splendor of the old tradition suddenly faced the demands and terrors of an age in which war was transformed by science. This was a new war in a new age. It was total, an absolute war, fought with new weapons of annihilation: airplanes, submarines, tanks, bombs and poison gas. In short, the war introduced the methods of wholesale destruction.

Arnold Toynbee believed that, between past and present, "1914 was the watershed date . . . much more than the outcome of the second war. Because the second was implicit in the first."

The Great War destroyed Victorian European civilization. Three imperial monarchies–the Romanovs in Russia, the Hohenzollerns in Germany and the Hapsburgs in Austria-Hungary–disappeared. (Two other empires, the Ottoman and the Manchu, also disappeared during the second decade of the century.) Most devastating of all, an entire European generation was lost: 37.5 million killed, wounded or missing. In the Battle of Verdun alone, the Germans and French each lost 300,000 men. In only one day, July 1, 1916, almost 20,000 young English volunteers were killed in the Battle of the Somme. By 1917, both the Germans and the Allies should have questioned the insane trench warfare with its fruitless human sacrifices. But by then the war had become a crusade for both sides, with "total victory" the only acceptable goal. By the end of 1918, the values of a settled civilization were gone.

The consequences of the war have reverberated throughout the 20th century. Indeed, in some ways the Western world never really recovered from that shattering. The wealth of the world, as it then existed, was destroyed to an unimaginable extent. The currencies of the major nations were devalued either during the war or in the years that followed. Trade routes were interrupted. Every great nation, except the U.S., had borrowed far beyond its capacity to repay. New concepts of government, alien to both culture and tradition, became established in three of Europe's major countries. New nations came into existence. When the war started, there were 17 nations in Europe; at war's end, 26. Accepted moral values were shattered, blind obedience to tradition and institution ended, the very fabric of civilized life destroyed, and the after shocks left no small amount of emotional and even psychological dislocation. ("Shell-shocked" is a phrase that entered the English language as a result of the war. Indeed, it was the need to deal with psychologically dislocated soldiers that brought Sigmund Freud his first limited measure of acceptance in the European medical community.)

One consequence of World War I ranks above all others. From the end of the Napoleonic wars in 1815 until 1914, the world maintained a certain equilibrium. Basic to such balance was the status of Great Britain, which, for a century, had been the dominant nation maintaining a relative balance of power. Britain supplied the world with most of its structure of international trade, including the unit of currency in which most trade was conducted. Britain, whose empire included Canada, Ireland, India, Pakistan, Bangladesh, Burma, Singapore, Malay States, Egypt, Sudan, Kenya, Nigeria, South Africa, Zimbabwe, Uganda, Australia and New Zealand, was the wealthiest nation, providing most of the capital for world development. Britain had the largest navy and largest merchant fleet. It was Britain that maintained a modicum of order under international law. Measured by the power of wealth, arms, trade or ideas, Britain was the center around which much of the world revolved.

After the war, Britain was broken and exhausted and no longer able to play its former role. A worldwide vacuum of power opened up. No one country stepped forward to do for the world after the war what Britain had done before. America was the only country that could have done so. We emerged from the war by far the world's richest and most powerful nation. Indeed, the hope that America would dominate and design the coming settlement of peace existed in Germany and Austria as well as in France and Britain. But America did not care for power, or perhaps more correctly, did not have the tradition of the use of power in world affairs. So we did not step in to fill the vacuum. Instead, President Wilson, who was no match for France's Clemenceau or Britain's Lloyd George, endorsed a disastrous Versailles Treaty and put forth the idea of a federated world represented by a League of Nations. Whatever the virtues or deficits of this idea, Congress rejected any notion of America's participation in the League of Nations, much less the assumption of a commanding world role.

The result was a world-embracing uncertainty. And out of the chaos of this uncertainty emerged Lenin and communism in Russia, the Great Depression, fascism in Italy, Hitler and Nazism in Germany, World War II and, eventually, the Cold War. The post-World War I slogan "Back to normalcy," was never to be realized.

In a commanding summary of the Great War, George Panichas wrote: "War generates habits of violence. It muddles human consciousness. It accentuates the ceaseless struggle between barbarism and its proper opposite, civilization. The Great War proved that the barbaric element, far from having been refined out of existence, remains a perpetual threat in a world of immense technological progress. Europe in the course of the war saw the deterioration of rational, civilizing values, particularly the value of life . . . [T]he very structure and consciousness of Europe crumbled."

It is not an exaggeration to suggest that future historians might some day point to the Great War as the central political-historical event of the Interregnum.

Chapter Five

First Articulations of the Interregnum

SUMMARY: Rise of American industry. First use of overhead cranes, power-driven hand tools, compressed air, conveyors such as gravity rollers. Rise of professional industrial engineers. Quality control is introduced. Emergence of the consumer society as wants become needs. Rise of public relations. Toynbee, Durant, Sorokin offer first expressions of historic seminal shifts taking place.

W orld War I hardly dented the great American economic and social expansion that was taking place. If anything, it spurred it on. By 1920, big businesses were, according to business historian Alfred D. Chandler, Jr., "integrated operating companies which used capital-intensive, energy-consuming, continuous or large-batch production technology to produce for mass markets."

New inventions were saving human labor and increasing productivity. Overhead cranes, power-driven hand tools, fork-lifts, compressed air, conveyors such as gravity rollers, new factory designs so that work would move smoothly along a conveyor belt rather than having to be carried from point to point–these and many more inventions changed the way America worked and goods were produced. After 1935, new machines were designed that would measure the exact thickness of a sheet of steel, that could discover the hidden flaws inside a mass of metal, or that would count and inspect goods coming off the assembly line.

Another invention, "quality control," reduced the number of defective parts, decreased costs and raised the status of the workman by giving him increased control over his own production. While the quality control of the 1930s would not look like much compared with today's standards, it was a vast improvement over the preceding two decades. Indeed, the output of the average U.S. worker more than doubled in the first half of the century. (It more than doubled again in the next 35 years.)

The cumulative effect of these inventions and new labor practices was to reduce the demand for unskilled labor and increase the demand for engineers and technicians. In 1900 America had some 11 million "common laborers." Fifty years later there were less than six million. In 1900 there were some 40,000 men classified as engineers. By mid-century that number had risen to 400,000. Indeed, in 1900 there was no classification of "chemical engineer." But in a five-year period after World War II, 15,000 people were trained as chemical engineers in America's universities.

These new engineers were changing the way America lived. In the 1940s the oil industry discovered that more than fuel came out of a barrel of crude oil, and thus the petrochemical industry was born. Synthetic rubber, fertilizers, detergents, nylon stockings, cosmetics and refrigerants began to flood the American market. In 1935, you didn't fly to Europe, you took a Cunard Line steamship, which was more like a huge floating hotel. A dozen years later one could easily fly from New York to London—even before the advent of the jet, which only entered commercial service in the 1950s.

These words do not begin to scratch the surface of the new inventions being made and the vast changes of life they created. Cortisone, antibiotics, tungsten carbide, radar, photosynthesis—these and countless other new products were transforming the way Americans worked and lived.

All but unnoticed at the time was a philosophical shift which gave rise to the "consumer economy." As early as 1899, economist Thorstein

Veblen had described the American ethos as "conspicuous consumption." But it was in the 1920s that the consumer society was really created, and this required a basic change of attitude. For, as Veblen had long since pointed out, what provides direction for the economy is *the value system of the culture* in which the economy is embedded, and America's burgeoning consumer society needed a value system which promoted an ethic of consumption of private goods.

Traditionally, Americans had concentrated on the making of durable, crafted goods that would last a long time. The consumer society requires exactly the opposite approach–the making of less durable goods which, in turn, would lead to the need for replacement. The emphasis shifted from *meeting* demand, to *creating* demand. As North Carolina's Thomas Wolfe had one of his characters say in a story of the changes reshaping America in the 1930s, *You Can't Go Home Again*, "Why, if we waited nowadays to sell a machine to someone who *needs* one, we'd get nowhere . . . We don't wait until he *needs* one . . . We make him see the need, don't we, Randy. We *create* the need." A good example of this approach was Alfred Sloan's innovations in marketing automobiles–the annual model change, constant upgrading of the product, efforts to associate it with social status and the deliberate inculcation of a boundless appetite for change.

This explosion of a consumer society was not seen as a blessing by everyone. In his *Capitalism, Socialism and Democracy* (1942), Joseph Schumpeter saw the capitalistic process "rationalizing behavior and ideas," and by so doing, Schumpeter believed, "metaphysical beliefs" and other ideas were drained as essential social supports. "The stock market is a poor substitute for the Holy Grail," he wrote. The ultimate conclusion of the trend Schumpeter noted was expressed in 1997 by the executive creative director of the New York advertising firm of Kirshenbaum Bond & Partners. "No one's really worrying about what it's [tasteless ads] teaching impressionable youth," *Business Week* reports him saying. "Hey, I'm in the business of convincing people to buy things they don't need."

Other critics thought it misleading to characterize the culture of consumption as a culture dominated by things. As Christopher Lasch wrote, the consumer lives "surrounded not so much by things as by fantasies." He lives in a world that "has no objective or independent existence and seems to exist only to gratify or thwart his desires."

Nevertheless, as the consumer society expanded, the new profession of advertising played a pivotal role. Advertising became the agent that created wants and desires where they had not existed before. As historian and former Librarian of Congress Daniel Boorstin has pointed out, whatever their eventual benefits to society, there was no public "demand" that created the telephone, automobile or television.

Inherent in the new consumer society was the belief that spending was more virtuous than saving, a total reversal of traditional American attitudes. In the 1870s a popular moralist, Samuel Smiles, expressed the ethic of saving in writing, "It is the savings of the individual which compose wealth–in other words, the well-being of every nation." But by the early 1920s, this attitude was reversed and installment buying and consumer credit were introduced. In the consumer society, the worth of an individual was not measured by what a person is as a human being or does as a profession, but by what goods are possessed or how much money that individual might have. As James Oliver Robertson notes in his history of American business, "If a 'rising standard of living' was the goal of American progress, then the standard of living needed to be defined as visible consumption." Or as C. Wright Mills wrote with a sharp irony in *The Power Elite*, there is only one completely acceptable goal in America. "That goal is money, and let there be no sour grapes from the loser." In the America of the 1990s, *Forbes* magazine's annual listing of the 400 wealthiest people indicates just how deeply money has become the American god and the highest measurement of value. In the *Forbes'* America, riches give a *sanction* to a person's efforts and existence. Thus *Forbes* was unable to decry the fact that by 1995, the average corporate chief executive officer raked in 145 times more pay than the average worker, up from 41 times more pay in 1960. Part of this increase clearly came from the benefits of firing workers, euphemistically termed "downsizing," in order to increase the value of corporate stock.

As vast changes took place in habits of production and consumption, so, too, were changes taking place in the role and management of the corporation. Gone were the days when one person such as a Morgan would be something very close to a supreme boss of much of American business. For one thing, the role of banks in business had changed, and corporations were not as dependent on them for financing as in earlier decades. Insurance companies, investment trusts, reinvested profits, the Reconstruction Finance Corporation all made corporations less dependent on banks for financing.

Another significant development was the change in the character of the American economy—from one of free enterprise to a "mixed" economy. The Securities and Exchange Commission, the Federal Trade Commission, the Budget Act of 1922, the Pure Food and Drug Act, state Fair Employment laws, fiscal policies to regulate prices, closer scrutiny by the IRS, regulation of ways goods may be advertised and sold, government control over what businesses a corporation could buy into, greater bookkeeping demands incurred by the need to collect withholding taxes or social security payments—these measures and many more meant that the modern manager was operating under a series of external restrictions, and doing so with an eye to the general welfare.

As corporations grew, as the government oversight of the economy expanded, it became clear that some mechanism which gave the public more information about corporations, the people running them and the products being produced was needed. Thus modern public relations was born.

Public relations is as old as the Republic. The first major public relations campaign in America took place when Alexander Hamilton, James Madison and John Jay—over the pseudonym of Publius—wrote a series of 85 letters to the public which explained the proposed new federal Constitution then being considered for adoption by the 13 States. These letters were published in New York newspapers between October 1787 and August 1788. The new charter of government had already been agreed upon by representatives of the states in Philadelphia in September 1787, but it needed the ratification of at least 9 of the 13 states to bring the new Constitution into effect. A clear-cut vote against the Constitution in any one of four key states, of which New York was one, would be enough to deny the new nation their hopes for "a more perfect union." Thus, on the initiative of Alexander Hamilton, a campaign was undertaken to educate and influence the mind of the New York public. The rest is history.

The first modern public relations campaign was launched by Woodrow Wilson in 1917 when he created the United States Committee on Public Information. Wilson's famous phrases disseminated by the committee–"Make the World Safe for Democracy," "The War to End Wars," "Open Covenants Openly Arrived At"–while appearing hollow in the light of subsequent history, at the time brought an enthusiastic response not just from Americans, but from other nations as well. It was a major public relations effort aimed at advancing democratic ideas throughout the world. As noted earlier, part of Wilson's objective was to offset the revolutionary ideas promulgated by Lenin and the Bolsheviks.

Edward L. Bernays served on President Wilson's committee. Bernays and others working with him recognized that understanding the public and responding to its hopes and needs were basic to any American institution's attainment of its goals. Accordingly, in 1919 Bernays set up office in New York, and in 1923 published *Crystallizing Public Opinion*, a book in which he defined and named a new profession, that of counsel on public relations. In Bernays's view, the new professional advises his client on policies and practices that meet social goals in accord with changing public desires. He also helps interpret his client to the public. Bernays saw the coincidence of the public and private interest as a basic tenet, and to attain success, a corporation must recognize and act on that creed.

In practical reality, however, the creed took second place to the pressures of necessity. Bernays was the first to diagnose how large groups could be manipulated, and to capitalize on the herd instinct that inclines people to follow so-called opinion leaders.

To implement these tactics, Bernays developed a vast array of tools. He flooded the media with an army of experts and opinion leaders. He organized pseudo trade associations to disseminate information favorable to his client. In fact, Bernays was the father of the "pseudo event" staged strictly for its publicity value.

Thus was born modern public relations. Throughout the 1920s and 1930s, this new profession became an increasing element in corporate planning. Most major corporations developed their own in-house staff, but many sought outside advice from the burgeoning Madison Avenue public relations firms.

Bernays probably would be most impressed with what passes for public relations today, for his own work was the genesis of today's instant public opinion polls, focus groups and "spin doctors."

Thus it was that public relations enabled the Great Expansion to bring America a degree of wealth and convenience beyond anything ever before experienced by the broad population of any society in history. Such new wealth and consumer convenience accelerated the shaping of a different America, and they brought forth the clearest descriptions to that point of the Interregnum that was well under way. Three assessments of the Interregnum were offered by Will Durant, Arnold Toynbee and Pitrim A. Sorokin.

According to Will Durant, author of the eleven-volume *The Story of Civilization*, writing in 1929, "Human conduct and belief are now undergoing transformations profounder and more disturbing than any since the appearance of wealth and philosophy put an end to the traditional religion of the Greeks . . ." Durant saw everything as new and experimental in contemporary ideas and actions. Nothing seemed established or certain any longer. "The rate, complexity and variety of change in our time," he wrote, "are without precedent . . . all forms about us are altered . . . All things flow, and we are at a loss to find some mooring and stability in the flux." This, in 1929.

In his 12-volume *A Study of History* (1934-1961), Arnold Toynbee assessed the factors contributing to the rise and decline of 21 civilizations. He sought to appraise each civilization in its widest circumstance, for he believed human affairs are not intelligible until they are seen as a whole. At the heart of Toynbee's survey was the question of how nations respond to successive challenges, be those challenges external or internal. For Toynbee, the challenge was, and still is, how to respond imaginatively to the two primary forces shaping the contemporary world–"democracy and industrialization." Successful response to these two challenges, Toynbee thought, could be claimed if the outward development brought greater degrees of "self-determination and self-articulation." In other words, material advance demands a corresponding advance in human character and spirit.

Pitrim A. Sorokin, who fled Lenin's Russia, was chairman of Harvard University's department of sociology and president of the International Institute of Sociology. During the late 1930s he prepared a four-volume survey of Western sociocultural trends which was published starting in 1937 under the title *Social and Cultural Dynamics*. Taken together, Toynbee's and Sorokin's studies represent two of the deepest and most exhaustive surveys of Western civilization published during the 20th century.

Sorokin noted that most analyses of the crisis facing Western nations tend to describe life in terms of opposite political or economic views–capitalism versus communism, democracy versus totalitarianism, nationalism versus internationalism, or Great Britain versus Germany. Sorokin saw the crisis not merely as an economic or political maladjustment, but as "a disintegration of a fundamental form of Western culture and society dominant for the last four centuries."

In Sorokin's view, Western medieval culture was a whole whose parts articulated the same supreme principle of true reality and value–"an infinite, supersensory, and superrational God." This world view began to decline around the end of the 12th century, and in its place emerged a new principle, namely, that the true reality and value are sensory–only what we see, hear, smell, touch and perceive through our sense organs. Sorokin termed this new principle as a *sensate* culture–a "sensory, empirical, secular and 'this-worldly' culture." The sensate culture, Sorokin believed, became the dominant Western principle somewhere around the beginning of the 16th century.

What is happening in the 20th century, Sorokin said, is the disintegration of the dominant sensate system of modern Euro-American culture. "We are living and acting," he wrote, "at one of the epoch-making turning points of human history, when *one fundamental form of culture and society–sensate–is declining and a different form is emerging."* What is emerging, Sorokin believed, is "a new integration as magnificent in its own way as were the five centuries of the sensate era."

Taken together, with whatever differences of opinion that are bound to attend analyses as sweeping as those given by Durant, Toynbee and Sorokin, these three giants of understanding provided three profound perspectives on the Interregnum as it was rapidly reshaping America.

Chapter Six

The Intellectualization of American Life

SUMMARY: Intelligentsia introduced into America in the 1880s from Russia. Young Intellectuals of the 1920s. The attraction of the Left. Emergence of conservative intellectuals in the 1950s. Science and technology as public culture. Scientists as the New Intellectuals. What happens to the intellectuals when robots become "the most intelligent life form on earth?"

America possessed no distinct intellectual class before the 1880s. Thomas Jefferson, Daniel Webster, Henry Clay, Robert E. Lee and Thomas Edison possessed intellects which, at a minimum, would compare favorably with the best of today's intellectuals, but none of them was what would be described as an "intellectual." In some ways, the difference between these men and today's intellectuals is one of the distinctive features of the Interregnum.

"Intelligentsia" is a Russian word which only entered the American lexicon after Russian Jewish immigrants began arriving in America during the last two decades of the 19th century. In its Russian meaning, intelligentsia describes "the strange hothouse development of a class without social roots and political responsibilities," in the words of cultural historian Christopher Dawson. The creation of the Russian intelligentsia was, to some extent, fed by the introduction of a Western rationalist, secular Enlightenment into a Russia whose historic impulses had always been shaped by the life-giving vastness of the land and by the Orthodox Church.

This new class of American was perhaps signaled in 1890 by the founding of the first graduate school in America, a school for political science at what was then Columbia College. Part of the mission of the new school was to train teachers in research and to form the minds of future politicians and civil servants.

Another indication of the emergence of a new class of American was the appearance in 1914 of *The New Republic*, a new type of magazine, one of opinion as well as of literature and the arts. The year 1922 saw the birth of two of America's best-known professional journals of considerable intellectual weight, *Foreign Affairs* and *Harvard Business Review.*

In the 1920s, the "Young Intellectuals" (described as "utopian, predominantly socialist, one who believes that the world can be reshaped by the power of intellect") were all the fashion. Many of America's intellectuals, such as Gertrude Stein, went to Paris in the 1920s–so-called "exiles" who wanted to escape American "commercialism and provinciality."

After the 1929 stock market "crash," some of these exiles returned home to seek common cause with America's "masses" who bore the brunt of the Great Depression. It is no surprise that many of the intellectuals of that era flirted with socialism or Marxism in the hopes of finding a suitable replacement for the capitalism they thought to have outlived its purpose. We've forgotten about it now, but there were many Marxist intellectuals in the halls of academia or serving as foreign correspondents abroad who were assured of the benevolent intents of such "agrarian reformers" as Mao Zedong, Stalin and, later in the 1950s, Castro. As Lionel Trilling noted, the character of the intellectual class was "through all mutations of opinion, predominantly of the Left."

Yet being of the Left in the 1930s is totally understandable. It was a time of crisis, and crisis engenders reconsideration of underlying assumptions. Capitalism appeared to be in a final collapse, thus forcing a whole generation to seek some "cause to believe in." As one writer noted, "One can have causes and passions only when one knows against whom to fight." So the need was to define the "enemy," any enemy–capitalism, monopoly, bourgeois culture and bureaucracy, religion, fascism, Stalinism. So a whole generation of writers–John Dos Passos, Reinhold Niebuhr, Max Lerner, Norman Podhoretz, Sidney Hook, Daniel Bell, Irving Kristol, Malcolm Cowley, Irving Howe, Saul Bellow–waged their war in the pages of the *New Leader*, the *Partisan Review* or *Dissent*.

But by the 1950s, the intellectual climate was changing, due in no small measure to the writings of English intellectuals such as George Orwell (*Animal Farm*, 1945, and *Nineteen Eighty-Four*, 1949) as well as to the terrors of Stalin and Soviet imperialism. A new climate was also due to the fact that capitalism in America had survived the Great Depression, produced the hardware to win history's greatest war and engendered a period of economic growth that was rebuilding Europe and Japan, as well as changing the face of America.

A new generation of American conservative intellectuals, led by William Buckley (*God and Man at Yale*, 1951) and his conservative journal, *National Review*, and quickly joined by the neoconservatives who had been idealistic socialists 20 years earlier, launched a sustained attack on liberal intellectualism. Over the course of four decades, this attack made a significant contribution to the rollback of the social engineering of the welfare state which had been the ultimate triumph of 20th century leftist intellectuals.

But despite the work of Buckley, Russell Kirk, George Gilder and a growing phalanx of other conservatives, something else was taking place that brought into question the very concept of an intellectual. In 1959, C.P. Snow, the English physicist whose 11-volume series *Strangers and Brothers* had analyzed power and the relation between science and the general community, wrote a book entitled *The Two Cultures*. Snow accused the literary intellectuals of the 1930s of co-opting the term "intellectual" so that it referred solely to "men of letters" as though there were no other type of intellectual. This implied that people in science, education or government were somehow not true intellectuals.

In his 1995 book *The Third Culture*, publisher John Brockman picks up on Snow's theme and announces that the traditional intellectual ("men of letters") has become increasingly marginalized. "Their culture," he writes, "which dismisses science, is often nonempirical. It uses its own jargon and washes its own laundry. It is chiefly characterized by comments on comments, the swelling spiral of commentary eventually reaching the point where the real world gets lost."

Brockman's thesis is that the "men of letters" are being displaced by "scientists and other thinkers in the empirical world who, through their work and expository writing, are taking the place of the traditional intellectual in rendering visible the deeper meanings of our lives, redefining who and what we are." While it is certainly true that in Europe secular thinkers such as Rousseau, Voltaire and the *philosophes* replaced the priests and clerics in rendering "visible the deeper meanings of our lives" and defining "who and what we are," the American tradition assigned that responsibility to religion up until our own time.

Brockman notes that throughout history, "only a small number of people have done the serious thinking for everybody else." What we're seeing now, he says, is "a passing of the torch from one group of thinkers, the traditional literary intellectuals, to a new group, the intellectuals [scientists] of the emerging third culture." Intended or not, Brockman is suggesting that the scientists are the ones doing the "serious thinking" for the rest of us today. No one could argue the fact that contemporary science is *very* serious thinking, far too serious, in fact, to be left to the scientists. For the primary thought of scientists is, not surprisingly, about science, with very little "serious thought" given to the human and social consequences of scientific achievement. To do this would require openness to the non quantifiable subjective side of life, something which does not come easily to either scientists or intellectuals.

World-renowned scientist and author Freeman Dyson decries what he sees as the intellectual "snobbism among scientists, especially the academic types." Intellectual snobbery concludes Dyson, "is a worldwide disease." In Harvard University's massive study of technology and society, Victor C. Ferkiss notes that despite its prominent role in technological society, "science will not be able to provide the new cultural orientations that will be needed. There is little evidence that any scientific world view is taking over the integrating function in our culture, or even that such a world view is commonly shared by those who call themselves scientists. . . ."

While there is evidence for Brockman's thesis that science has become the "public culture," it could hardly be argued that scientists are America's only intellectuals. In the last 50 years the intellectualization of American life can be seen in the spawning of "think tanks," public opinion polls, new job categories such as the research assistant, TV's "talking heads," newspaper "commentary and analysis," "experts" on every aspect of life, Ph.D. mathematicians hired by Wall Street firms to design investment programs so complex even the firms' CEOs can't understand them, the intellectualization of mainstream religious denominations which has given rise to the evangelical church, and, finally, in the ubiquitous "Opinion" section in virtually every Sunday newspaper. What has happened to Harvard University is another indicator of the intellectualization of America. In Freeman Dyson's words, Harvard doesn't "care about the undergraduates. It's essentially a graduate school; the undergraduates are left to sink or swim." And so the intellectualization of American life would appear to have become the basis of the "Information Society."

What is more, the intellectualization of American life raises the question of what is happening to time-honored wisdom and common sense. Instincts and institutions developed since prehistory now seem superseded by "scientific research." Thus *The Washington Post* of September 10, 1997, carries the front-page headline "Love Conquers What Ails Teens, Study Finds." The $25 million study sponsored by the National Institutes of Health informs us that "family relationships are critical in raising healthy children . . . Teenagers who have strong emotional attachments to their parents and teachers are much less likely to use drugs and alcohol, attempt suicide, engage in violence or become sexually active at an early age." The results of the study, we are assured, "will continue to be analyzed in increasing detail over the next decade." How, one may ask, did the human race manage to come this far without the benefit of such studies?

It is just such intellectualization of elemental life processes that leads psychologist Eugene C. Kennedy to write of the "overintellectualization of life" in America that causes man to lose touch "with the values that make him truly human," and that has created "an age in which man's loneliness and alienation have been identified as something like a national epidemic." Deep down inside, Kennedy writes, "man is groaning for something more than cold, clear knowledge . . ." We are searching, he says, "for a center of gravity in a world that is moving too fast."

The ultimate challenge to the intellectual, as well as to the scientist and all the rest of us, will come when computers and robots become "the most intelligent life form on earth," when "they will not only tolerate but love us—even as they threaten to displace us as the dominant form of life on Earth," which, we are confidently told by scientists at Carnegie Mellon University's Robotics Institute and elsewhere, will take place before the passage of another half century.

What such efforts tell us is that *the intellectualization of life in America during the 20th century has led to the intellectuals of science becoming the contemporary social engineers.* They pursue their aims to a degree far beyond the wildest intentions of the social engineering of an earlier generation of intellectuals, and without the slightest public discussion about the consequences of their research. The new social engineers evidently "find it impossible to believe it makes sense to continue, as human beings, in our exact same form" (Hans Moravec, formerly of Carnegie Mellon University), and they want "to produce something that goes beyond ourselves" (Danny Hillis, pioneer of massively parallel processing for computers, and a Disney Fellow and vice president of Disney Imagineering).

We now stand at a point beyond the ability of unaided intellect to establish either order or meaning for the world that intellect has created, and this is perhaps the central challenge of the Interregnum.

Chapter Seven

The Great Depression

SUMMARY: Profile of the Depression. The Depression's causes. Smoot-Hawley Tariff bill. The Hoover response. Roosevelt and a sense of hope. In 1974, former FDR assistant says that "practically the whole New Deal was extrapolated from programs that Hoover started." A moral depression as well.

In 1929, roughly 97 percent of American families had incomes below $10,000. An income of $2,000 was regarded as the minimum income needed to meet life's basic necessities, yet 60 percent were below that poverty line. It was a degree of simplicity in terms of material possession which we are unable to imagine today.

The events of October 1929 are well known and represent the most devastating economic crisis of the Interregnum thus far. During the market plunge, $30 billion in paper values–an amount larger than the national debt at that time–vanished into thin air. The Dow Jones industrials plunged from a 1929 high of 381 to a 1932 low of 41, about a point above where the average began in 1896. General Motors common stock went from just over 72 in 1929, to just below 8 in 1932. United States Steel went from over 261, to 21. By the middle of 1932, American industry was operating at less than half its maximum 1929 volume. National income fell by 38 percent. Total wages paid out in 1932 were 60 percent less than in 1929. Over 5,000 banks had closed their doors since 1920. Twelve million Americans, every fourth person in the labor market, were unemployed. In 1933, 2,000 rural schools did not open for the fall semester, thus throwing 200,000 teachers out of work and 2.3 million children out of school. In 1935, the Social Security Act established a federal payroll tax to finance a cooperative federal–state system of unemployment insurance. In the industrial world as a whole, some 30 million people were without jobs.

Prices of farm products fell by half. In early 1933 machine tool orders were one-eighth their 1929 level. Crude oil was selling for 5 cents a barrel. It was a terrifying collapse of the market economy that had been established during the 19th century.

The causes of the Great Depression are still argued today, but most experts agree that the roots of the crash lay in the profusion of debt that resulted from World War I. Long after he had left the White House, Herbert Hoover, who all through the 1920s had warned, passionately and insistently, against the dangers of easy money and stock market speculation, wrote: "In the large sense the primary cause of the Great Depression was the war of 1914-18." Writing in 1939, the great economist Joseph Schumpeter observed: "Depressions were actually impending or in progress in 1914 . . . [P]ublic expenditure turned them into prosperity first and created untenable situations afterward."

The Great Depression was essentially a collapse of inflated asset values. The most important were Wall Street stocks, German war-reparations obligations and the British pound. The overvaluing of all these assets was sustained by credit from the U.S. financial system. One result was overinvestment and underconsumption.

In *A Monetary History of the United States*, Milton Friedman and Anna Schwartz cite the contraction in the money supply as the primary cause of the Great Depression. Between 1929 and 1933, the money supply shrank 36 percent. Part of the problem was that at the time it wasn't really known how drastically the currency was contracting. The "money supply" did not include bank deposits, and it was in bank deposits where liquidity was vanishing as banks failed. By 1933, 11,000 banks had become insolvent, causing many critics to blame the Federal Reserve for not doing its job.

Certainly a major factor exacerbating what at the time was a recession was passage of the Smoot-Hawley Tariff Bill, signed into law in 1930. Despite the warnings of over a thousand economists and the protests of some 35 nations, the Smoot-Hawley bill raised tariffs to their highest levels in history and helped spread the Depression in Europe. Consequently, because other nations could not sell their goods to America, they were denied the necessary finance to buy American products. So the Depression deepened. By 1934, Secretary of State Cordell Hull had persuaded Congress that such high tariffs were making the Depression worse and should be replaced by mutual tariff relaxation. Thus Congress passed the Reciprocal Trade Agreement Act, giving the president the power to negotiate trade pacts without advice or consent of the Senate.

Other causes might include the loss of European markets and the inability of European nations to continue repayment of their war debt. Historian Frederick Lewis Allen suggests that the market crash happened "because of an appalling breakdown of the fiduciary tradition." Businessmen had become "bemused with paper values—with the piling up of speculative or artificially generated wealth which had little relation to the production of goods." Another historian, James Truslow Adams, wrote in 1931: "Having surrendered idealism for the sake of prosperity, the 'practical men' bankrupted us on both of them."

When the 1929 crash came, President Hoover initiated a three-pronged program to sustain demand and keep the economy moving: (1) more public works spending; (2) low interest rates to ease business investment and home-building—mortgage money could be had at 5 percent; (3) keeping wages high to prevent a collapse of consumer purchasing power.

Hoover persuaded Congress to enact a tax cut, persuaded business and labor leaders to hold the line on prices, wages and capital spending (he actually exacted promises from corporate leaders not to reduce wages, a promise which was broadly kept until 1932), and got the Federal Reserve to ease credit by lowering the interest rates from 4 percent to 1.75 percent, the lowest on record. As the Depression deepened, in 1931 he organized the Reconstruction Finance Corporation

(RFC), whose loans to banks and railroads did much to save the financial system. In 1932, the RFC's capital was increased by almost 100 percent to $3.8 billion. Hoover cut taxes heavily, deliberately running up a sizable deficit in an effort to reflate the economy. He gave farmers $500 million through the Agricultural Marketing Act, and added another $100 million in 1930. Government spending on public works under Hoover was increased to the extent that more major public works were started in Hoover's 4 years than in the previous 30. The San Francisco Bay Bridge, the Hoover Dam, and the Los Angeles Aqueduct were all started under Hoover.

In the beginning, Hoover's moves seemed adequate. The economic situation was serious but not disastrous. In 1930, after the stock market crashed and the first wave of plant closings and layoffs had occurred, most banks were still solvent. But in 1931, just when the U.S. Depression should have been bottoming out, the whole world's economy collapsed, taking the U.S. with it. The 1931 European financial crisis pushed the Great Depression in the U.S. into a new phase. Another 3 million workers lost their jobs, and the nation began to lose hope. New leadership was clearly needed.

Franklin Delano Roosevelt came to office in 1933 asserting his belief that "the only thing we have to fear is fear itself." Where Hoover was a somewhat dour engineer, Roosevelt was a politician with a keen sense of the public pulse. He laughed and seemed to enjoy life. In fact, he was the first president to deliberately flash a smile whenever possible. He was also the first president to understand the political significance of radio, and his 1928 speech nominating Al Smith at the Democratic Convention was the first major political speech geared to the radio audience rather than the audience in the convention hall.

Roosevelt's first congressional session saw a spate of bills passed by Congress, including the Emergency Banking Act, which proclaimed a "Bank Holiday," thus closing the nation's banks. This was followed by the Emergency Banking Relief Act, which allowed the banks to reopen under presidential powers to safeguard depositors and shareholders. Soon to follow was legislation creating the Civilian Conservation Corps, the Tennessee Valley Authority, and the U.S. Employment Service. The

Glass-Steagall Banking Act instituted various banking reforms, including creation of the Federal Deposit Insurance Corporation (FDIC).

While Roosevelt sought ideas from every quarter, the New Deal was, to some extent, a vast expansion of programs begun under Hoover. In fact, in 1974, Rexwell Tugwell, a leading light of FDR's "braintrust," noted in an interview, "We didn't admit it at the time, but practically the whole New Deal was extrapolated from programs that Hoover started."(1) Evaluating the Hoover-Roosevelt effort to deal with the Great Depression, Walter Lippmann wrote in the *Yale Review* in 1935, "The policy initiated by President Hoover in the autumn of 1929 was something utterly unprecedented in American history. The national government undertook to make the whole economic order operate prosperously . . . the Roosevelt measures are a continuous evolution of the Hoover measures."

The Great Depression was not just an economic catastrophe; it was a social and political cataclysm of unimaginable proportions. As Arthur Schlesinger, Jr. writes, the Great Depression exposed "the pretension that democracy would guarantee prosperity. A third of the way into the century, democracy seemed a helpless thing, spiritless, paralyzed, doomed." It was only World War II that finally ended the Great Depression. Even then, not until 1954 did the stock market regain its 1929 level.

The Great Depression's toll on the human spirit was poignantly described by Thomas Wolfe in *You Can't Go Home Again:*

> What happened in Libya Hill [the story's locale] and elsewhere has been described in the learned tomes of the overnight economists as a breakdown of "the system, the capitalist system." Yes. it was that. But was also much more than that. In Libya Hill it was the total disintegration of what, in so many different ways, the lives of all these people had come to be. It went much deeper than the mere obliteration of bank accounts, the extinction of paper profits, and the loss of property. It was the ruin of men who found out, as soon as these symbols of their

outward success had been destroyed, that they had nothing left–no inner equivalent from which they might now draw new strength. It was the ruin of men who, discovering not only that their values were false but that they had never had any substance whatsoever, now saw at last the emptiness and hollowness of their lives. Therefore they killed themselves; and those who did not die by their own hands died by the knowledge that they were already dead.

The effect of the Great Depression on American cultural life and thought was significant. Writers such as James T. Farrell and Waldo Frank produced a radical fiction commonly known as "proletarian literature." That such literature was of a Marxist orientation is not all that surprising, given the question in the minds of many people as to whether capitalism had a future. The greater surprise is that "American literary communism" failed to make deeper inroads. The Great Depression authors who are remembered as the century comes to a close are writers such as John Steinbeck, Edmund Wilson, Charles Beard and Thomas Wolfe.

The consequences of the worldwide Depression were many, not least of which was the rise of Hitler and World War II. But at home, perhaps the major consequence was the permanent alteration of the nature of the American economy and an expansion of the role of government in the affairs of commerce.

Chapter Eight

Management—A New Profession

SUMMARY: The emergence of business schools. Wallace Donham inaugurates Harvard's "case method." In 1920s, Donham writes two articles in *Harvard Business Review* stressing importance of change as a new factor in civilization. Berle and Means write of the shift from individual ownership of corporations to publicly owned companies. Peter Drucker first to analyze corporation as an institution in need of the discipline of management. Importance of Drucker's writings. Continued "crisis of legitimacy" facing professional management. Deming and quality. Emphasis on excellence.

For centuries before the Interregnum began, the institutions of the Catholic Church and the army were the two models of organization in Western society. The business organization, which emerged just as the Interregnum started, is the one new social invention to be added to these historic forms. As America's national economy was formed and needed to be serviced by an organization capable of operating on a continental scale, as immigrants flocked to America during the first two decades of the century, as new inventions provided more jobs and higher incomes, and as a consumer society began to emerge, how to manage the business organization became an increasingly important question.

It had been Robert E. Lee who, as president of Virginia's Washington College (now Washington and Lee University), had first proposed professional business training for college students. The industrial civilization he saw emerging would need to be properly managed. The trustees of the College, however, turned Lee's proposal down for lack of funds. While the University of Pennsylvania established the Wharton School of Finance and Economics in 1883, it was John D. Rockefeller who enabled the University of Chicago to found a School of Business to train professional business managers. Almost three decades later, Harvard University founded the Harvard Business School and, under the direction of Wallace B. Donham, inaugurated what became known as Harvard's "case method."

Dean Wallace Donham was a remarkably farsighted man. In a series of articles in the *Harvard Business Review* in the late '20s and early '30s, he offered his view of what was happening to America, what he saw as the role of business leadership, and thus the type of business training Harvard Business School ought to provide its students. Donham wrote of the importance of change as a new factor in civilization and the necessity not so much of our learning how to deal with successive changes as they occur, as of our learning "general principles which may enable us to deal more effectively with change itself–constant change– in ways which may give us a more stable basis for society and for its continuous progress. . . ."

Donham stressed the need to address the implications of a rapidly changing environment. Since these changes result mainly from the control over nature through scientific and industrial developments, and since the "creative scientists have lost control of the consequences of their thinking," Donham posited that the solution to the problems involved must be sought in the leadership of an enlightened business community.

To produce this leadership, Donham proposed a business training that would include three broad categories: "thorough intellectual training which will enable the student to think broadly and soundly about the problems he must face in business; depth and perspective on vital social problems which will enable him as he practices his profession to think of both present and future with a clear conception of their significance; and preparation for the moral issues which will constantly present themselves to him in practice." *(Wallace B. Donham, circa 1927.)*

One of the moral issues to which Donham referred was the relationship between the business corporation and society at large. A vast change in this relationship was taking place, and nowhere was this change more clearly perceived than in *The Modern Corporation and Private Property*, published in 1932 by Adolf A. Berle and Gardiner C. Means. Berle and Means wrote that the development of big business corporations "created economic empires" and "delivered those empires into the hands of a new form of absolutism," which was quite the opposite of traditional American individualism. What concerned them was the "translation of perhaps two-thirds of the industrial wealth of the country from individual ownership to ownership by the large, publicly financed corporations." Corporations had now grown too large for an "owner" to manage, and this divorce of ownership from control, they maintained, introduced "a new form of economic organization to society."

Fifty years later Peter F. Drucker was to write that professional management "still faces a severe crisis of legitimacy because it is no longer grounded in yesterday's economic power, that of the capitalist owner, and is not grounded in anything else so far."

In some ways, Peter Drucker follows in the tradition of Wallace Donham. Both men exhibit an exceptionally wide-ranging grasp of history, both discern the character of the changing times in which they live, both see the corporation as a social institution, and both project a world outlook.

But Drucker took Donham's work further, and he was the first to analyze the corporation as an institution in need of the discipline of management. Thus the first "management" book was Drucker's *Concept of the Corporation*, based on research at General Motors in 1943 and published three years later. While many books existed on advertising, industrial production and sales training, no one had considered how a business was organized and structured, how it functioned, and what its basic tasks and problems were. *Concept of the Corporation* was the first work to consider decentralization as a principle of organization, and it put Drucker out front in arguing that America has moved to a society where the major social tasks are carried out by a new institution–the industrial corporation.

Drucker followed *Concept of the Corporation* with a stream of books arguing the need for a new theory of organizations. What gives an organization its legitimacy? How does an organization decide what its objectives should be? How does it mobilize its objectives, priorities, strategies and assignments for performance? How does it measure whether it performs? How does it cultivate productivity? How does it achieve and manage growth? How does it nourish and administer its primary resource–knowledge? And how does an organization relate to its changing global environment? The elements Drucker pursues relate to all institutional entities. What are the requirements of a knowledge organization? What are an organization's moral and political dimensions? How does it anticipate and limit its impacts on people and the larger environment? How does it discharge its social task? Agree or disagree with him, no other writer has addressed the extent of complex issues confronting the modern organization as has Peter Drucker.

Born and raised in pre-World War I Vienna, a journalist for a Frankfurt newspaper in the early 1930s, a securities analyst for an international bank in London in the mid-1930s and a writer of world renown since his arrival in the United States in 1937, Peter Drucker is one of the genuine "giants" of the second half of the 20th century. Few men have so dominated their discipline as Drucker has dominated, indeed virtually defined, the profession of management. And not only in America. An entire generation of Japanese managers owes its training and expertise to Peter Drucker. An article in *Forbes* described Drucker as "perhaps the most perceptive observer of the American scene since Alexis de Tocqueville." Drucker, however, would certainly forgive *Forbes* for ignoring Lord Bryce and *The American Commonwealth* (1888). Adrian Wooldrige, West Coast bureau chief of the *Economist*, wrote that Drucker "is one of the few thinkers from any discipline who can reasonably claim to have changed the world: the inventor of privatization, the apostle of a new class of knowledge workers, the champion of management as a serious intellectual discipline."

As Peter Drucker, who has taught political science, philosophy, religion and Oriental art as well as management, has written (as of 1998) 32 books and thousands of articles, it is impossible to summarize his writings. But three statements particularly suggest the scope and depth of his thinking.

In *Management: Tasks, Responsibilities, Practices* (1973) Drucker wrote:

> Management may well be considered a bridge between a civilization that is rapidly becoming worldwide and a culture which expresses divergent traditions, values, beliefs and heritages. Management must become the instrument through which culture and diversity can be made to serve the common purpose of mankind.

In *The New Realities* (1989):

> Management is what tradition used to call a liberal art— "liberal" because it deals with the fundamentals of knowledge, self-knowledge, wisdom, and leadership; "art" because it is practice and application. Managers draw on all the knowledges and insights of the humanities and the social sciences—on psychology and philosophy, on economics and history, on the physical sciences and ethics. But they have to focus this knowledge on effectiveness and results—on healing a sick patient, teaching a student, building a bridge, designing and selling a "user-friendly" software program.

In 1987, Jonathan Peterson of *The Los Angeles Times* interviewed Drucker on his seventy-eighth birthday. In that interview Drucker described management as

> . . . no less than the nature of man, the nature of God, and–believe me–the devil, too. When you're dealing with man, you're dealing with good and evil.

Such a statement is consistent with Drucker's beliefs for at least the past half-century. In 1957, he wrote: "[T]he individual needs the return to spiritual values, for he can survive in the present human situation only by affirming that man is not just a biological and psychological being but also a spiritual being, that is creature, and existing for the purposes of his Creator and subject to Him."

In the final years of the century, Peter Drucker was still going strong. In a 1997 *Harvard Business Review* article, he argues that the "dominant factor for business in the next two decades . . . will be demographics." The key factor for business "will be the increasing *under*population of the developed countries," who are, Drucker says, "in the process of committing collective suicide." The citizens of the developed countries "are not having enough babies to reproduce themselves." Thus the only possible comparative advantage for the developed countries is in the supply and quality of a country's knowledge workers.

In a 1998 *Fortune* article, Drucker argues that the "worst trend in management is those enormous millions paid to people at the top when they lay off 12,000 people. You have no idea how contemptuous upper-midlevel managers are of those people." In a *Forbes* article the same year, Drucker criticizes "the inward focus of management" which has been aggravated by the rise of information technology. Management, he says, does not need more information about what is happening inside the corporation. It needs more information about what is happening outside. "I have yet to hear of one [conference on information] that even raises the question: 'What outside data do we need, and how do we get them?'"

Many have come, made their contribution, and departed. Peter Drucker, who describes himself as a "social ecologist concerned with man's man-made environment," has endured. Drucker's own view of himself is simple: "I just look out the window and see what's visible–but not yet seen."

Few others have equaled Drucker's influence, but one who has is Edwards Deming. Deming came out of the army after World War II, and began preaching the gospel of quality to American management who, by and large, shunned Deming and his statistical control methods. Deming's theory was simple: Build quality in at the start rather than check it at the end of the production process. American management was in the midst of the "built-in obsolescence" attitude and in no mind to make quality the primary consideration. So Deming went to Japan, where he trained a generation of managers in total quality management, the results of which by the 1980s forced American management to take Deming seriously. Ironically, American companies began adopting Toyota's "just in time" inventory process, which had been pioneered by Henry Ford in the 1920s.

The underlying issue of management's legitimacy, which had been discussed by Berle and Means in the 1930s and Drucker in the 1980s, still remains. And nowhere is it reflected more than in business education. Countless studies, from Chicago Business School's Leon Marshall in 1928, to Derek Bok's 1979 critique of Harvard Business School, basically reflect Gordon and Howell's 1959 report that "business schools have not yet reached agreement as to what their objectives should properly be and how these objectives might best be attained."

This uncertainty in business education, obviously, derives from an equal uncertainty in corporate management itself. The central schism was expressed by Donham in the 1920s: What is the primary responsibility of the manager? Is it to increase the shareholder's investment? Is it simply to coordinate a rationalized production process as efficiently as possible? Or is it, as Donham thought, to provide broad direction to the changes in society which managers are generating through their enterprises, while at the same time managing–for a profit–an enterprise that meets a legitimate material need of humankind? Clearly, in the era of "slash and burn" downsizing and CEO salaries at astronomical multiples of worker compensation, the question of responsibility for the broad changes corporations are engendering is not yet a high priority in America's boardrooms.

What is increasingly accepted, however, is a broad agreement on what it takes to excel in an increasingly competitive global market. As Peters and Waterman point out, such excellence requires superior quality and service, the centrality of growth and profits, an emphasis on risk and possibility, attention to details, the primacy of people and the need for individual challenge and growth, clear goals and a sense of common effort in attaining them, a worldwide outlook, and a perspective beyond immediate economic goals.

Such a management ethos increasingly pervades not only manufacturing and service corporations, but the management of nonprofit organizations as well. Certainly a significant management challenge of the coming decades will be to see such an ethos reshape the management of government affairs at all levels.

Chapter Nine

The March of Equality

SUMMARY: Brief profile of African Americans, 1900-1950. Impact of Great Depression on blacks. Advances of the 1940s. Blacks and World War II. In 1951, Ralph Bunche awarded honorary degrees from thirteen universities. Advances of the 1950s. Thurgood Marshall and the NAACP. Brown v. the Board of Education. Rosa Parks, Martin Luther King, Jr. and the Montgomery bus boycott.

One of the most significant advances of progress during the Interregnum has been a broader and more generous answer to the ancient question, "Who is my neighbor?"

"The problem of the twentieth century," W.E.B. Du Bois observed in 1900, "is the problem of the color line." In the year he wrote, there were 9 million African-Americans in America, and almost 90 percent of them lived in the South, mostly in the *rural* South. Needless to say, conditions were deplorable. Over 40 percent were illiterate. In 1900 it was estimated in Alabama that out of 181,471 African American males of voting age, only 3,000 were registered. Lynchings were numerous, 115 in 1900 alone. The million or so African Americans who lived outside the South tended to fare better, partly because the wage average was higher in the North and West, but also because the schools were better. This said, even in the North and West there was no pretense of equality.

Ever since the end of the Civil War, those southern African Americans who could afford to do so moved to other parts of the country. But what had been a trickle for some 50 years suddenly became a flood in 1915. World War I created a demand for unskilled workers in northern factories, and southern African Americans rushed to seize the opportunity. Philadelphia, Detroit, Chicago and Harlem absorbed thousands of African Americans seeking both a job and better living conditions.

But as the African American population of the North swelled, the same sort of prejudice that had been most acute in the South began to surface. Job and housing discrimination spread. In the mid-1920s the Ku Klux Klan flourished in northern cities which had hardly known the KKK existed. One realizes the depth of bigotry they faced in reading F. Scott Fitzgerald's 1921 remark, "The negroid streak creeps northward to defile the Nordic race."

Then came the Great Depression, and its impact on African Americans was disastrous. African Americans were last to be hired and were the first to be demoted or lose their jobs. The northern migration continued, not because of jobs but primarily because there was a better chance of getting on relief in the North than in the South. In 1935 in Mobile, Alabama, the median African American family earned only $481 during the year, contrasted with $1,419 for median whites. In that same year, almost half the African American families in the North were on relief!

Change for African Americans came with the approach of World War II. As military orders were filled, new jobs were created and the general wage level rose. Even so, when African Americans were drafted into military service, they were segregated and assigned menial duties. But the uneasy American conscience was at work, and many whites agitated against the segregation in the army and in some war industries. Despite lingering cries for "white supremacy" in some southern areas, increasing number of whites were making a conscientious effort to find, by quiet accommodation, a way beyond the racial division that had so plagued America.

The change that took place was not widespread, but it was significant. The year 1940 saw the first African American achieve the rank of general in the U.S. Army, as well as the first African American to be honored with an "Oscar" at the Academy Awards. In 1944, the first African American to become a State Department official was appointed, and so was the first African American correspondent to be accredited to the White House. In 1948, the first African American tennis player competed in the U.S. Indoor Lawn Tennis Association championship. The next year the first African American midshipman graduated from Annapolis, and the U.S. Congress saw the first African American congressman ever to head a standing congressional committee. In Atlanta America's first radio station to be owned and operated by African Americans went on the air.

So the 1940s brought changes that might have seemed impossible just a decade earlier. Eleanor Roosevelt commented on the change as it was reflected in president Roosevelt's inauguration of 1945. She noted that blacks and whites mingled together at the inaugural reception, a fact that drew virtually no comment from the press. Had the same thing happened 12 years earlier at the 1933 inaugural reception, Mrs. Roosevelt said, almost every newspaper in the country would have reported it.

In the 1948 presidential election, over a million southern African Americans voted. The Air Force and Navy officially ended segregation. The Supreme Court declared unlawful various practices that had kept African Americans from the voting booth or from educational opportunity. Reported lynchings of African Americans, which had averaged 12 a year in the 1930s, fell to a total of 13 between 1945 and 1950, which, even so, was a sign of lingering inhumanity in America. African American figures such as Duke Ellington, Marian Anderson, Jackie Robinson, Louis Armstrong, Roy Campanella and Joe Louis became revered national heroes. In 1947, Jackie Robinson broke segregation in professional baseball. In the spring of 1951, Dr. Ralph J. Bunche, who, as the American mediator in the Middle East and one of the country's foremost diplomats, was awarded honorary degrees by no less than 13 educational institutions. In 1953, the NAACP succeeded in driving "Amos 'n Andy" off TV, thus ending a long-held white stereotype of African Americans. By the early '50s, there were 94,000 African American students in American colleges and universities. It was not uncommon to see an African American policeman in a southern town arrest a white lawbreaker.

The 1950s saw other gains for African Americans. The first African American to represent the United States at the United Nations assumed his duties, Ralph J. Bunche became the first African American to be awarded the Nobel Peace Prize, the national tennis tournament of the U.S. Lawn Tennis Association saw the first African American woman compete, and professional hockey welcomed its first African American player. The second half of the decade saw the first African American airline stewardess and the first African American pilot on a scheduled passenger airline, the first African American baseball umpire in the major leagues, the first African American minister of an all-white congregation, the first African American page of the Supreme Court, the first African American sub-cabinet member, the first major league baseball team (Brooklyn Dodgers) to have more African Americans than whites on the team, the first African American Catholic bishop, and the first African American Air Force general.

But these advances, as impressive as they seemed at the time, were individual achievements. The social structure and legal basis of racism remained.

At least four factors began to change this institutional racism. First, it was sinking into the American consciousness that African Americans who had risked their lives for freedom during World War II could not be denied freedom at home. Second, social and demographic changes were altering the context within which racism was practiced. Third, pressure for desegregation from the National Association for the Advancement of Colored People (NAACP) and other civil rights groups began to mount. Finally, the Supreme Court changed the laws of the land.

No one was more influential with the Supreme Court than Thurgood Marshall. While Martin Luther King, Jr., roused the conscience of America, it was Thurgood Marshall who, more than any other individual, caused the legal basis of institutional racism to be dismantled.

As chief counsel for the NAACP, Marshall led the fight in the 1930s and 1940s against the "separate but equal" doctrine laid down by the Supreme Court some 30 years after the Civil War. Marshall's success led to the Supreme Court decision in 1950 to order the state of Texas to admit African Americans to its all-white law school. The same day, the Supreme Court barred the state of Oklahoma from segregating its graduate school of education.

Marshall, the NAACP and grass-roots groups then went on to challenge the very core of institutionalized racism in America, the public school system. By 1953, five suits reached the Supreme Court challenging school policies in South Carolina, Kansas, Virginia, Delaware and the District of Columbia. The most famous of these suits was *Brown v. the Board of Education of Topeka.*

In 1954, the Supreme Court announced that by a unanimous vote, it was overturning de jure racial segregation in America's public schools. Said Chief Justice Earl Warren, who was pivotal to the Court's unanimous decision, "In the field of public education, the doctrine of 'separate but equal' has no place. Separate educational facilities are inherently unequal." Thus was nearly 60 years of legally sanctioned injustice ended. Thus had Thurgood Marshall not only won his greatest legal victory, but he had helped spark one of the greatest transformations of cultural attitude and social practice ever to take place in America. His ultimate recognition was to be the first African American to become an associate justice of the Supreme Court.

The end of the "separate but equal" fallacy was only one of the many battles for equality being fought. In 1953, African Americans boycotted the buses in Baton Rouge and forced the city to let riders, regardless of race, be seated on a first-come first-served basis. In 1955, Rosa Parks refused to move to the back of the bus in Montgomery, and Martin Luther King, Jr., led the famed Montgomery bus boycott.

In 1956, the Supreme Court ruled the Montgomery City ordinances concerning seating on buses violated the 14th Amendment. Such discriminatory practices were stopped, and Martin Luther King, Jr., sat next to a white man in the front of a bus, which doesn't seem like much today, but was a milestone at the time. It was in 1957 that President Eisenhower sent federal troops into Little Rock to enforce the Supreme Court ruling outlawing segregation in public schools. That same year Eisenhower signed the first civil rights bill to pass into law in 87 years.

These gains notwithstanding, no one, least of all the African Americans, thought historic injustices had been totally compensated and discrimination fully eliminated. Yet nearly 40 years after the *Brown v. the Board of Education* decision, one of America's most celebrated African American authors of works on slavery and freedom, Harvard sociologist Orlando Patterson, would offer this assessment of American race relations: "The sociological truths are that America, while still flawed in its race relations . . . is now the least racist white-majority society in the world; has a better record of legal protection of minorities than any other society, white or black; offers more opportunities to a greater number of black persons than any other society, including all those of Africa. . . ."

As if to exemplify Patterson's words, two images suggest how far America had come. Roy S. Johnson, the black editor-at-large of *Fortune* magazine (August 4, 1997), describes those wielding "The New Black Power," who, he says, "are power brokers in the executive suite." Telling the story of African Americans who hold positions such as the managing director of Morgan Stanley or the CFO of Disney, Johnson writes that they "have achieved levels in business beyond anything their parents dreamed." The second image is Cheryl D. Mills, a 33-year-old female, African-American deputy White House counsel, standing in the well of the United States Senate, addressing 100 senators on behalf of President Clinton, a white, southern male.

America has come so far, and yet there's still so far to go.

Chapter Ten

World War II

SUMMARY: Japanese and German moves in the 1930s. American reaction to war outbreak in 1939 one of extreme caution. America moves from idealism to pragmatism regarding a new war. The human, financial, material dimensions of the war. Britain and France lose empires. Europe's loss, America's gain in scientific talent. Rise of the Soviet Union as a world power. The Holocaust. Arrival of "total war." Home front work enhances role of women. War ends the Great Depression. G.I. Bill lays basis of "knowledge society." Decline of "higher sensibilities" in war's aftermath. The end of idealism.

The Second World War was actually a continuation of the First World War, and taken together, they may ultimately be seen as the most barbaric and traumatic global catastrophe of the Interregnum.

World War II erupted in 1939, but the causes had been mounting for years. In 1931, the Japanese invaded Manchuria. In 1935, Italy overran Ethopia. In 1936, Germany entered the Rhineland, and two years later Hitler entered Austria and occupied part of Czechoslovakia. In the face of these invasions, Great Britain and France did nothing, and America was so detached from world events that she was hardly aware of what was taking place. Thus, in September 1939, after making an alliance with Stalin, Hitler attacked Poland, and Europe was embroiled in its third war in 69 years.

America's reaction to the onset of the war was one of extreme caution. The country was overwhelmingly in an isolationist mood. The Great Depression was far from over, and a large number of people felt that America's entry into World War I had been the great blunder of their parents' generation. Indeed, when a 1937 Gallup Poll asked the question, "Do you think it was a mistake for the United States to enter the [First] World War?" *70 percent* answered "Yes."

So when war finally came to America after the Japanese attacked Pearl Harbor in 1941, there was little crusading spirit. Gone were the idealistic slogans–"Make the world safe for democracy!"–such as had animated Americans in 1917. There was no popular song in World War II comparable to World War I's "Over There." It was much more of a practical attitude–"Let's get the job over with."

The dimensions of World War II are almost incomprehensible. Sixty-one countries comprising 1.7 billion people (three-quarters of the world's population) were involved. More than 110 million people worldwide were mobilized for military service (12.25 million in the U.S.). The war cost over $1 trillion, more than the combined cost of all other wars in history (the U.S. spent $341 billion). Over *60 million* people died (the U.S. suffered 292,131 battle deaths).

When the killing and carnage were over, Great Britain and France had lost their empires (as had Holland) and were no longer world powers. As the war ended colonialism, it opened up an era of national independence such as the world had never known. It inaugurated the Atomic Age, an era when, for the first time in history, humanity possessed the capability of rendering the earth uninhabitable. It brought the Soviet Union to a place of world power she never before had enjoyed. It ended American isolationism and gave America a relative geopolitical preponderance of economic, political and military power not possessed by one nation perhaps since the Roman Empire. And of enormous significance, the way in which the war was ended laid the groundwork for a struggle between the Soviet Union and the Western democracies, a conflict which was to dominate America's mind and energies for the next 44 years.

Countless historians have written about the many political and economic factors that combined to bring about the Second World War. But if there was any one main cause, it would have to be the psychological change that took place in the German people during the first quarter of the 20th century, a shift that had its origins in the last third of the 19th century. Somewhere along the way, Germany replaced Luther with Faust, and the result was a certain psychic inflation, an overreaching for Germany's "place in the sun." That shift played a major part in establishing the psychological and emotional climate which accepted Hitler, a demonstrated psychopath, as the leader of Germany.

Hitler was the product of far more than just an inequitable Versailles treaty or the Great Depression. He was the product of a Germany that, despite the carnage of World War I, still harbored inflated dreams of empire. Hitler was not a conventional leader in the same sense Churchill, Roosevelt or even Mussolini were leaders. Hitler was a mythic hero, a savior figure, a personification of psychic elements deep within the soul of the German people. As william L. Shirer wrote in *The Rise and Fall of the Third Reich*, "Hitler's sickness was contagious; the nation was catching it, as if it were a virus." Hitler projected his own repressed shadow, as well as that of the German people, onto other races and nations. Such a projection of inferiorities formed the basis of his theory of a master race. Hitler was an extreme case, but similar shadow projections are found in virtually all the ethnic and national conflicts of the 20th century.

The Jewish people, of course, were nearly exterminated as a result of this shadow projection. One cannot talk about World War II without considering the Holocaust, the systematic killing of some 6 million Jews in Europe. Slaughter of large numbers of people was not new to the 20th century nor was it unique to the Germans. Zbigniew Brzezinski, former National Security Advisor to president Carter and one of America's most knowledgeable authorities on geopolitics, in his 1993 book *Out of Control*, estimates that Stalin caused the deaths of 30 million Russians; that at least 40 million Chinese were killed during Mao

Zedong's experiment with Communism; and that during the 20th century as a whole, no less than 167 million people "were deliberately extinguished through politically motivated carnage."

What is particularly incomprehensible about the Holocaust is not only the attempt to methodically eradicate an entire ethnic group (Hitler had explicitly defined this as an objective as early as 1928), but the inhuman scientific exactitude with which one of Western civilization's most cultured nations, the country that produced Luther, Bach, Beethoven, Kant, Goethe and Schiller, approached the "final solution." It is only if we understand the psychopathic underpinnings of Nazism that we are able to perceive the German rationale for their dehumanization of the Jews. For in becoming Faust, Germany suffered the consequences of its pact with the devil. In this, Germany represented the Faustian tendency that had existed in all Western nations and is so evident today.

This said, slaughter is slaughter, whether it's 6 million Jews in crematoriums, or an estimated 5 million German Christians who died resisting Hitler, or the Rape of Nanking, or who knows how many Japanese women and children (80,000 in one night) deliberately targeted by American fire bombs, or 135,000 men, women and children killed by American and British bombers in the firestorm engulfing Dresden, or 100,000 killed by the atom bomb in Hiroshima.

The fact is that the 20th century initiated the concept of "total war," something quite different from Clausewitz's strategic 19th century objective of destroying "the enemy's fighting forces." Total war had been initiated by the British during the Boer War at the start of the 20th century, and it resulted in the insane fact that in modern war, there are no civilians. Thus, for the first time in modern Western history, elements of World War II were systematically waged against the enemy's civilian population.

There were many results of World War II, but one stands above all others. Untold human and material wealth was destroyed, ravaging the fabric of collective mores and retarding the progress of civilization by decades, if not by generations. This is so despite the acceleration of technological development resulting from wartime R&D, for far more was destroyed by the war in human, moral and spiritual terms than was gained by new technology. It is not possible to have 60 million people–greater than the population of France–slaughtered in a little over five years–almost twelve million a year–without altering the course of civilized life. After the horror and nightmare of the Holocaust and the atom bomb, where was the collective sanction for the essential moral and spiritual underpinnings of what once was called Christendom? Such a question is not as academic as it might appear, for subsequent events have shown the Holocaust to be only one example of the apocalyptic nature of the turmoil now taking place in humanity's collective psyche.

Another result was the countless European scientists, such as Einstein, who sought refuge in America, thus raising America's scientific research capability to a height and quality perhaps never again to be equaled. (An estimated 1,100 German scholars moved to the United States, including over 100 physicists.) The Manhattan Project (atomic bomb) alone compressed into five years of research, engineering and manufacturing experiment and development what might otherwise have taken a generation to accomplish. Although Alexander Fleming had discovered penicillin in 1928, it was not until the war came that penicillin was produced in quantity for medical use. In fact, much if not most of the fundamental scientific work out of which grew the new wartime products such as radar was conducted by European scientists. What the United States contributed was a capacity for the organization of research, the ability to set up quick production lines, and energy for executing large projects at high speed.

Next to the 19th Amendment in 1920 giving women the right to vote, the war did more to enhance the role of women in society than did any other event in the 20th century; women flooded into the workplace vacated by men going off to Europe or Asia. Half of all the workers in American aircraft factories were women; by 1942, one out of three American workers was a woman.

The war expanded the power and role of government even beyond anything seen during the Great Depression. Indeed, it finally ended the Great Depression by more than doubling the dollar value of goods and services produced between 1939 and 1945 (1939–$91 billion; 1945–$215 billion). In 1946, at the historic Bretton Woods conference in New Hampshire, global economic institutions were created which were completely new in mandate and outreach.

Certainly one of the greatest domestic results of the war was the G.I. Bill of Rights, which provided government financial assistance for millions of returning veterans to pursue a college education. As a result of the G.I. Bill, millions of Americans who, prior to the war, would never have had either the inclination or the finances to attend college, now had the opportunity to do so. It is no exaggeration to suggest that the education offered by the GI Bill of Rights provided the intellectual and theoretical foundations for the "knowledge society" which emerged in the 1950s.

Arnold Toynbee points out that the war raised the Soviet Union to a military level where, for the first time since 1683, the West was confronted by a non-Western protagonist of equal strength. Between 1683, when the second Ottoman assault on Vienna was defeated, and 1945, the West as a whole was so overwhelmingly superior in power that nobody could challenge the Western powers outside their own territory. This power monopoly came to an end in 1945, and from that date until the demise of the Soviet Union in 1991, the West was confronted by relatively equal strength, or at least enough nuclear strength to offset any military advantage the West might have enjoyed.

World War II yielded thousands of heroes, but one person stands out above all others as the epitome of resistance to Hitler and his barbarism. Chosen by *Time* magazine as the man of the half-century (1950), Winston Churchill, prime minister of Great Britain from 1940 to 1945 and again in 1951, ranks as perhaps the greatest figure of the 20th century. Soldier, painter, author, bricklayer, orator, historian, parliamentarian, recipient of the Nobel Prize in literature, and statesman, Churchill's indomitable spirit held Britain together and defied a seemingly invincible Hitler until America finally entered the war.

Wars alter the course of nations in basic ways. It is not that a nation is on one course–interrupted momentarily by a war–and then that nation picks up where it left off and continues on as if nothing had happened. Wars put a nation on a totally different course.

Massive conflicts such as the 20th century's two world wars alter nations so fundamentally that only decades later can the effects be evaluated. It's not only a question of lost lives, destroyed physical assets or changed geopolitical relationships. War summons forth great energies; some would even say the most heroic energies a people are capable of achieving. Thus, after all great wars, there is a psychological release, a relaxation of effort and a decrease in civil authority, as well as a lessening of the influence of religious belief and moral code. People think differently about life after experiencing the terror and incomprehensibility of war's carnage. Young men who have been fighting far from home, away from the grounding and guiding influences of family and community, change their values and mores and are different people on their return home. It happened after the Civil War as well as after World War I. Those higher collective sensibilities of life that constitute civilized existence, especially manners, culture and aesthetics, tend to find their hold on a people diminished. Thus in the three-and-one-half years of World War II, Americans became a different people, and America a different country.

John W. Aldridge captured something of the sense of post-war America in his 1970 book *In The Country of the Young*. For Aldridge, "life in America had become frozen at the level of utilitarian existence." Reliance on the utilitarian, on "social engineering," has led to a style of life antagonistic to aesthetic and civilizing standards. The American ethos (dream) in the years following 1945 was based on "higher incomes, bigger houses, better cars, and more and more goods and services." It was a specious siren, which could only generate an inner emptiness, for such an ethos lacked the standards and the discipline that alone give permanence of culture or value to existence.

Perhaps the most significant long-term effect of the 20th century's two world wars is the loss of idealism in the Western world. The senseless carnage of World War I that eliminated a generation, and the incomprehensible horror of World War II which brought the world to the brink of self-destruction, have fostered a belief in disbelief by liberal intellectuals and an attempt to revivify some lost greatness by conservatives. Neither effort offers a forward-reaching vision for a new phase of human existence. "Progress" lost any practical meaning–other than producing more consumer technology–in light of the barbaric savagery of all sides in both wars. In this sense, the march of science replaced the faith of idealism in the imagination of America and the Western world. World War II certainly saved Europe and Asia from domination by dictatorship, but it also extinguished any belief in the possible "perfectibility of man," which had been the theme of the Enlightenment and the hope of centuries.

Chapter Eleven

Changing Cultural Patterns

SUMMARY: Different definitions of culture. American cultural cracks already apparent in 19th century. The psychological significance of *Moby Dick*. Spiritual malaise reveals exhaustion of traditional American culture. Fitzgerald and disillusion with American Dream. Rejection of the dominant American credo. The Armory show and the arrival of modernism. What was modernism? The enduring culture of the 1930s. The end of American innocence.

In considering the Interregnum, it is important to look at shifting cultural patterns, for never before has a culture changed so radically within such a relatively short space of time. By surveying the culture, we approach the artistic expressions of the Interregnum, and we even draw nearer to its psychological underpinnings.

"Culture" must be clarified here, as the word has collected a variety of interpretations. In its popular use, culture can mean pretty much whatever one wants it to mean. It has become any chunk of social reality you like or dislike. Exporting "American culture" includes "Levis" and "Coke," as well as "Bevis and Butt-head." "Corporate culture" defines the social and operating attitudes prevailing in a particular business, usually codes established by management and having little to do with aesthetic taste.

In anthropology, culture traditionally means the way of life of a human society, transmitted from one generation to the next by language, by symbolic media and by experience. All cultures have included at least four elements, without which no culture can exist: (1) social organization, (2) adaptation to a physical environment, (3) a way to "make a living," and (4) some system of values and accepted standards of behavior. Absent any one of these, culture collapses.

Jacques Barzun, former dean of faculties at Columbia University and former president of the American Academy of Arts and Letters, says culture means "the traditional things of the mind and spirit, the interests and abilities acquired by taking thought; in short, the effort that used to be called cultivation–cultivation of the self." To Barzun, culture is to educate the mind and spirit, to elevate one's self to a higher plane of understanding and sensitivity. Thus in most civilizations throughout history, the role of culture has been to cultivate the higher attributes of life–courage, nobility of spirit, generosity, self-restraint–to encourage wholeness of personality and to link the individual with some transcendent vitality. Part of the practical function of culture has been to help the human soul discriminate between what is beautiful and what is ugly, as well as between what is good and what is evil. The best art is continually at work educating the spirit of the age, offering up forms of life and civility in which the age is most lacking.

In *Culture and Anarchy*, which stands as one of Europe's most authoritative commentaries on culture, 19th century English poet Matthew Arnold described culture simply as "the study of perfection." Arnold believed a link exists between culture and religion. Religion, he wrote, "is the greatest and most important of the efforts by which the human race has manifested its impulse to perfect itself." Goethe went so far as to say that man "is only creative when he is truly religious; without religion he merely becomes repetitive and imitative."

The English cultural historian Christopher Dawson, in his 1947 *Gifford Lectures*, took Arnold's thought even further. "Throughout the greater part of mankind's history," Dawson wrote, "in all ages and states of society, religion has been the great central unifying force in culture." Indeed, the origin of the great cultures of the world has always been some spiritual impulse. Dawson reflects the Greek and Roman belief that art is a divine process, that the function of art is a spiritual act. Plato, it will be remembered, equated the study of art with the study of moral value. The renowned Hellenist Sir Gilbert Murray described the three major goals of Greek culture primarily in spiritual terms–humanizing the brutal masses, effecting universal concord, and proclaiming a unified world. As Murray wrote:

"This is the true message of our Hellenic and European tradition. Serve humanity; glorify God; go forth, not so much to convert, but to contribute. Live in the service of something higher and more enduring, so that when the tragic transience of life at last breaks in upon you, you can feel that the thing for which you have lived does not die."

Given this interpretation, the true gauge of a people's spiritual condition is not so much how many profess belief in a deity or attend a house of worship; rather, it is the tone and quality of their culture. Culture speaks to the overarching question of how people live together. At the deepest level, it reflects a people's spiritual and psychological orientation, a subject we'll consider later.

While these comments may appear far removed from "Baywatch" or "Seinfeld" reruns, they're important to an understanding of what's happening to American culture today, for our culture is primarily drawn from two sources: our European heritage, which includes the Classical Tradition; and our own experience of life. Dante, Milton, Shakespeare, Bach and the Bible were the cultural underpinning for educated Americans of the 18th and early 19th centuries. Lincoln categorically states that the Bible and Shakespeare were his two primary sources of education. In some circles in earlier times, it was taken for granted that to be educated meant to be versed in Cicero, Virgil and Plutarch which would be read in the original Latin and Greek.

By mid-19th century, American culture began to exhibit divergent strands. Melville and Poe looked into the darker side of life, finding a sense of the catastrophic and morbid. Others, while living in the same historical context, expressed the promise and possibility of exploring a new continent. No one exemplifies this more than Walt Whitman, who saw in America's future "the promise of thousands of years, till now deferr'd." The landscapes of Durand, Cole, Church, Moran and Bierstadt offer inviting opportunities of distant horizons. They portray ethereal qualities, almost spiritual essences. This is not surprising, as Americans such as Thomas Jefferson, James Fenimore Cooper, Ralph Waldo Emerson and Walt Whitman had long thought the sheer magnificence of America's seemingly infinite wilderness would produce a person of higher spiritual sensibilities than was produced by the atmosphere of the Old World. They believed, as F. Scott Fitzgerald later wrote, that "man must have held his breath in the presence of this continent . . . face to face for the last time in history with something commensurate to his capacity for wonder." (Fitzgerald was wrong, of course. Since he wrote that, our capacity for wonder has infinitely expanded as we have entered deeper and deeper into the mysteries of the cosmos.)

Yet what seems striking about mid-19th century American culture is the absence of depiction of the century's greatest crisis, the Civil War. As *Time* magazine's Robert Hughes comments, "The sense of pity, fratricidal horror and social waste that pervades the writing of the time, like Walt Whitman, and is still surfacing thirty years later in Stephen Crane's *Red Badge of Courage*, is only to be *seen* in arranged battlefield photographs like those of Mathew Brady—never in painting." Never in painting, that is, unless one visits the immense cycloramas in Atlanta and Gettysburg which, while perhaps not timeless art, depict the carnage of the greatest war ever fought in the Western hemisphere.

If a spiritual impulse is the initial impetus to a culture, it expresses itself over time in contemporary life. Gradually, over generations, even centuries, institutions take shape informed by an inner dynamic. In this way, the structures of civilization are built. And so it was with Western civilization and America; in one way or another, the spiritual impulse of Christianity provided the belief, assurance, moral anchorage, and sense of transcendent meaning that were ultimately expressed in forms of law, family, government, education and social relationships.

When such a spiritual impulse runs its course and starts to wane, or is challenged by new scientific information, then the beliefs that held civilized life together, as initially expressed, begin to lose their force, their coherence. The spiritual impulse and the culture lose their organic connection. This loosening process may be played out over decades, or even generations, but gradually the clear distinctions that had shaped the society–distinctions of national meaning, of family upbringing, of educational level, of social convention, of legal status, and especially of moral code–those distinctions become blurred and lose their clarifying force. Vastly different cultural patterns emerge. A people leave the old civilization, but a new one has not yet formed. This is the essence of an interregnum.

Something like this was taking place in America in the early years of the 20th century. It was seen in many small and large patterns. Conspicuous consumption was replacing thrift and decorum. More and more people turned to a psychoanalyst rather than a priest when they had personal problems. Progressive education rejected established educational traditions. A vaguely defined humanism spread a sort of a religion without theology. The dance craze of the Jazz Age reflected a desire to overthrow convention. Sexual "freedom" was advocated in order to soften the perceived confinements of Puritanism. Divorce became more accepted. Politeness, a social tool essential for regulating human conduct and relations, began to erode. Writers such as H.L. Mencken scorned religion and moral propriety, while Ernest Hemingway became the prophet of a "lost generation," a theme given expression in his *The Sun Also Rises*–a story of "the courage to endure rather than the courage to do," as one critic put it. A blurring of moral and, eventually, aesthetic distinctions took place as the ethos and social norms of an earlier way of viewing life began to dissolve.

Taken in its totality, this movement was a limited rejection of the dominant American credo–the belief in the certainty and universality of moral standards, the inevitability of progress and the primacy of traditional literary culture. This rejection was partially based on the mid-19th century intellectual atmosphere of the time–science, industrialization, exploitation of earth's bounties and a Christianity that had moderated some of what might have been considered its "sharper edges." Personifying this new "American relativism" was William James, possibly the greatest figure of American intellectual life in the first decade of the 1900s. James, who had a fascination with mediums and communing with the dead, embodied an acceptance of intuition and faith, as well as a certain skeptical practicality and materialism. This was a long way from the strict Puritanism of an earlier century. Author of *Principles of Psychology*, James founded the school of philosophy known as "Pragmatism," America's only major indigenous philosophical school and a philosophy well suited to the emerging age of technology. James, who was a "generalist" who fulminated against doctoral academic degrees, believed that the truth of a proposition is judged by its practical outcome. His "radical empiricism" rejected all transcendental principles. In one sense, James, who died in 1910, came closest to forging a synthesis of the old and the new beliefs that were vying for the American soul. He was a man who best embodied, in the words of one historian, "all that men of good will expected from the twentieth century."

A foreshadowing of a significant change of temper in American attitudes and culture could be seen as early as 1851 with the publication of Melville's *Moby Dick*, generally considered America's greatest novel and widely acclaimed throughout Europe at the time of publication as the American *Faust*. Indeed, spiritual alienation expressed in the opening pages of *Moby Dick* echoes the first portions of Goethe's *Faust*.

Moby Dick is far more than the absorbing story of a half-crazed sea captain chasing a "great white whale," as Edward F. Edinger explains in his *Mellville's Moby-Dick: A Jungian Commentary*. As a work of art, *Moby Dick* makes manifest the collective *Zeitgeist* of industrial America taking shape in the mid-19th century. Indeed, Captain Ahab's ship, the Pequod, is little more than a floating factory for the manufacture of whale oil and other whale-derived products. Just as the Native Americans considered it safe to kill particular buffaloes only if they maintained a reverent relationship to the "great buffalo," so whalers felt free to hunt whales as long as they held to their reverent attitude toward the sacred white whale, the one whale who will not permit himself to be captured. Thus, for those who understood the whaling culture, an assault on Moby Dick was nothing less than an attack on the very concept of the sacred.

Edinger shows how, on a psychological level, *Moby Dick* tells us that the "eternal images" of the soul–those images that had been contained in the prevailing symbol system of religion–no longer resonated in the depths of the American soul with the same intensity. Consequently the soul was submerging itself in the unconscious in search of a new container for its transpersonal symbols. Melville uses the symbolism of the sea voyage to represent the isolated individual's journey into his own depths. Thus *Moby Dick* suggests that some basic change in attitude toward life was already starting in mid-to-late-19th century America.

The changing temperament moved to center stage in 1913, when the first modern art exhibit in America opened in the 69th Infantry Regiment Armory in Manhattan. This was possibly the most significant art exhibit in America in the 20th century, and it drew over 100,000 viewers in the first month. Gone were the expressions of harmony and the monumental interpretation of a Raphael, the richness and humanity of a Rembrandt, or the transcendent themes of Church and Cole. In their place were more than 1,300 hundred paintings of Picasso, Matisse, Duchamp and many other European artists who fought to free art from the world of human affairs and, eventually, from visual reality itself.

Whereas a Titian or a Rembrandt concerned himself with the deep human qualities of the individual being, as portrayed in the magnificent faces of Titian's *Portrait of Francesco Marie della Rovere* or Rembrandt's *Aristotle Contemplating the Bust of Homer* (or his many self-portraits), human individuality is much less in focus in Renoir and Monet who were more concerned with tone, color and the play of light on the surface of objects, and it's gone alltogether by the time one arrives at Klee or Picasso. In essence, we see the gradual disappearance of the human being as a subject of art, as industrialism, urbanization and a rationalized social order replace an earlier agricultural period with its emphasis on the instinctiveness of nature. As one of the founding fathers of abstract art, Wassily Kandinsky, said, it was "as if I saw art steadily disengaging itself from nature."

In any event, the 1913 Armory show in New York signaled the arrival of *modernism*, which is not to be confused with the Modern Age, as a shaping force of American culture.

Inasmuch as modernism has been such a dominant impetus for 20th century America, it's worth looking at modernism as an artistic expression and at its deeper meaning. In its simplest sense, "modern" comes from the Latin *modo*, which means "of today" or what is current. Modernism's century was roughly from 1850 to 1950, and perhaps its heyday was between 1880 and 1930. It was based, in part, on the change in the temporal and spatial perception of motion and height that took place in the 19th century. For the first time, man could travel faster than on foot or horseback. Also for the first time, man could rise thousands of feet in the sky by balloon. These two possibilities gave people a new sense of their changing relationship to the landscape. New topographical patterns never before known became apparent.

This new perspective coincided with a broader awareness of Einstein's theory of relativity, which influenced a significant number of artists and intellectuals. A tendency existed to equate the relativity of physics with a relativity of standards or attitudes in the human world of art, manners and morals. As a result of the merging of all of these developments, modernism insisted on the meaninglessness of appearances, and it sought to uncover the substructure of the imagination.

At its heart, modernism was the cultural expression of the belief that life had lost its mystery, that men, not gods, can rule the world, that tradition must yield to experimentation in every aspect of life, and that at the core of life there is nothing, just the void of nihilism. Modernism, wrote the American literary critic Irving Howe, is "an unyielding rage against the existing order." The emphasis of modernism was a repudiation of the past, the belief that only the present has authority. Modernism's instrument in philosophy was criticism, its instrument in politics was revolution, and in art its instrument was the avant-garde.

The thrust of modernism was to substitute the aesthetic for the prevailing moral and spiritual order. Art increasingly assumed the role formerly assigned to religion. According to its adherents, modernism demanded liberation from all inner restraint, and the destruction of all prevailing forms. The aesthetic expression of this view required the attempt to eclipse distance, whether aesthetic, social or psychological. It held that experience is the touchstone of life, that tradition is to be negated, that art must pursue the infinite along all paths, even of eroti-cism, cruelty and terror. Modernism separated the aesthetic from tradi-tional moral norms. *Time* magazine's Robert Hughes suggests that modernism gave art "the necessary metaphors by which a radically changing culture could be explained to its inhabitants." Abstract paint-ing was a break with belief that a picture must represent a landscape, a person or a still life. The pure form of abstract painting, it was believed, would show the way to a world of pure spirit, manifesting, as Russia's Kazimir Malevich wrote, "The spiritual, therefore the divine, the universal."

One of the earliest spokesmen for modernism was Sergei Diaghilev, the famed impresario of the *Ballets Russes*. Said Diaghilev in a 1905 speech: "We are witness of the greatest moment of summing-up in history, in the name of a new and unknown culture, which will be created by us, and which will also sweep us away. That is why, without fear or misgiving, I raise my glass to the ruined walls of the beautiful palaces, as well as to the new commandments of a new aesthetic."

In hindsight, we see that, despite modernism's fresh perspective and energy, its major failure was that it never understood the universal function of tradition. Tradition is not a sentimental clutching to the past. Tradition presupposes the reality of what is timeless, of what en-dures through all ages. Tradition is the carrying forward of those atti-tudes and forms that human experience has taught us are the highest levels the human spirit can attain. Modernism waged relentless war against tradition, and, consequently, against the transcendent impulses tradition manifests and without which no society can endure.

The advent of modern art drew varied reactions. Theodore Roosevelt, who at the time was the most admired person in America, wrote in a report titled *A Layman's Account of an Art Exhibition*: "It is vitally necessary to move forward and to shake off the dead hand of the reactionaries. And yet we have to face the fact that there is apt to be a lunatic fringe among the votaries of any forward movement. In this recent exhibition [the Armory show] the lunatic fringe was fully in evidence, especially in the rooms devoted to the Cubists and the Futur-ists, or Near-Impressionists."

The Spanish philosopher Ortega y Gasset expressed perhaps a more focused view in his 1925 book *The Dehumanization of Art*. In Ortega's view, modern art was "avoiding living forms . . . a thing of no transcendent consequence." With the advent of cubism and surrealism, Otega thought, the distinction between the trivial and the important disappears. In the view of Thomas Mann, one of the great figures of 20th century European literature, the trivialization of art is indicative of a culture which trivializes God.

Toynbee expressed concern that "this generation is ceasing to cultivate its aesthetic sensibilities on the traditional Western lines." Toynbee lamented that we "have willfully cast out of our souls the great masters who have been the familiar spirits of our forefathers." Such abandonment of traditional artistic technique, in Toynbee's view, is "manifestly the consequence of some kind of spiritual breakdown in our Western Civilization." His conclusion was that "the abandonment of a traditional artistic style is an indication that the civilization associated with that style has long since broken down and is now disintegrating."

But there may be a dimension in abstract art that its critics didn't fully evaluate. It is a psychological fact that the artist has at all times been the instrument and spokesman of the spirit of his age. As the German artist Franz Marc, who died in the First World War, said, "The great artists do not seek their forms in the mist of the past, but take the deepest soundings they can of the genuine, profoundest center of gravity of their age."

The *Zeitgeist* of the Western world during the early years of this century was described by Bernard S. Myers in *Art and Civilization*. Myers, who served as a consulting editor for *The Encyclopedia of World Art*, writes of "the extremely strained conditions of the early twentieth century, a tense, nervous, doom-foreboding atmosphere [that] had its inevitable effect on the arts." The crises of the beginning of this century, Myers writes, "the social unrest, revolution, and threats of war–seem to have catalyzed artistic techniques. The fragmentation of reality and space tensions of Cubism," Myers continues, "the warlike dynamism of Italian Futurism, the tortured colors and forms of Expressionism, the chaotic impulses of English Vorticism, are evidences of what was happening in the minds of artists." The feeling of "imminent catastrophe" that was prevalent caused a "flight from every-day reality [which] reached its first climax in the early part of this century." As part of the psychology of the time, "this flight appeared in the wildness of the Fauves, in the form analysis and destruction of the Cubists and Futurists, and in the self-destruction of the Expressionists . . . The out-of-jointness of the times was proclaimed by artists, writers and musicians, who were led further and further along the path of experimentation and subjective exploration."

The French painter Fernard Leger drew a clear link between art and the increasing industrialization of the Western world. "The age I live in," he said, "surrounds me with manufactured objects . . . If the whole way of painting has changed, it's because modern life has made this necessary . . . The condensation of the modern picture, its diversity, its dislocated forms—all result from the tempo of modern life."

Joseph Conrad, in his 1915 book *Victory*, saw the age as one "in which we are camped like bewildered travelers in a garish, unrestful hotel." Conrad's assessment of his times used such phrases as "the growing murderousness of the world . . . the erosion of the ancient edifices . . . the collectivist discipline."

Paul Klee, one of the commanding figures of early 20th century art, drew an even more succinct parallel between art and the spirit of an age. Wrote Klee in 1915, just as the battles of Marne and Gallipoli were introducing the terror of a new mechanized warfare, "The more horrifying this world becomes, the more art becomes abstract; while a world at peace produces realistic art."

The psychological atmosphere described by Myers, Conrad and Klee can readily be seen from the perspective of nine decades, but for politicians such as Theodore Roosevelt and others, it must have been virtually impossible to exhibit the same sensitivity to the emotional climate of the times as did the artists, writers and musicians.

Wassily Kandinsky notes in his essay "Concerning Form" that "great abstraction" and "great realism" have "always been present in art; the first was expressed in the second. Today it looks as if they were about to carry on separate existences." Aniela Jaffe, the Swiss psychologist, suggests that such separate existences are seen first, in Kazmir Malevich's 1913 painting of a black square on a white ground, which is the "great abstraction"; and, second, in Marcel Duchamp's exhibition of a bottle rack on a pedestal, which is the "great realism." Jaffe suggests that both these elements represent the two extremes of abstract art.

These two extremes, the naked object (matter) and the naked nonobject (spirit), Jaffe writes, point to "a collective psychic rift" that first appeared in the Renaissance "when it became manifest as a conflict between knowledge and faith." As Cartesian rationalism and the scientific method further removed man from his instinctual foundation, "a gulf opened between nature and mind, between the unconscious and consciousness." These opposites, Jaffe concludes, "characterize the psychic situation that is seeking expression in modern art." With these comments, Jaffe is expressing the very core, both culturally and psychologically, of the Interregnum.

In terms of our culture, there is no longer a "conflict between knowledge and faith." Knowledge has clearly won. The result, playwright and president of the Czech Republic Vaclav Havel reminds us, is that "we live in the first atheistic civilization in human history," a civilization which proudly asserts "that man is capable of knowing everything, describing everything and doing everything."

This loss of a collective spiritual orientation, which, from a psychological viewpoint is the loss of life's highest value, was increasingly reflected in early 20th century art. "Heaven is empty," Kandinsky wrote in *On the Spiritual in Art*. Nonetheless, Kandinsky turned against 19th century scientific materialism and positivism. Experiencing the "soul" and the spiritual dimension of art became his primary artistic goal, an effort that culminated in his 10 "Compositions," the greatest of which was Composition VII, completed in 1913. What Kandinsky may or may not have realized is that the very fact that he *consciously* sought the spiritual in art suggests that his search was no longer connected psychologically to that primal spiritual impulse which had given birth to, and which had informed, Western civilization.

Other artists took different approaches, such as the Italian painter Giorgio de Chirico, who declared that "Schopenhauer and Nietzsche were the first to teach the deep significance of the senselessness of life, and to show how this senselessness could be transformed into art . . . The dreadful void they discovered is the very soulless and untroubled beauty of matter."

When such an attitude prevails, destruction and dissolution actually become an art form. The goal of art appears "to be no longer the making of things but their unmaking," in Barzun's words. Travesty, ridicule and shock become high art. As Christopher Dawson wrote, "When the prophets are silent and society no longer possesses the channel of communication with the divine world, the way to the lower world is still open, and man's frustrated spiritual powers will find their outlet in the unlimited will to power and destruction." A few years before Dawson's time, D.H. Lawrence had written in *Women in Love*, "There is a phase in every race . . . when the desire for destruction overcomes every other desire." Or, as Dostoyevsky put it in *The Brothers Karamazov*, "Is there beauty in Sodom? Believe me, that for the immense mass of mankind beauty is found in Sodom."

The giant figure of modernism, of course, was Pablo Picasso. Perhaps no other figure has been so dominant in 20th century art. Picasso once told the French cultural historian Andre Malraux that he [Picasso] had no need of "style" because his "rage" would "become the prime factor in the style of our time." From the psychological standpoint, jagged edges, such as characterize Picasso's painting, symbolize rage, anger or anxiety. Indeed, rage has become a dominant motif of later 20th century culture.

One of the greatest expressions of Picasso's rage was "Guernica," his masterpiece depicting the carnage of the Spanish Civil War in 1936. Commenting on this painting, Alfred H. Barr, of New York's Museum of Modern Art, noted that Picasso's piece was not only of superb technical skill, but that above all, "it represents, or symbolizes, a society in the throes of destruction, as convincingly as Raphael's School of Athens represents a society in perfect equilibrium." Barr observed that Picasso was "not usually concerned with beauty so much as with power and intensity."

That sentence alone suggests a break with the underlying purpose of art as expressed throughout Western history.

Picasso's insight that people did not expect to receive consolation and exaltation from art was amplified in psychological terms by C.G. Jung. Jung wrote that Picasso's art no longer followed the traditional artistic ideas of goodness and beauty, but instead followed "the demonical attraction of ugliness and evil." From a psychological viewpoint, Jung said, the main characteristic of Picasso's art "is one of fragmentation, which expresses itself in so-called 'lines of fracture'—that is, a series of psychic 'faults' which run right through the picture."

Given the sentiments expressed by figures like Klee, Kandinsky and Picasso, it is not too difficult to understand what was in Oswald Spengler's mind when he wrote *The Decline of the West*. It was not the carnage of World War I that turned Spengler into what some people consider a raving pessimist. He actually wrote his two-volume work before the war started. Spengler simply believed that somewhere after 1800, the West had passed its life-creating cultural stage and was now in the autumn of its existence as a culturally creative community. He saw the future in terms of a "world-historical phase of several centuries." In point of fact, it is increasingly obvious that we have indeed entered such an age.

The development of modernism was given a powerful boost by the cultural aftermath of World War I. The war was far more than a military or geopolitical event. It was a decisive cultural and psychological event as well. The war offered horrific evidence that the Western world could not protect civilization from its own arrogance and evil impulses. Wrote English author Leonard Woolf, "In 1914 in the background of one's life and one's mind there was light and hope; by 1918 one had unconsciously accepted a perpetual public menace and darkness and had admitted into the privacy of one's mind or soul an iron fatalistic acquiescence in insecurity and barbarism." Historian Mark Sullivan used other words to describe America after World War I: "Lack of equilibrium . . . half-blind, half-deaf, and chronically dazed . . . a fundamental alteration . . ."

Many years later, the eminent historian William McNeil was to write: "In retrospect it now seems obvious that the institutional frame of Western society, as imperfectly readjusted during the nineteenth century to accommodate modern industrialism and democratic notions, had begun to heave and crack even before 1914.(2) The war of 1914-1918 set great chunks of habit and custom adrift like Arctic sea ice in the spring; each floe solid and recognizable in itself, like the wine bottles and guitars of a Picasso painting, and each one liable to drift–like the same bottles and guitars–into quite extraordinary juxtapositions with other shifting fragments of the disintegrating past."

Five years after the war ended, in 1923, T.S. Eliot published *The Waste Land*, described by Woolf as "the poem that had greater influence upon English poetry, indeed upon English literature, than any other in the 20th century." In Edmund Wilson's words, Eliot's poem "enchanted and devastated a whole generation." Rich in scholarship and spare in hope, *The Waste Land* reflected a "heap of broken images" for a generation whose idealism lay buried in the mud and trenches of France. James Atlas, an editor of *The New York Times Magazine*, suggests the revolution in language and writing exemplified by Eliot, Joyce, Proust and others was a response to the "social disintegration" left in the war's aftermath.(3)

The broken images of *The Waste Land* were followed by a different set of disillusioning images in F. Scott Fitzgerald's classic, *The Great Gatsby*, published in 1925. *The Great Gatsby*, the story of the corruption of the American dream, was America's first celebrated statement of disenchantment with the possibilities that Walt Whitman and others had seen in the American future. Many of America's more privileged people agreed with Daisy as she said, "I'm pretty cynical about everything . . . I think everything's terrible anyhow . . . Everybody thinks so–the most advanced people." This was written in 1925, when the stock market was booming, America's consumer market was expanding as never before and the "American Century" was in its ascendancy. As with many great works of literature, *The Great Gatsby* was not a smashing success when it was published. Critics called it "second rate" (after 15 years it had sold only 24,000 copies), and when Fitzgerald died in 1940, *Gatsby* was out of print. It was only in the 1950s that it became the classic it is today (which may tell us something about the '50s).

However, *The Great Gatsby* marks a distinct change in the tone of American culture. Gone is the sense of optimism and of life's possibilities that had marked much of the century before. As Rollo May has written, the "Jazz Age was the first throes of collapse of the American dream. *The structure of myths on which America had existed for four centuries was now thrown into radical transition.*" Fitzgerald's biographer, Andrew Le Vot, argues that the meaning of *The Great Gatsby* is clear, "that it is not men who have abandoned God, but God who has deserted men in an uninhabitable, absurd material universe."

America's new literary sensibility was one of doubt and disillusion representing, as Fitzgerald put it, a generation "grown up to find all Gods dead, all wars fought, all faiths in man shaken." Sinclair Lewis lampooned Main Street, while Gertrude Stein announced from the comfort of Paris that "the future is not important any more." As one historian noted, "to have a literary conscience was to take a bleak view of American life, human life in general, and the way the world was going." Difficulty itself had become a primary virtue.

W.H. Auden, the Pulitzer Prize-winning English author who became an American citizen, looked back on American literature produced in the two decades following *The Great Gatsby*. In 1948, Auden wrote, "Coming from Europe, my first, my strongest, my most abiding impression is that no body of literature, written at any time or in any place, is so uniformly depressing." Henry May has described this period as an "age of disillusion."

Nonetheless, this age of disillusion produced a new form of American popular art which would maintain its momentum through the 1950s–the Broadway musical. The Gershwin brothers, Cole Porter, Jerome Kern, Rodgers and Hart, Irving Berlin, Sigmund Romberg and Oscar Hammerstein produced music with a uniquely American tone, vitality and sensitivity. George Gershwin wrote what still stands as perhaps the quintessential American composition, *Rhapsody in Blue.*

The 1930s, despite the Great Depression, saw an explosion of creative expression, which included what still stands as some of America's most authentic culture. In 1930, Sinclair Lewis became the first American to win the Nobel Prize in Literature. For sheer pathos, few writers can equal John Steinbeck who, in the 1930s alone, wrote *Tortilla Flat, Of Mice and Men* and *Grapes of Wrath*. In 1936, Margaret Mitchell published *Gone with the Wind*, which, three years later, was made into what became one of America's most enduring movies. Dashell Hammett wrote *The Maltese Falcon,* which influenced mystery writing for decades to come. Pearl Buck published *The Good Earth*, for which she won a Pulitzer Prize as well as a Nobel Prize for Literature. Damon Runyon, William Saroyan, John O'Hara, Ogden Nash, John Dos Passos and Ayn Rand all broke into national awareness in the 1930s. And Carl Sandburg published *Abraham Lincoln: The War Years*, which won the 1940 Pulitzer Prize.

In 1931, the *Star Spangled Banner* was officially adopted as the U.S. national anthem. And it was in 1939, just as America was about to exit the Great Depression and enter World War II, that Irving Berlin released "God Bless America," sung by Kate Smith. Few songs have so gripped the national emotions as did Berlin's paean to the virtues of America.

In the theater, the 1930s produced Erskine Caldwell who wrote *Tobacco Road*, Lillian Hellman, who wrote *The Children's Hour*, and Orson Wells, who directed an all-black cast of *Macbeth*. Thornton Wilder's 1938 classic play *Our Town*, which won a Pulitzer Prize, expressed some of the enduring realities of human existence:

everybody knows in their bones that something is eternal, and that something has to do with human beings. All the greatest people that ever lived have been telling us that for five thousand years, and yet you'd be surprised how many people are always losing hold of it. There's something way down deep that's eternal about every human being.

"Big Bands" broke on the scene with Benny Goodman, Tommy and Jimmy Dorsey, Artie Shaw and Glenn Miller. Harry James hired a young vocalist named Frank Sinatra. Richard Whiting and Johnny

Mercer wrote a new kind of music for America–the musical scores for movies. Count Basie and Ella Fitzgerald contributed a new rhythm to the ever-expanding popular taste. Radio City Music Hall opened in New York, while Eugene Ormandy, conductor of the Philadelphia Orchestra, raised the orchestra to international status. The School of America Ballet was founded, as was the summertime Berkshire Festival in Tanglewood.

In Hollywood, Shirley Temple captured the nation's heart singing "On the Good Ship Lollipop," and in 1937, Walt Disney filmed *Snow White and the Seven Dwarfs*. It was 1939, however, that was the greatest year of Hollywood's Golden Age. In a single year Hollywood gave America *Gone with the Wind*, *The Wizard of Oz*, *Wuthering Heights*, *Drums Along the Mohawk*, *Stagecoach*, *Goodbye, Mr. Chips* and *Mr. Smith Goes to Washington*.

In newspapers, comic strips such as "Blondie," "Dick Tracy" and "L'il Abner" were introduced. Radio became a new source of entertainment for millions with programs such as *Fibber McGee and Molly, The Bob Hope Show,* and *Jack Benny*. In 1938, *Invasion from Mars*, a radio show produced by Orson Wells, caused panic when listeners thought the broadcast was a valid account of an attack from Mars. In 1939, television was introduced and the first baseball game was aired.

In the visual arts, in 1930 Grant Wood exhibited what has become one of America's most famous paintings, "American Gothic," while Edward Hopper produced masterpieces of bleakness and loneliness, not unknown attributes to the millions in the throes of despair caused by the disappearance of hope for work and its rewards.

The uncertainty and turbulence of the 1930s brought other tones and voices to the American cultural scene. In 1933, 11 years after its initial publication in Europe, James Joyce's *Ulysses* was finally permitted publication in America, an event which was in keeping with the increasing literary preoccupation with the subjectivity of the individual. In the words of one historian, *Ulysses* "marked not merely the entrance of the anti-hero but the destruction of individual hero-ism as a central element in imaginative creation." The traditional novel was a story of time against the background of permanence. But as James Atlas of *The New York Times* suggests, in the hands of Joyce and his contemporaries, "literature became a means of regis-tering states of mind rather than telling a story." The anti-hero is not concerned with the story of one's obligation to one's fellow man, but rather with what is owed to one's self. As Goethe said to Eckermann, "Epochs which are regressive and in the process of dissolution are always subjective, whereas the trend in all progres-sive epochs is objective."

Edwin Muir points out in his *Essays on Literature and Society* that writers such as Henry Fielding and Jane Austen had lived in an order in which everybody possessed "the feeling for a permanence above the permanence of one human existence, and believed that the ceaseless flux of life passed against an unchangeable background." The history of novels such as *Ulysses* and other modern novels, George Panichas points out in *The Reverent Discipline*, is "in essence the history of the mutation of this concept; it is the history of . . . the total rearrange-ment of society."

The nation's readiness to absorb *Ulysses* reflected a change in the American temperament; we became fascinated with the darker side of human nature as portrayed in a new genre of literature–the murder mystery–as well as in the radio program *The Shadow* ("Who knows what evil lurks in the hearts of men? The Shadow knows."). The word "shadow," denoting the dark side of human character, had recently been introduced into popular usage by Jung. And it gives a certain perspective to realize that an America ready for murder mysteries or for *Ulysses* was an America in need of the self-help therapy represented in the 1936 publication of Dale Carnegie's *How to Win Friends and Influence People*, the book that launched half a century of therapeutic self-help literature.

Despite the agony and despair of the Great Depression, and de-spite the mounting tensions in Europe, the 1930s produced a body of distinctly American culture, which may eventually be seen as the most lasting corpus of American culture produced in the 20th century.

Thus it was that the vast cultural tone of modernism spread across America and, in one sense, became the culture of the Interregnum. It's a shift that Henry May has termed "the end of American innocence."

Chapter Twelve

The Interregnum's Spiritual and Psychological Context

SUMMARY: A new worldview emerges. Impact of Nietzche. Lippmann and the "acids of modernity." Rationalization–the substitution of a technical for a natural order. Rise of a scientific and rationalistic culture. The struggle of science and religion. The Bible and historical accuracy. The Western discovery of Eastern spirituality. Freud and discovery of the personal unconscious. Jung and a psychological interpretation of history.

At the very heart of the Interregnum has been perhaps the most all-encompassing spiritual and psychological reorientation of the past two millennia. These twin reorientations began generations ago, they turn our life upside-down and their reorientation will continue to do so far into the future.

As the psychological and spiritual origins of a majority of Americans spring from our European heritage, it is to Europe we must look for the initial changes. Such changes help us understand what was happening to America and Europe beneath the surface of events in the first three decades of the 20th century, three decades that launched developments that have shaped our world ever since.

Changing Spiritual Patterns

Beginning in the mid-19th century, a new way of seeing the world began to open up, a perspective outside the Christian context, a perspective that is only now coming into its fullest expression.

In France, Courbet's Realism art exhibition created a new art which broke with established forms. Baudelaire's 1857 *Les Fleurs du mal* marked the beginning of modern literature. That same year Wagner composed *Tristan und Isolde*, considered by many to be the beginning of modern music. Darwin published *On the Origin of Species by Natural Selection* in 1859, which challenged organized religion's view of our human origins. We've already mentioned Melville's *Moby Dick*, which is as much a psychological document as it is a literary masterpiece. Shaw, Ibsen and Poe all offered new perspectives for interpreting the world. Marx published *Das Kapital* in 1863, which offered a radically different view of the historical economic process, and which laid the groundwork for 20th century Marxism and communism.

One of the most dramatic manifestations of this new way of seeing the world was expressed in 1883 in *Thus Spake Zarathustra*, a book by Nietzsche which announced his contention that "God is dead." This thought was not particularly new with Nietzsche, as the "metaphysical void" had already troubled the minds of many 19th century French and German poets. Indeed, even by 1850, Lord Tennyson, Britain's Poet Laureate, had warned of "the secular abyss that is to come." So it is clear that during the 19th century, much of Western thought and culture became secularized.

Although not many Americans in Omaha or San Jose read or cared about Nietzsche, he had a powerful effect on America's intellectual class. Yet it would be a mistake to try to draw a direct line of cause and effect between Nietzsche and the general secularization of America's culturally creative minority. It wasn't just Nietzsche who affected them. Many other forces, such as Freud's dismissal of religion as a "delusional remolding of reality," influenced a generation of American artists and intellectuals.

But Nietzsche is important, as he represents a landmark in the religious thought of Western civilization. What was he actually saying? Not that the Creator had died. Rather, he was saying that the spiritual impulse of Christianity had ceased to be the inner dynamic of Western culture; that the God who had been fixed and defined in terms appropriate 2,000 years ago no longer resonated at the deepest, life-giving levels of the Western psyche. He was talking about what happens when a society loses its unifying center of values. He warned that man's great advances in technique, without a parallel advance in ethics and self-understanding, would lead to nihilism.

The condition Nietzsche described profoundly affected some of America's "best and brightest." The impact of scientific rationalism on American intellectual circles was such that Walter Lippmann, perhaps America's preeminent 20th century writer-philosopher, writing in 1929, asked "whether the modern man possesses any criterion by which he can measure the value of his own desires, whether there is any standard he really believes in which permits him to put a term upon that pursuit of money, of power, and of excitement which has created so much of the turmoil and the squalor and the explosiveness of modern civilization."

Lippmann was talking about the dissolution of the religious myth that had contained Western society for some two thousand years. Nothing is more disorienting to a society than to lose its containing myth. ("Myth" is used here not in its current popular meaning of falsehood, but as a metaphor for life's transcendent reality.) At its core, that containing myth is the agency that provides life with a sense of order and with its highest meaning.

Others saw the same process of dissolution through a different lens. Joseph Campbell, author, educator and preeminent authority on the underlying meaning of world myths, wrote in the 1970s, "One would never have thought when I was a student back in the twenties, that in the seventies there would be intelligent people still wishing to hear and think about religion. We were perfectly sure in those days that the world was through with religion. Science and reason were now in command."

Campbell was not an insignificant figure. His understanding of religious symbolism is unsurpassed. Like Lippmann, he became a giant in his field. Their views represent what thousands of America's best and brightest believed. Indeed, we cannot understand our own time without appreciating such views.

Two particular developments coincided with this changing attitude toward religion, both helping to cause it, and resulting from it.

First, as Campbell said, science and reason were now in command. Science was giving an empirical interpretation of life that seemed to contradict much of what religion represented. The new scientific culture was an immense complex of technique and specialization without any internal guiding spirit or moral standard. The standard was efficiency. A technological civilization is a purely external order; it brings no inner moral gauge to the individual. It became a secularized scientific world culture, which is a body without a soul.

Religion, on the other hand, increasingly maintained its separate existence as a spirit without a body. America experienced a social schizophrenia which divided the soul between a non moral scientific will to power served by techniques devoid of guiding principles, and a religious faith and moral idealism which may have comforted the individual, but had minimal power to influence the course of events. The result has been that absent any commonly accepted spiritual orientation, America's new scientific powers were primarily directed to serve an economic consumerism, which people increasingly turned to in an attempt to fill an inner emptiness. In its baldest terms, America accepted a scientific secularized belief, coupled with a subordination of man to economic ends. Materialism became life's guiding principle.

Another aspect of the rise of science and rationalism was that various scholars, starting in Germany in the 19th century, began to look at the Bible in terms of its historical accuracy. Up until then, most people were inclined to be literalists, to accept a literal interpretation of the scriptures.

However, with rationalism and a new interest in scientific accuracy, in the latter half of the 19th century and continuing on to today, questions were raised about contradictory facts in the New Testament, and about stories which seem to defy the laws of both science and common sense. The reaction to the Bible seems to have gone from unquestioning acceptance to unquestioned skepticism, without ever pausing for consideration of the symbolism the Bible might represent. Considered from the standpoint of rationalism, Christian symbolism may not seem to represent external truth. But its psychological validity is not in dispute, for it served as a source of many of the more charitable and noble instincts of Western Christendom.

A second development was the Western discovery of Eastern thought and religion. At least since Alexander the Great, the West had known about the existence of Indian and Chinese sages and of Buddhism. But such awareness was somewhat shallow and confined to a small coterie of the more educated.

One of the consequences of the European global expansion that started in the 15th century was that for the first time, the West began to see Christianity within the comparative context of all world religions. This new knowledge started in the late 18th century, when the British were first exposed to Sanskrit literature. Then, between 1876 and 1910, some 50 of the Sacred Books of the East were published in English in Oxford.

In 1929, Richard Wilhelm, the German author and director of the China Institute in Frankfurt, translated the *I Ching* or *Book of Changes* into German, and it shortly made its way into English. Educated Americans were soon attracted to compelling Chinese modes of thought. While the Western mind carefully sifts, weighs, selects, isolates and classifies, the Chinese picture of life encompasses everything down to the minutest nonsensical detail, because all of the ingredients make up the observed moment. An alluring sense of wholeness entered America's awareness. This reeinforced the earlier exposure to Lao Tzu's *Tao de Ching, The Tibetan Book of the Dead,* the *Upanishads,* and Suzuki's *Introduction to Zen Buddhism,* all of which fed the searching minds of Americans whose traditional faith was being eroded by "the acids of modernity," in Lippmann's phrase. Indian gurus such as J. Krishnamurti opened windows of new possibility for many. As Anne Morrow Lindbergh wrote, "To listen to [Krishnamurti] or to read his thoughts is to face oneself and the world with an astonishing morning freshness." And in 1935, Arnold Toynbee went so far as to suggest that the influence of Eastern religion and thought on the West would be one of the most significant developments of the century.

Part of America's attraction to Eastern concepts was–and still is–a growing disenchantment with the reductive emphasis of Western science and rationalism. As a *New York Times* reviewer wrote about the *I Ching*, it offered Americans "a relation between the individual and his worlds undreamed of in the schemes of social engineers."

One result of the contact with Eastern religion was a move to synthesize the underlying realities of all spiritual belief and practice. Perhaps the best known of these efforts was Aldous Huxley's 1944 publication of *The Perennial Philosophy*. Rudiments of the Perennial Philosophy, Huxley wrote, "may be found among the traditionary lore of primitive peoples in every region of the world, and in its fully developed forms it has a place in every one of the higher religions." Huxley's book sought to present "this Highest Common Factor," which, he said, "is primarily concerned with the one, divine Reality substantial to the manifold world of things and lives and minds." He was quick to add that the nature of this one Reality is such that it can only be apprehended "by those who have chosen to fulfill certain conditions, making themselves loving, pure in heart, and poor in spirit."

The Psychological Reorientation

Underlying the spiritual shift taking place in America was a significant psychological reorientation. Part of the reason for this change was the major advances in psychology that took place in the early part of the 20th century. This raises the vital importance of psychology in understanding the Interregnum, for the mind is the foundation of human awareness and activity. The psyche–which includes consciousness and unconsciousness–is the instrument, the lens through which we perceive all reality. No assessment of the Interregnum is complete without such an understanding.

Psychology ("the study of the soul") first emerged as a separate and distinct discipline of life in the 18th century. It was Christian von Wolf (1679-1754) who, in his 1732 publication of *Psychologia Empirica*, was the first to speak of an "empirical" or "experimental" psychology. It was no accident that this happened just at the moment when the totality of the medieval world view was breaking down, and what had been known as natural philosophy was breaking into the separate parts of economics, sociology, psychology and philosophy. The impetus behind Thomas Aquinas's effort to bring all knowledge into a Christian synthesis had reversed direction.

"Psyche," the Greek word for "soul," was associated with consciousness throughout most of Western history. It was Sigmund Freud who first discovered the personal *un*conscious as an empirical, living aspect of the psyche. Freud, whose writings found a receptive audience earlier and more widely in America than in Europe, applied to the study of the mind the same rational and reductive methods scientists applied to the study of natural phenomena. He believed the study of a patient's dreams revealed what was happening in the patient's unconscious mind. Freud's psychoanalysis resulted from his belief that neuroses and psychoses were based on forgotten psychic traumas in early life–representing undischarged emotional energy, which Freud said was primarily sexual in nature–the well-known "Oedipus complex." Freud believed it was necessary to make a "dogma" of his sexual theory because it was the "sole bulwark of reason" against a possible "eruption of the black flood of occultism," Freud's term for religion.

In a bizarre turn of events, it may have been Hitler who ultimately provided the chief impetus to Freud and psychoanalysis in America. The great majority of psychoanalysts in Europe were Jewish, and citizens of Germany or Austria. As Hitler extended his rule after 1936, hundreds of Freud's disciples fled to the United States.

Given Freud's views of religion, it's not too surprising that the first translation of his writings was into Russian, and that the Bolsheviks were the first government to recognize psychoanalysis as a science. Professor Martin Miller, a historian at Duke University, notes that the

"Russian psychoanalysts were seeking a way to make Marx and Freud compatible. They wanted a collective psychology."

The second giant figure of early 20th century psychology was the Swiss psychologist C.G. Jung. Jung recognized Freud as the genius who had discovered the reality of the personal unconscious, but by 1912, Jung had accumulated a vast amount of psychological data that confirmed his earlier doubts about Freud's psychoanalysis and caused him to break with Freud. Whereas Freud saw the unconscious as a repository of repressed desires, Jung saw the unconscious as something of far greater importance, not only to the individual, but also to the whole course of human history.

Jung's immediate contributions to psychology are well known. *Extravert, introvert, archetype, individuation, complex, shadow, anima* and *animus, synchronicity, the collective unconscious,* and the *Self* are all words derived from Jung's experience that entered the general vocabulary. Much of the analysis of personality types done by corporate human resource departments today is based on Jung's delineation of the thinking, feeling, sensing and intuitive types of personality.

But Jung's work was of a far larger dimension than is generally understood. If we limit Jung simply to being a "psychologist," we miss the historic significance of his epochal work. In fact, in order to gain a full comprehension of the Interregnum, one needs a passing acquaintance with the significance of Jung's research and work, which offer a profile of the underlying human forces at work for the past century.

Jung and the 20th Century

Perhaps there is no one "right" way to assess the past. Because we each view events through the unique lens of our psyche–and no two psyches are the same–we differ in our interpretation of events. That is why historians, given the same data, will arrive at different interpretations of both cause and implication.

It was given to C.G. Jung (1875-1961) to articulate an interpretation of history that has moved our understanding onto a different plane. Like Gibbon, Tocqueville and Toynbee, Jung was a unique observer of events. In the 23 volumes which include his collected works, letters, interviews and autobiography, Jung offered the first comprehensive psychological interpretation of history. Most people have simply not read enough of Jung to appreciate this fact. Included in his research are probes into the turning points of the 20th century; the meaning of events that gave rise to Hitler, the psychological causes of the welfare state, and the genesis of the Cold War.

Never before had such a perspective been articulated, and through it we have gained an understanding of the continuing forces that were set in motion at the birth of human history. Trained as a psychiatrist, Jung was more than that. Psychiatry was an instrument of his work, but not the work itself. Of Swiss-German origin, Jung developed what some believe to be the broadest and most comprehensive view of the psyche ever offered. He articulated a fully developed theory of the structure and dynamics of the psyche in both its conscious and unconscious aspects, a detailed theory of personality types and, perhaps most of all, a full description of the universal, primordial images deriving from the deepest layers of the unconscious psyche. He called these primordial images *archetypes of the collective unconscious.* The latter discovery enabled Jung to describe striking parallels produced by individual dreams and visions, and by the mythologies of all ages.

The concept of the collective unconscious gives depth psychology an added dimension. It takes the theory and practice of psychotherapy and relates it to the whole history of the evolution of the human psyche in its various manifestations of art, myth, culture and religion. Jung thus offered a practice of psychology that was not only a therapy for neurosis but also a technique for psychological development applicable to every individual. For the individual, Jung declared, is the carrier of civilization.

Most historians have offered us a chronicle of the economic, political, technical and cultural aspects of the life of nations. On the whole, they have assumed that the inner subjective realm of the life of past ages was either much the same as today's subjective life, or not really relevant to the course of events.

Jung took a different view. He saw the individual as the being at the very heart of history. He saw the so-called "great" events of the world more as consequences than as causes. "In the last analysis," he wrote in 1933, "the essential thing is the life of the individual. This alone makes history, here alone do the great transformations take place, and the whole future, the whole history of the world, ultimately springs as a gigantic summation from these hidden sources in individuals." In Jung's view, in our most private and subjective lives, "we are not only the passive witness of our age . . . but also its makers. *We make our own epoch.*" [Emphasis added]

To more completely grasp how individual subjectivity has shaped events, Jung undertook a massive study of the history of the development of the mind. He wanted to understand and feel the inner life of earlier ages, for his research had led him to believe that each of us carries within us all the psychic residue of the past. He pushed his research back not only to Greek, Egyptian or Sumerian eras, but back into the mists of the prehistory of Neolithic culture, to the man who represented the original pattern of creation. His conclusion was startling: that beneath our conscious intelligence, each of us carries with us the evolved intelligence of humankind–the "collective unconscious." Each carries the remnants of that time when nature, not man's ego-consciousness, was in charge. This, Jung said, is "the two-million-year-old man that is in us all," a concept he expressed in a *New York Times* interview in 1936.

As Jung studied the history of the mind, he saw patterns that appeared to be common to every culture ever known. As Anthony Stevens points out in *The Two-Million-Year-Old Self,* all human communities, however "primitive," have always had laws about property, rules governing courtship and marriage, rules of etiquette prescribing forms of greetings and modes of address, cooperative labor, gift-giving, the performance of funeral rites, the recital of myths and legends, procedures for settling disputes, taboos relating to food and incest, dream interpretation, etc.

Jung defined all such patterns of behavior as evidence of what he termed "archetypes," or universal motifs stemming from the collective unconscious. These archetypes speak to us through our dreams, religions and myths. An archetype is neither passive nor inert, but a dynamic, autonomous agent that directs our actions in ways of which we are not aware. In Jung's view, what you and I experience in life is not determined solely by our personal history or conscious inclination. It is also shaped by the collective history of the human species as a whole, a history that is biologically encoded in the collective unconscious. This is the area where, as Laurens van der Post has written, "all men are one, where the brotherhood of man already exists." While we've learned volumes about the workings of the brain since Jung's time, he still stands as the 20th century's foremost researcher into the reality of the collective unconscious.

To more fully appreciate how this collective history has expressed itself in different cultures at different times, Jung traveled widely. In 1909, on his first visit to America, he analyzed the dreams of African American patients in St. Elizabeth's Hospital (for mental patients) in Washington, D.C. Jung uncovered motifs in the dreams of these patients that were identical with patterns found in Greek mythology. This experience corroborated his view of the existence of a "universally human characteristic," an archetype.

In 1912, Jung lectured at Fordham University in New York. While he marveled at the energy of Americans, and the power and scale of the civilization which that energy was building, he also saw a danger. In an interview with *The New York Times*, Jung suggested that whatever a man builds has the ability to destroy him; and that America was facing "a moment in which it must make a choice to master its machines or be devoured by them." As we consider the 21st century, more than one person is asking whether we do, in fact, control our machines or whether our machines control us.

In North Africa in 1920, Jung studied Europe from the perspective of a so-called "less-developed" people. He was struck by the slow tempo of North African life, so different from the "god of time" that governs the European (America is implied). This deliberate tempo, Jung reasoned, allows the North African to live a more instinctive emotional life, a life of greater intensity. He wondered whether the rationality of the

European, only achieved in recent centuries, had been gained at the expense of his vitality.

Jung was once again in America in 1924, this time in New Mexico visiting the Pueblo Indian chief Ochwiay Biano (Mountain Lake). His dialogues with the chief, which Jung recorded in his autobiography *Memories, Dreams, Reflections*, gave Jung his first picture of how non white people view the white man. The whites, Ochwiay Biano said, "are always seeking something. What are they seeking? The whites always want something; they are always uneasy and restless. We do not know what they want. We do not understand them. We think they are mad."

"Why is that?" asked Jung.

"They say they think with their heads."

Jung showed his surprise at this answer and asked Ochwiay Biano what he thinks with.

"We think here," the chief replied, indicating his heart.

Jung was deeply struck, and later recorded, "What we from our point of view call colonialization, missions to the heathen, spread of civilization, etc., has another face–the face of a bird of prey seeking with cruel intentness for distant quarry–a face worthy of a race of pirates and highwaymen."

But Jung was to learn another lesson from Ochwiay Biano. While he had not expected the chief to talk about religion, a subject which Pueblo Indians are reluctant to discuss with anyone, least of all a white man, the chief himself opened the door.

"The Americans want to stamp out our religion," he said. "Why can they not let us alone? What we do, we do not only for ourselves but for the Americans also. Yes, we do it for the whole world . . . If we did not do it, what would become of the world?"

Jung sensed that Ochwiay Biano was beginning to touch on the sacred mysteries of his people. "After all," the chief continued, "we are a people who live on the roof of the world; we are the sons of Father Sun, and with our religion we daily help our father to go across the sky. We do this not only for ourselves, but for the whole world. If we were to cease practicing our religion, in ten years the sun would no longer rise. Then it would be night forever."

Suddenly Jung understood the source of the dignity and composure of the individual Pueblo Indian. He is a son of the sun; his life is cosmologically meaningful, for he helps the father and preserver of all life in his daily rise and descent.

Jung later recorded, "The idea, absurd to us, that a ritual act can magically affect the sun is, upon closer examination, no less irrational but far more familiar to us than might at first be assumed." Our Christian belief, Jung noted, is "permeated by the idea that special acts such as certain rites or prayer or a particular morality can influence God." That man feels capable of formulating a relationship to the overpowering influence of the Creator, and that he can render something which is essential even to God, Jung wrote, "raises the human individual to the dignity of a metaphysical factor. Such a man is in the fullest sense of the word in his proper place."

Jung's visit to Kenya and Uganda in 1925 was to give him a new understanding of the consequences of Western colonialism. He asked a medicine man about his dreams and the role they play in the life of his tribe. "In the old days," the medicine man replied, "the medicine man had dreams, and knew whether there is war or sickness or whether rain comes and where the herds should be driven." But since the whites were in Africa, he said, no one had dreams any more. "Dreams are no longer necessary because now the English know everything." Jung realized that the medicine man had lost his *raison d'etre*. The divine voice which had counseled the tribe was no longer needed because "the English know better." In effect, the primal expression of the natural human spirit–which the African manifests–had been crushed by the imposition of Western rationalized modes of thinking and administrative structures.

But East Africa was to offer Jung one of his deepest insights into the meaning of human existence. Visiting the Athi Plains, one of Kenya's great game reserves, he was overpowered by the silent sight of the broad savannah unfolding across the horizon; the gazelle, antelope, zebra and warthog grazing, moving forward like slow rivers. This was the "stillness of eternal being," the world as it had been before humans achieved a conscious state.

As he experienced this stillness, Jung envisioned the cosmic role of man. "Man is indispensable for the completion of creation, for it is man alone who gives the world its objective existence." Without that existence, he wrote, life would progress through hundreds of millions of years in the night of non being. It is human consciousness that creates objective existence and meaning. "As far as we can discern, the sole purpose of human existence is to kindle a light in the darkness of mere being." The human being, said Jung, is the conscious awareness of the Earth, and perhaps of the Universe.

In 1918, as Jung studied the meaning of the dreams of his European patients, he recorded his observations of the "beast" that was ready to break out "with devastating consequences" as "the Christian view of the world loses its authority." He noted that especially in his German patients, he found "peculiar disturbances," images of violence, cruelty and depression which could not be ascribed to their personal psychology, but appeared to represent something in the collective German psyche. Accordingly, Jung, who as a Swiss-German was part of the German culture, turned his attention to the state of mind then prevailing in the German nation. His conclusion was that the "dechristianization of man's view of the world" was resulting in an uprush of unconscious forces representing "all the powers of darkness."

From the standpoint of psychology, Jung saw Christianity and all religions as "psychotherapeutic systems in the truest sense of the word, and on the grandest scale. They express the whole range of the psychic problem in mighty images; they are the avowal and recognition of the soul." All religions, in one way or another, he said, contain images that symbolize the conscious realization and fulfillment of an integrated personality. Loss of the spiritual connection to the soul, to a transpersonal realm, creates a "psychic split" or neurosis. Further work with patients from many European countries as well as America showed Jung that this state of mind was by no means limited to Germany, but was increasingly representative of Western man.

Thus Jung began to correlate the diminishing hold of Christianity on the Western mind and culture with the rise of psychology. There appeared to be a specific relation between the two phenomena. Why was it, he wondered in 1928, that "the discovery of psychology falls entirely within the last decades?" It could only be, he concluded, that "a spiritual need has produced in our time the 'discovery' of psychology." Formerly, people felt no need of psychology, as does modern man. "All through the Middle Ages," he told a New York meeting in 1935, "people's psychology was entirely different from what it is now." Psychologically, Christianity was a projection of the God-image in the unconscious, an image that is the ordering symbol of the psyche. But as Western man has become more and more rational, believing himself to be free from "superstition," the archetypal contents expressed by Christianity have come loose from their moorings. The result is widespread alienation; more precisely, modern man has put himself at the mercy of the psychic "underworld." As rationalism and scientific understanding have increased, so has man's world become more dehumanized. Technology, which has diminished our contact with nature, has also decreased the emotional energy that the nature connection supplied. Contemporary man, Jung wrote for the *Europaische Revue* in Berlin, "has lost all the metaphysical certainties of his medieval brother, and set up in their place the ideals of material security, general welfare and humanitarianism." In Jung's view, Western man had replaced his spiritual faith in the kingdom of God with a secular belief in the welfare state. In psychological terms, modern man has replaced an integrated personality with an over reliance on ego-consciousness.

Jung offered what stands as one of the most fundamental evaluations of Germany in the 1930s and the rise of Hitler. He noted that 20th century sophistication believes the modern world to be reasonable, basing this view on rational economic, political and cultural factors. But beneath the thin veneer of so-called Christian civilization exists another world of unconscious psychic forces, one of which, in the German psyche, is represented by Wotan, the ancient god of storm, rage and frenzy (which embodies the instinctual and emotional aspect of the unconscious). While there were many Christians in prewar Germany, Jung noted that "the god of the *Germans* is Wotan and not the Christian God." Today's rationalized mind may dismiss gods as primitive imagination or fancy, yet gods, in point of fact, have always personified psychic forces. Dismissing them as "unreal" hardly lessens their power as psychic factors in shaping reality. They just continue to act without our awareness.

So it was in 1936 that Jung wrote about the god of storm and frenzy which had seized the German people. "A hurricane has broken loose in Germany while we still believe it is fine weather," he wrote in Zurich's *Neue Schweizer Rundschau*. What struck him about the German phenomenon was that " . . . one man, who is obviously 'possessed,' has infected a whole nation to such an extent that everything is set in motion and has started rolling on its course towards perdition." What Jung saw happening in Germany was the collectivization of the spirit, a regression to the pre-Christian Germany of Europe's "tribal" past. The individualized man who was the product of Christianity was being taken over by a collective demonic spirit embodied in Hitler.

Notwithstanding Jung's comments, in 1936 Hitler's doctor invited him to come to Germany to analyze the *Fuhrer*, an invitation Jung speedily declined. Although he never met Hitler, Jung had seen him in person and had formed a clear diagnosis of his psychological state. In Jung's view, Hitler suffered from "hysterical dissociation of the personality," a condition exemplified by "auto-erotic self-admiration and self-extenuation, denigration and terrorization of one's fellow men, projection of the shadow, lying, falsification of reality, determination to impress by fair means or foul. . . ."

In a 1938 interview with Hearst's *Cosmopolitan*, Jung expressed the view that Hitler was able to maintain control of the German people for over a decade because he was "the mirror of every German's unconscious . . . the loudspeaker which magnifies the inaudible whispers of the German soul." One would have thought, Jung suggested, that the bloodbath of the First World War would have been enough. But that was not the case, as reality had been completely blotted out. Jung concluded that interview by saying, "America must keep big armed forces to help keep the world at peace, or to decide the war if it comes. You are the last resort of Western democracy."

After the war, Jung pondered the deeper meaning of the catastrophe that had taken place. Not simply the more obvious factors of the effects of the Versailles Treaty, or the isolationism of America, or the Great Depression, or Chamberlin's folly at Munich. Jung was probing the deeper psychological level which, in the end, determines human activity.

And thus, in one of the most profound analyses of World War II, he wrote in 1945 in the *Neue Schweizer Rundschau* (Zurich) that "the German catastrophe was only one crisis in the general European sickness." Well before Hitler, and even before World War I, Jung wrote, there were symptoms of the mental changes taking place on the continent. "What is wrong with our art," he asked, that most delicate instrument for reflecting the national psyche? "How are we to explain the blatantly pathological elements in modern painting? Atonal music?" That is a question that merits considerable reflection, for it comes from one of the most skilled psychiatrists of the 20th century.

In part, Jung wrote, this condition was the result of the fact that the "medieval picture of the world was breaking up and the metaphysical authority that ruled it was fast disappearing . . ." When a psychological projection, such as the God-image, ceases to be a living reality for a people, he explained, that projection goes back into the unconscious; the psychic God-image is a dynamic part of the psyche's structure. But the deflation of the God-image as a vital factor had left the Western world in a metaphysical vacuum. "This, then, is the great problem that faces the whole of Christianity: where now is the sanction for goodness and justice, which was once anchored in metaphysics? Is it really only brute force that decides everything? Is the ultimate authority only the will of whatever man happens to be in power?"

As the questions Jung was asking in 1945 remain at the core of the Interregnum, it is fitting to close this chapter with his own words:

> Everything possible has been done for the outside world:
> science has been refined to an unimaginable extent,
> technical achievement has reached an almost uncanny
> degree of perfection. But what of man, who is expected to
> administer all these blessings in a reasonable way? He has
> simply been taken for granted. No one has stopped to

consider that neither morally nor psychologically is he in any way adapted to such changes. As blithely as any child of nature he sets about enjoying these dangerous playthings, completely oblivious of the shadow lurking behind him, ready to seize them in its greedy grasp and turn them against a still infantile and unconscious humanity. . . .

The question remains: How am I to live with this shadow? What attitude is required if I am to be able to live in spite of evil? In order to find valid answers to these questions a complete spiritual renewal is needed. And this cannot be given gratis, each man must strive to achieve it for himself. Neither can old formulas which once had a value be brought into force again. The eternal truths cannot be transmitted mechanically; in every epoch they must be born anew from the human psyche.

Answering these questions may well determine what purpose and meaning we give to the 21st century.

Chapter Thirteen

Summary of 1900-1950

SUMMARY: 1950 and the loss of optimism. America–another Carthage or Greece? What makes civilized life possible? Expansion of the social agenda. Summation of the first half of the 20th century.

Beyond the many obvious material differences between the America of 1900 and of 1950, two differences of attitude stand out. In 1900, America was a nation of optimistic, relatively unsophisticated people of modest means who, whatever hardships they had known, saw in America the chance of a better life. As the president of Stanford University, David Starr Jordan, expressed it in his turn-of-the-century book *The Call of the Twentieth Century*, "The man of the Twentieth Century will be a hopeful man. He will love the world and the world will love him." Whether this man was someone newly arrived from Ireland or Italy, or whether he was someone moving West for a new opportunity, this 20th century man was a part of an America still in the process of "becoming."

By 1950, that process of becoming had matured to the point where America had "become," and the national mood was different. While perhaps not wealthy by today's standards, America had risen to be the wealthiest nation the earth had ever known. Whether it was the debilitating effects of this abundance, whether it was the rationalizing effects of intellect, whether it was the slippage of moral code . . . whatever it was, a different voice was now heard. Harvard University's president, A. Lawrence Lowell, gave expression to this new voice when he asked "whether America was becoming another Carthage, with its commercial civilization which left no mark on history, rather than becoming another Greece, with its respect for learning, philosophy and the arts."

Author Bruce Bliven, in his 1951 book *Twentieth Century Unlimited*, said the major difference between the America of 1950 and the America of 1900 was "the alteration in the moral climate from one of overwhelming optimism to one which comes pretty close to despair." Historian Frederick Lewis Allen asked in 1951 whether "our technological and economic triumphs are barren because they have brought us no inner peace."

This new mood did not suddenly materialize out of thin air in 1950. As the Interregnum had proceeded during the first half of the century, doubts about the path America was on were expressed by many of America's most perceptive voices.

In 1932 the Japanese invaded Manchuria, and Austrian-born Hitler received his German citizenship so he could become Chancellor the following year. In that year American historian James Truslow Adams (who was the first to use the phrase the "American Dream") identified one of the great problems of the world as "how to preserve, in a mechanized and democratic order, those higher human values which have been slowly evolved in the past 2000 years." Adams questioned how America would make "a deep and radical adjustment to a changed social environment without sinking into a new dark age as a period of transition."

In 1940, as Radio Corporation of America (RCA) built the first electron microscope and Vought-Sikorsky made the first successful helicopter flight in the U.S., British author John Buchan looked at America and pondered the technological world that was emerging. He wondered what it would eventually be like. "In such a world," he wrote, "everyone would have leisure. But everyone would be restless, for there would be no spiritual discipline in life. Some kind of mechanical philosophy of politics would have triumphed, and everybody would have his neat little part of the state machine. Everybody would be comfortable, but since there could be no great demand for intellectual exertion, everybody would be also slightly idiotic. Their shallow minds would be easily bored, and therefore unstable. Their life would be largely a quest for amusement. The raffish existence led today by certain groups would have become the normal existence of large sections of society." Buchan described it as a "de-civilization, a loss of the supreme values of life."

In 1942, as Fermi split the atom and the first computer was developed, author Herbert Agar asked whether America was losing the very conditions that make civilized life possible. In Agar's view, a "social order without moral purpose fails to sustain life." Agar was concerned that "the Western world has talked as if civilization were a by-product of economic progress." Civilization, Agar argued, requires the discipline and standards with which to judge the value of thought and action. In the end, he wrote, civilization "rests upon power to discriminate in the name of moral values."

So this was one difference of attitude between the America of 1900 and 1950.

Another difference stood in contradiction to those who felt a sense of gloom. It was well expressed by Frederick Lewis Allen: "During the half century the answer to the ancient question, 'Who is my neighbor?' received a broader and broader answer." This answer expressed itself in a markedly expanded sense of public obligation, an obligation taken for granted today. Look at what happened in fifty years: Child labor laws, pure food and drug laws, public health service, expanded educational opportunities for almost everyone, unemployment insurance, women's rights, workmens' compensation, minimum wage, retirement insurance, health benefits, collective bargaining, criminal parole and probation, equal opportunity codes, equal rights laws, voter's rights laws to name just a few. True, all of these benefits were first enacted in some other country, but the record shows they all were enacted in America in the first 50 years of this century. That is a significant expansion of our attitude about our obligation to each other as citizens and human beings.

In summation,
during the first half of the 20th century . . .

- We consolidated incorporation of the remaining continental territories into the U.S. and, in effect, completed the building of the nation;
- We absorbed 20,203,879 immigrants, mostly from Europe;
- We finished the transition from an agricultural to an industrial society, from a rural to an urban nation;
- Our population doubled, and life expectancy jumped from 49 to 68 years;
- We changed our mode of living from a stationary to a mobile existence;
- We shifted our economic base from one of laissez-faire to a mixed economy;
- We invented the world's first Consumer Society where "wants" became "needs;"
- We moved labor-management relations from bitter antagonism to collective bargaining;
- Through radio and television, we created the age of instant global information;
- Our national debt skyrocketed from $1 billion to $257 billion (nominal dollars);
- We altered the status of women more fundamentally than it had been altered in any comparable half-century in the past one thousand years;
- We moved from being *a* world power to being *the* world power;
- Although it's hard to quantify, along with our European cousins, we may have experienced a greater diminishing of the Christian faith as the foundation of collective belief than had taken place in any other 50-year period in Western history;
- We inaugurated the age of flight, thus shrinking time and space to a degree never before experienced;
- Our culture lost its anchorage in traditional inner symbols of psychological wholeness;
- We developed management of large institutions as a new professional discipline;

- We created an intellectual class which, by and large, accepted the power of reason as life's highest authority;
- Our relations between the sexes underwent greater redefinition than in any other period of our history up to that time;
- We developed the possibility of destruction on a scale never before envisioned by the human mind;
- We developed the theoretical scientific basis for computers and for the information technologies of the quantum age;
- We discovered and explored the workings of the unconscious psyche and its relationship to all other aspects of human life;
- We gave our people a level of affluence and comfort probably not even enjoyed by royalty in past ages;
- We preserved Europe and Asia from military domination by Germany and Japan;
- We probably used up more natural resources than had been used by the whole of humanity in all prior history; and
- We absorbed more people from more parts of the world, giving them fresh opportunities in life, than had any other nation in history over a comparable period.

In short, more people experienced greater change in their attitudes and habits of living in a shorter space of time than had any people on the face of the planet up to the 20th century.

Chapter Fourteen

The Context

SUMMARY: The appearance of a new phase of history. Drucker defines the "postmodern" era. A new geopolitical pattern. The changing nature of change. The shifting information environment. Science's new assumptions. Major Western intellectual themes evaporate. A single human community as the defining reality. Mumford's response to the transformation of civilization.

By the 1950s, it was clear to thoughtful people that America and the world had entered a new stage of history. It was more than just a "postwar" period. It was something qualitatively new. We had entered the heart of the Interregnum.

This new phase seemed somehow to have come unhooked from the past. It was free-floating into a new dimension where the ground rules were unknown, where relationships lacked definition, where beliefs fragmented, and where historic forms of governance appeared threatened by population mass, new technology and seemingly unlimited possibilities. It was a new world shaped by different dynamics.

In the mid-1950s, Peter Drucker took a look at these new dynamics and defined their essential features. While Drucker is known primarily as an authority on management, he has few peers in his 60 years of writing on the scope and nature of the Interregnum's "new realities" reordering America and the world.

By 1950, Drucker contended in *Landmarks of Tomorrow* (1957) that the Modern Age had come to a close, and America had entered a postmodern world with its new concepts, capacities, realities and worldview. It was a world without any integrated order of values and perceptions, and thus it lacked a distinct character. Until such an order of values and perceptions was identified, the world could only be defined as "post" something else rather than with a definitive contemporary name.

At heart, as Drucker wrote, a worldview is the result of a common experience. It is a foundation for artistic perception, philosophical analysis and technical vocabulary. The new worldview Drucker saw unfolding was first and foremost "post-Cartesian." For 300 years, Drucker asserted, the ideas of Rene Descartes determined what problems would appear important to Western life; they delineated the scope of modern man's vision, his basic assumptions, and above all, his concept of what is rational and plausible. The best-known formulation of Descartes's axiom was given by the Academie Francaise: "The certain and evident knowledge of things by their causes."

That the whole is the sum of its parts had been an axiom of arithmetic for almost 2,000 years before Descartes. But Descartes implied that the whole is determined by the parts, and thus we can know the whole by identifying and knowing the parts. Through his Analytical Geometry and its quantitative logic, Descartes provided the method to make his axiom effective in organizing knowledge. Reality was what could be seen, quantified, and verified by repeated experiment. As one scientist later summarized Descartes, "I know what I can measure."

The new worldview that was shaping the future, Drucker wrote, had moved from parts to patterns, from cause to configuration. He pointed out how psychology talks about "gestalt"; social science speaks of "culture" and "integration"; the business enterprise talks of "management" and "automation." Government talks of the "political process," while engineering speaks of "systems" and "quantum." Even education refers less to "grammar"–the study of the parts of speech–and more and more about "communications." These new concepts, Drucker maintained, conform to a new assertion, that the parts exist in contemplation of the whole–a view that quantum physics has made today's conventional wisdom but which was not so widely accepted at the time Drucker wrote.

Moreover, Drucker contended, "causation," the unifying axis of the Cartesian worldview, had disappeared. Underlying the new concepts is a unifying idea of order. It is not causality, but "purpose" that infuses the new concepts. He went so far as to declare that "the elements . . . will be found to arrange themselves as to serve the purpose of the whole." Quoting Edmund W. Sinnott's *The Biology of the Spirit*, Drucker wrote: "Life is the imposition of organization on matter." This purpose, Drucker wrote, is in the configurations themselves; it is not metaphysical but physical, not purpose *of* the universe but purpose *in* the universe.

In addition to purpose, the new worldview, Drucker declared, assumes *process*. Every one of the new concepts embodies process in the idea of growth, development, rhythm or becoming.

Although we have abandoned the Cartesian worldview, Drucker wrote, we have not, so far, developed a new synthesis, new axioms of meaning, order and inquiry. As our knowledge advances, it becomes more specialized rather than more general, a fact Drucker thought proves that we still lack a philosophical integration appropriate to the world that is emerging. For the first time in perhaps 700 years, the unity of the universe is gone for Western man. Lacking such a synthesis, he said, we are in intellectual and aesthetic crisis in every area of life.

In the final chapter of *Landmarks of Tomorrow*, Drucker returns to the problem that occupied Henry Adams 50 years earlier: the question of knowledge and power. Knowledge and power, Drucker maintained, had changed their very meaning, and as a result, *the meaning of man is changing*. As 20th century man has achieved the knowledge and power to destroy himself both physically and morally, a new dimension has been added to human evolution. Knowledge and power, Drucker acknowledged, have been problems ever since the Garden of Eden. But now they are at the center of human existence.

Only two or three generations ago states Drucker, knowledge was essentially a private affair. Science was the pursuit of knowledge for the sake of knowledge. "Today science, whether we like it or not, is increasingly the pursuit of knowledge for the sake of power. No concept of knowledge we possess faces up to this new reality of human existence."

In the final passages Drucker writes:

> The problem created by the breakthrough of scientific knowledge to the core of human existence is not political. It is spiritual and metaphysical. It poses the question: What is the meaning of knowledge and power? Knowledge and power being specifically human among the attributes of the creature, the question really is: What is the meaning of human existence and of human spirit? These questions are as old as man. But absolute knowledge adds to them new urgency and new depth. . . .
>
> If we do not know what power is for, we cannot say what its limits are. If we do not specify its proper use we will not be able to stop its abuse
>
> Both knowledge and power, traditionally ends in themselves, must now become means to a higher end of man. Both knowledge and power must be grounded in purpose—a purpose beyond the truth of knowledge and the glory of power. We must demand that both control themselves, direct themselves, limit themselves in and through the purpose for which they accept responsibility.

Much of what Peter Drucker articulated in *Landmarks of Tomorrow* has passed into the stream of common understanding despite the fact that we have yet to come to terms with its implications. But what he wrote was far from conventional wisdom in the 1950s.

Against the background of Drucker's analysis, certain major trends of the second half of the 20th century stand out. In assessing the trends, the *scale of observation* we employ is crucial. If we evaluate what's happening to America within the frame of reference of the four-year presidential election cycle, we'll arrive at one conclusion. If we widen our frame of reference to encompass a decade, say the 1960s or the 1980s, we'll reach another conclusion. If we broaden our frame of reference still further, say, to the whole of the 20th century, which was Drucker's context, or even to the past five centuries, we'll arrive at an altogether different judgment. For it is as Goethe wrote: "He whose vision cannot cover / History's three thousand years, / Must in outer darkness hover, / Live within the day's frontiers." It is only against the widest scale of observation that we begin to have a basis for assessing the megatrends that have been shaping the global landscape and altering the daily existence of every person on the planet.

Such megatrends include:

A new geopolitical pattern. We are at the end of a 450-year period when the nations bordering the Atlantic Ocean dominated world political, economic and military affairs. Non-Western nations are now major players. For the first time in modern history, China and Japan have larger economies than any European nation.

In fact, for the first time in 500 years, Europe is no longer a formative force in shaping global affairs. Europe has assumed an inward posture trying to define its own 21st century. Vaclav Havel notes that the restructuring now taking place in Central Europe and the Eurasian landmass might be "as extended and complex a process as the creation of a Christian Europe" in the centuries following the Roman Empire.

A new historical epoch is emerging in which the realization of national aspirations is no longer solely a national event. The 20th century has brought to a close distinctive national histories, and all events are now merged into a worldwide process.

Part of this change entails the end of the world political, economic and military predominance America enjoyed roughly from 1945 to 1973. We are not, as is often claimed, the world's sole remaining superpower. True superpower status entails political and economic as well as military power. The superpower standing we enjoyed in the late 1940s and 1950s enabled America to restructure the world trade and financial system, create global economic institutions, and launch the Marshall Plan. Our political power enabled President Eisenhower to force Britain and France out of the Suez in 1956. Today, we are clearly the world's sole military superpower, but we no longer have the relative economic and political preponderance of just a few decades ago.

The nature of change itself is being altered. For the past 500 years, the West has been the primary agent of change in the world. Now, the ability to create change–as well as the attitude that change is desirable–is a global possession. So today we have economic, technological, social, political and cultural change taking place simultaneously from India to Mexico, from Egypt to Kajikistan. Planetary change, potentially affecting the physical balance of all life on the planet, now reaches into every aspect of individual human activity, and has become a social and psychological dynamic with a force and magnitude never before experienced.

It is as J. Robert Oppenheimer, father of the atomic bomb, has written: "One thing that is new is the prevalence of newness, the changing scale and scope of change itself, so that the world alters as we walk in it, so that the years of man's life measure not some small growth or rearrangement or moderation of what he learned in childhood, but a great upheaval."

This is a reversal of history. Throughout history, in all civilizations, *continuity* rather than change has been the desired state of affairs. No society on the planet knows how to live with constant, radical change. It has never been done before.

What we've created with our emphasis on constant change is a *clash of different time scales.* The time scale created by technology clashes with the time scale required by natural life. Unhurried time is essential for growth. Yet speed, which is the obliteration of time, is increasingly necessary for the modern economy. Some people suggest that we've moved out of the age of speed and have entered the era of "real time." They say we now have a single "world time."

Severe change has psychological effects about which we know very little. Among other things, severe change weakens, or even destroys, tradition. For tradition is the outward expression of those inner collective images that form the cohesion of civilized life. Tradition is an expression of the life of human instinct. Age-old convictions and customs are deeply rooted in the instincts, and if they get lost, the conscious mind becomes severed from the instincts and loses its roots. Any society that loses its traditions weakens its psychological moorings. So constant change, as a desired principle, however convenient in the short term, cannot anchor a civilization for long.

At some point, acceleration of time and change beyond a people's capacity for assimilation generates counter-productive effects. Such results destroy existing structures while undermining the very goals to be achieved.

The information environment in which the individual lives is being radically altered. Throughout history, the transmission of information, ideas and images took place slowly, taking generations, even centuries, to move around the world. Such a slow pace of information travel gave people time to adjust psychologically to a new information environment.

Today we zap information, ideas and images across the globe in nanoseconds. People have no time to adjust, no time to shape the new information into any coherent meaning. If one were to read the entire edition of the Sunday *New York Times*, one would absorb–or be exposed to–more information in that one reading than was absorbed in a lifetime by the average American living in Thomas Jefferson's day. Microsoft's CD-ROM encyclopedia has surpassed all printed encyclopedias in sales. This is the greatest shift in the presentation of encyclopedias since Diderot published the first encyclopedia over 300 years ago.

This flood of information is going to increase. Intel is installing computers in the National Laboratories capable of cracking speeds of 1 teraflop, or one trillion calculations a second. They're already planning for computers capable of 10 teraflops, and even 100 teraflops.

Boundaries are disappearing. One consequence of the new communications ability is that we're zapping all the artificial boundaries that have been erected over centuries. Throughout history, national, cultural and ethnic boundaries helped define a person, group or nation. Now these boundaries are collapsing. While cultural and national groupings will continue to exist, they no longer form the outer limits of a people's psychological awareness.

This collapse of boundaries is bringing with it a redefinition of nationhood. It's happening everywhere—in Russia, Central Europe, Germany, South Africa and India. Such boundary erosion is changing the demographic composition and cultural underpinnings of America. Before 1960, for example, 80 percent of the immigration came from Europe. Since 1960, 80 percent has come from places other than Europe. Miami is now the northernmost city of Latin America. Dade County, Florida, copes with 123 nationalities in the school system. Chicago has more Muslims than Methodists, more Hindus than Presbyterians. In another decade, America will have more Muslims than Jews. By 2025, Spanish may be the standard language of the average person in Southern California, with English as the language of the professional or wealthier class. Already, public opinion polls show that the majority of people in California feel a closer affinity with the nations of the Pacific Basin than with the states on the Eastern seaboard.

No one suggests that the nation-state is about to disappear. But as people's awareness and experience expand, so does their collective sense of identification. Early Americans had a fierce adherence to their state. Virginia and Massachusetts meant more than did the larger concept of the United States. The most distinguished American general of the 19th century, Robert E. Lee, declined to lead his nation in war in order to lead his state.

It might well be that the most sharply defined sense of American identity showed itself in the century between 1850 and 1950. In terms of a "collective soul," that period may actually have been the true "American Century." Indeed, it should be asked whether today's multicultural, multiethnic America is bound together more by mutual interests than by shared convictions.

On the personal level, the old boundaries no longer supply a relevant psychological border providing individual identity. Thus the question of *identity* has become a basic issue for everyone. People ask, "With whom do I identify? Who is my group? Indeed, do I even have a group any longer?"

The answer, of course, is that all the old classifications of identity are being subsumed into a larger whole. From Alaskan Inuit to New York intellectual, from Southern Baptist to Parisian nihilist, from Muslim fundamentalist to European neofascist, what each person faces is the need to adjust to dissolving traditional borders and boundaries of identification. "East is East, and West is West," but the two *are* meeting, Kipling not withstanding.

The assumptions underlying almost 400 years of science are yielding to new assumptions. The scientific enterprise was built on three Cartesian assumptions: (1) There is an objective universe that can be explored by methods of scientific inquiry; (2) Anything scientifically "real" has basic data that are physically observable–that is, measurable; and (3) Scientific investigation consists of reducing complex phenomena to their more elemental parts.

These three assumptions, the bedrock foundation of three centuries of science, are giving way to new assumptions. Quantum physics tells us that what we think of as an objective experiment doesn't exist; the person making the experiment affects the character and outcome of the experiment. Quantum physics further suggests that consciousness is not the end-product of evolution; rather, some elemental form of consciousness may have been here first. Consciousness may be causal, not epiphenomenal.

The reductionist assumption may also be yielding its place in the scientific method. The Cartesian approach did more than simply break down scientific investigation into its discrete parts. The reductionist assumption also separated the whole panorama of existence into isolated segments. What once was encompassed in Natural Philosophy became economics, psychology, sociology and the sciences. By adhering to immutable laws, it was believed, the direction of these segments could be predicted and controlled.

We have now come to the end of this 300-plus-year-old reductionist theme as a valid perspective of life. We suddenly see that all things
are interconnected—a view held in the West from sixth century BC
Greece up to the time of Descartes. It becomes clear that we can understand a particular phenomenon only if we look at it in relationship
to the totality of which it is a part.

This new science, a science of *interconnections*, of relationships, is
superseding three centuries of a science of materialism.

*The sheer number of people on earth drives virtually every issue America
faces—economic growth, protection of the environment, migration, water scarcity
and global political stability.* Eighteen percent—almost one-fifth—of all the
people who lived in the past 2,000 years are alive today. It took millions
of years for the population to reach one billion in 1800. The second
billion was added in the next 130 years. Thirty years later we were up
to three billion. Fourteen years after that we hit four billion. The fifth
billion mark was reached in 12 years; and the sixth billion increment
will have been reached in an 11-year span.

One consequence, urbanization, means that the mayor of a city
such as Mexico City presides over a population greater than the combined populations of Norway, Sweden and Denmark. The mayor of
Los Angeles has a more complex management job than did Henry VIII
governing England. The mayor of Chicago presides over a political
jurisdiction that, in terms of people, is larger than the political jurisdic-
tions governed by Washington or Jefferson.

*We are in the midst of the largest migration in history—from the country
to the city.* By 2050, the planet will house 10 billion people, a billion of
whom will live in 50 Asian megacities of more than 20 million residents
each. Such megacities are beyond the concept of nation; they are regional hubs of global commerce and transport. Such a vast shift of
Earth's population from the country to the city raises the specter of the
slow death of the village culture throughout the planet. The technical
advances in agriculture are so great that some experts believe it prob-
able that, by and large, the peasantry could cease to exist in 100 years.

*Of all the themes that have dominated Western life for the past two
centuries, only one—freedom—remains as an energizing force.* Few people

any longer believe in *reason* as the ultimate authority in ordering human affairs. Faith in the *perfectibility of man*–the cornerstone of the Enlightenment–fell victim to the wholesale slaughter of two world wars. Belief in *utopias* has vanished. *Socialism* is discredited. *Marxism* remains only as an intellectual toy in Western universities. *Communism* has been buried. *Fascism* enlists no loyalties. *Radicalism* has degenerated into spastic anger without any program.

Liberalism, having won historic gains, now languishes in exhaustion. *Conservatism* has a political agenda, but it still has to find a way to make that agenda be seen as a vision of a highly uncertain future rather than simply a nostalgic relic of the past. While *capitalism* continues as an economic program–with distinct mutations in different parts of the world–few look to capitalism to provide any larger significance to human life.

The *avant-garde* vanished long ago. *Modernism* has deconstructed. *Postmodernism* wallows in an anarchy of conflicting styles and attitudes.

Nationalism–in the 19th century sense of constituting the outer limits of a people's political awareness and allegiance–is on the wane. What surfaces in places such as Bosnia, Georgia or Tajikistan is not historic nationalism, but an old ethnicity that cries out for a new expression.

Science continues its unabated march, but hardly anyone believes science will bring the promised land. Even confidence in *progress* has substantially waned. Indeed, most of the social agenda that constituted the faith in progress has now been enacted into law. Progress has achieved its earlier goals and now needs redefinition. Thus it's not surprising that political leaders no longer speak of progress. Politicians speak only of "change" and "solving problems."

The danger now is that people will believe there is nothing big left to believe in, that ideals are a sham, and that short-term self-interest is the only realistic goal. We are in danger of enshrining pragmatism and efficiency as the grand themes of life.

Yet the great concepts that gave birth to Western civilization are now going global. Beliefs and institutions that evolved in the West are now being absorbed by the rest of the world. Indeed, the term "Western" no longer defines a geographical area. It now represents a condition of universal political and technological aspiration. The most obvious examples are representative government and free economic markets. In 1997 alone, China conducted the largest experiment in democracy in world history when 700 million peasants voted in municipal elections for the first time in China's history.

Other Western ideas going global include the significance of private property, the sanctity of the individual, equality before the law, universal education, human rights, the equality of women, and science as the engine of social growth, to name only a few.

While Western nations had generations to assimilate these ideas, they are being force-fed to Asia and Africa in a matter of a few decades. Whether or not Western ideas, not originating in the substrata of the unique Asian and African psychology, will ultimately take permanent root remains to be seen.

Finally the defining reality of our time is the awareness of the human community as a single entity—commonly referred to as "globalization." The basic referent is no longer my tribe, my nation, or even my civilization. In this new era, as Brian Swimme writes in *The Universe Is a Green Dragon*, we are incorporating the planetary dimensions of life into the fabric of our economics, politics, international relations and culture. For the first time in human history, we are forging an awareness of our existence that embraces humanity as a whole. What is emerging, Swimme concludes, "is a new context for discussion of value, meaning, purpose, or ultimacy of any sort."

These, then, are some of the contemporary currents shaping the Interregnum. They're by no means the only megatrends at work, but they are among the most readily visible.

Such world-transforming developments naturally pose the question, "What does this mean for us? How are we to respond?"

Lewis Mumford in the mid-1950s offered one of the most profound responses to this question. Mumford, author and social commentator, saw America and the world as standing on "the brink of a new age: the age of an open world." Like all great transformations,

Mumford said, this new era would take the form of "a new picture of the cosmos and the nature of man."

Lewis Mumford is probably best remembered as a commentator on architecture and city planning. But just as Drucker was far more than an authority on management, Mumford's expertise was far broader than the design of urban spaces. In a series of essays in the mid-1950s, Mumford assessed the relationship between the knowledge-power complex and individual social structure with a depth of insight that is as valid today as when he wrote.

Mumford's appreciation of technology was the basis of his critique of what America was doing with that technology. "For me, as for the most ardent apologist for the machine," he wrote in 1954, "the automaton is Western Civilization's decisive answer to the problem Aristotle propounded–on what terms can human slavery be brought to an end?"

He then went on to warn, "Civilization begins by a magnificent materialization of human purpose: it ends in a purposeless materialism." His concern was that America was developing technology without considering the human and social implications, without understanding how this technology was affecting us as human beings. He noted, for example, that during the 20th century, science and technology had transformed war from "a limited order of destruction and violence, directed toward limited ends–which had been the historic conduct of war–into systematic and unrestricted extermination not only of enemy troops and war-making capability, but also of women, children and nonmilitary property."

Such a change, he thought, reflected not only the enhanced power of technology, but also "a basic change of human attitude toward life itself." Human life–women and children–had become expendable to a degree never before accepted in civilized society. Thus it is, Mumford thought, that "power and order, pushed to their final limit, lead to their self-destructive inversion: disorganization, violence, mental aberration, subjective chaos." He saw this tendency "already expressing itself in America through the motion pictures, the television screen, and children's comic books."

Thus while Mumford welcomed the new technologies he saw coming on stream in the 1950s, he also suggested the new human responsibilities such technology demanded. "The test of maturity, for nations as for individuals," he wrote, "is not the increase of power, but the increase of self-understanding, self-control, self-direction, and self-transcendence." Having developed powers of total destruction, Mumford thought "social and personal development must take precedence" over pursuit of unlimited power and profit. "Not the Power Man, not the Profit Man, not the Mechanical Man, but the Whole Man" must be the "central actor in the new drama of civilization."

This sense of the Whole Person was central to Mumford's thinking, as he thought the world had entered a new phase in which "the destiny of mankind, after its long preparatory period of separation and differentiation, is at last to become one." Such a unity was not essentially political, but had to begin with the individual. It required the "creation of unified personalities, at home with every part of themselves, and so equally at home with the whole family of man, in all its magnificent diversity." For Mumford, nothing less than "a concept of the whole man–and of man achieving a consciousness of the cosmic and historic whole–is capable of doing justice to every type of personality, every mode of culture, every human potential."

In his book *Transformations of Man* (1956), Lewis Mumford defined what still stands as a challenge to America at the beginning of a new century:

> What is ideally desirable, at this stage of man's development, does not exist in any past form of man, either biological or social: not cerebral man, muscular man, or visceral man: not the pure Hindu, the pure Mohammedan, the pure Christian, nor yet the pure Marxist or the pure Mechanist: not Old World man or New World man. The unity we seek must do justice to all these fragments, and be ready to include them lovingly in a self that shall be capable of transcending them. Any doctrine of wholeness that does not begin with love itself as the

symbol and agent of this organic creativity can hardly
hope to produce either a unified self or a unified world:
for it is not in the detached intellect alone that this
transformation must be effected.

Peter Drucker and Lewis Mumford were only two of the voices
who, in the 1950s, suggested that what was happening to America and
the world was not just some minor adjustment to a postwar atmosphere. Rather, America and the world, despite the preoccupation of
the Cold War, had embarked on a new journey, the underlying concepts and realities of which seemed virtually disconnected from the first
half of the century and all history that preceded it. This was indeed the
Age of the Interregnum.

Chapter Fifteen

The 1950s—Hinge of the 20th Century

SUMMARY: Archibald MacLeish and America's misreading of the Communist challenge. Rollo May's America. The Consumer Society–Phase II. The knowledge worker and postindustrial society. A torrent of new technology. A new culture. World War II's aftermath alters the moral ethos. The frenzy of Joseph McCarthy. Korea. America and world responsibility.

If the Interregnum represents a period between two ages, no decade of the 20th century represents the hinge on which a new age was swinging open than does the 1950s. While the 1960s may have been more explosively dramatic, it was the '50s that most exemplified the underlying shift from one age to another that had been taking place throughout the 20th century.

Conventional wisdom, of course, pictures the '50s as a placid, uneventful decade, presided over by the benevolent father figure of Dwight Eisenhower. Explosive economic growth, to be sure, but essentially the *Leave It to Beaver* or the *Ozzie and Harriet* decade. A decade of secure jobs, suburban homes, paternal corporations and, generally speaking, a sense of optimism and security about the future. And, yes, a decade of resistance to communist expansion in Europe and across the globe.

That's still the view of the 1950s held by many Americans today. But what was the view held by Americans as the decade unfolded?

We've already heard the judgments of people such as Peter Drucker and Lewis Mumford. What about others?

In the view of Archibald MacLeish, former librarian of Congress, undersecretary of state and Pulitzer Prize-winning poet, America was in grave danger of confusing the challenge of communism with the deeper crisis of history he felt the nation faced. It was not a crisis in international relations, he wrote in the *Atlantic*, "but a crisis in civilization, a crisis in culture, a crisis in the condition of man." That crisis had not been precipitated by the rise of communism, which was, in point of fact, one of its consequences.

The great nations of the world, MacLeish believed, had been the nations which proposed, the nations which asserted and affirmed something large and bold. Resistance to the Soviet Union, in and of itself, while vitally essential, was not a grand theme for a great people.

The crisis facing America, wrote MacLeish, was to create "a world of individual men, whose relation to each other, in the freedom of their individuality, will create a society in which each can live as himself." It was a crisis of the individual, of the ability to be "as whole and individual human beings answerable to their conscience and God." Americans needed to undertake "moral action at the highest level" to affirm the "revolution of the individual which was the vital and creative impulse of our national life at the beginning of our history. . . ."

Rollo May, one of America's leading psychologists, saw the crisis of the individual in another light. In 1952, only seven years after the greatest military triumph in history, May wrote that the "chief problem of people in the middle decade of the 20th century is emptiness." This emptiness, May said, "has now moved from a state of boredom to a state of futility and despair which holds promise of dangers." In May's view, "our middle of the twentieth century is more anxiety-ridden than any period since the breakdown of the Middle Ages." We are anxious, May said, because "we do not know what roles to pursue, what principles for action to believe in. Our individual anxiety, somewhat like that of the nation, is a basic confusion and bewilderment about where we are going." May concluded that "we live at one of those points in history when one way of living is in its death throes, and another is being born." The Interregnum, although May didn't call it that.

As if to provide an antidote to May's diagnosis, Norman Vincent Peale published *The Power of Positive Thinking* in 1952. Peale's book was a forerunner of the self-help literature that is so prominent in our bookstores today.

Daniel Bell described America in the 1950s as a nation of individuals who have "grown more estranged from one another. The old primary group ties of family and local community have been shattered; ancient parochial faiths are questioned; few unifying values have taken their place." Most important, Bell noted, the critical standards of an educated elite no longer shape opinion or taste. As a result, he wrote, "mores and morals are in constant flux, relations between individuals are tangential or compartmentalized, rather than organic." Because of all this, Bell concluded, the individual "loses a sense of self. His anxieties increase. There ensues a search for new faiths . . . a substitute for the older unifying belief that the mass society has destroyed."

Such views suggest a different picture of America in the 1950s than the prevailing mythology suggests.

But the truth is that Americans were too busy savoring the fruits of victory to consider such questions as were raised by MacLeish or May. America after World War II was not interested in issues of purpose and ultimate ends; she was absorbed with satisfying immediate wants. The 1950s became a transforming decade for the country, a period when aggressive materialism shaped both perception and reality.

America's consumer society had begun to emerge in the 1890s, prompting Thorsten Veblen to coin the phrase "conspicuous consumption" in 1899. But it was in the 1950s that the consumer society came to full flower, that the myth of "growth" became the civic religion. The consumer society became the "throwaway society," and "planned obsolescence" became the order of the day. The GNP shot up from $286 billion to $506 billion in a decade. Credit cards were introduced, and in a four-year period, consumer credit ballooned 55 percent. The Dow-Jones industrial index went from 216 to 618, and individual shareholders nearly tripled. Author John O'Hara described America as "the new expense account society." The "affluent society" had arrived, J.K. Galbraith told America in his 1958 best-seller, *The Affluent Society*, and now that the difficulty of production had been "solved," the only question left was the equitable distribution of wealth, a question Galbraith said could readily be solved by the legacy of John Maynard Keynes.

Archibald MacLeish saw the new consumerism through another lens. Americans were, he wrote, ceasing to think of themselves as "proudly self-governing makers of a new nation, and were instead becoming a society of consumers; recipients–grateful recipients–of the blessings of a technological civilization." This new condition showed in our discourse: We no longer spoke of the "American Proposition," but now boasted of "the American Way of Life."

In 1956, for the first time in America's history, the majority of American workers were not engaged in the production of tangible goods, but in administration and services. Postindustrial society was born, in large measure thanks to the G.I. Bill of Rights, which was creating the knowledge worker such a postindustrial society required.

At the same time, the era of great urban centers of culture came to a close. After the 1950s, Boston, Chicago, Philadelphia and New York all ceased to grow. People moved west and south, and the era of Suburban America emerged, as shown by the doubling of the suburban population between 1950 and 1970. The development of suburbia–spurred in large measure by the G.I. Bill–created the nuclear family, diminished the extended family and forever altered the structure of family life on which America had been built.

In 1950, the semiconductor chip was invented. Four years later, GE bought a Univac from Sperry Rand in the first private computer sale. The transistor, having been invented by Bell Labs in 1947, introduced the phenomenon of "miniaturization," a process that has been a primary impulse of economic growth for the past three decades. By 1956, the term "artificial intelligence" was coined, and research began in Britain on the use of computers to simulate the intelligence of humans.

Another milestone was the creation of the model of the molecular structure of DNA. The possibility of genetic engineering was now at hand. Humans would soon, in part, be able to control evolution.

In 1954, the Supreme Court outlawed segregation by race in America's public schools. Three years later, President Eisenhower sent federal troops into Little Rock to enforce the new law. In the following decade, African Americans made more progress than in the 90 years that followed the Civil War. Contrary to the benign, passive president Eisenhower was said to be, he was one of the most successful presidents of the second half of the century. In 1950-1952, the risk of a major war was palpable. Eight years later, equilibrium had been reached where each side knew the rules and limits, and alliances had been settled across the globe. Eisenhower put holding down inflation above social spending, as he felt that responsible fiscal policy was the only sure social security. Thus the Eisenhower years were some of the most prosperous—in real terms—of modern times.

In 1957, the Soviets launched *Sputnik I*, and the Space Age took on geopolitical dimensions.

We don't think about it today, but it was in the 1950s that U.S. industrial competitiveness met its first postwar challenge. The Volkswagen "Beetle" replaced the Ford as the "world car," and in 1956, for the first time in the history of the automobile, America imported more cars than we exported.

The 1950s produced the first TV generation, causing our children to be raised in a different context, with wider horizons at earlier ages than any prior generation. In 1948, 172,000 American households had television sets. Four years later, 15.3 million households had TV. In 1956, Chet Huntley and David Brinkley started the first TV news, broadcasting a 15-minute program that lasted until the format was expanded to 30 minutes in 1963. With the arrival of television, parents lost effective control of the information environment within which their children grew up. Television seemed to extend communication geographically, but as this happened, the depth and quality of personal and family communication diminished.

Completely unnoticed at the time was the change of the function of the American university. From its inception, the purpose of a university had been teaching, with research as a subordinate activity. The 1950s solidified a reversal of these functions. Research became the primary focus of major universities, with teaching relegated to a secondary position, frequently attended to by a graduate student. Education focused on process and seemed to lose sight of purpose.

Not only did the function of the university change, but the size radically expanded. Thousands of veterans, who in all likelihood would not have gained higher education had it not been for the war and the G.I. Bill, enrolled.

The H-bomb was produced, and the world's first generation to grow up under the threat of possible extinction of the human species wrestled with new psychological pressures.

The moral ethos of America radically shifted during the 1950s. What modernism and an existential vacuum did to the Jay Gatsbys of life in the 1920s now spread to the broader mass of "middle America." Who knows how many of the millions of veterans of World War II, having experienced the ultimate life-and-death challenges of war, abandoned previous attitudes toward sex, loosening the bonds of family cohesion. The so-called "sexual revolution," which actually started in the 1920s, accelerated in the '50s. Invention of the "pill" quickened the change in mores. Alfred Kinsey's report on *Sexual Behavior in the Human Female*, appearing in 1953, told America that nearly 50 percent of all middle-class women had experienced premarital intercourse, while 26 percent had committed adultery by age 40.

All this was exemplified by the 1953 publication of *Playboy*, a magazine of hedonism, eroticism and cynicism that never could have found a mass readership in an America of just a few decades earlier. Books such as *Peyton Place, Lolita* and *Lady Chatterley's Lover*, ripe with graphic sex, began to flood the bookstores by 1956. Such fare caused Henry Luce to observe in *Life* in 1955, "Our artists and our novelists have disintegrated the human personality into the most miserable shreds of degradation."

Not to be outdone, Hollywood came out with films exploring themes of adultery (*From Here to Eternity*, 1953), homosexuality (*Compulsion*, 1958) and abortion (*Blue Denim*, 1959). Such themes seem tame by today's standards, but they shook the accepted ethos of America when they appeared in the 1950s.

The character and tone of culture changed in the 1950s. Arthur Miller's Willie Lohman typified the times. Willy "never knew who he was," says his son Biff. With J.D. Salinger's *Catcher in the Rye*, a new sort of character entered American literature: the alienated adolescent, a theme which was given life by James Dean in the 1955 film *Rebel Without a Cause*, and which has been a staple of America's culture ever since. Allen Ginsberg, symbol of the "Beat Generation," declaimed his poem "Howl" in San Francisco. Jack Kerouac published *On the Road*, which opened with a paean to alienation: "I first met Dean not long after my wife and I split up. I had just gotten over a serious illness that I won't bother to talk about, except that it had something to do with the miserably weary split-up and my feeling that everything was dead." Beyond Kerouac came Camus, Beckett, Sartre, existentialism and the "School of the Absurd," which became dominant in literature, cinema and philosophy. It was as Archibald MacLeish wrote: "[T]he notion propagated, largely in France, after the Second World War, that Aristotle had somehow died in that great disaster, and that truth to life was no longer the criterion of art because life was no longer the criterion of anything–life had been found out at last–life was absurd."

In art, Abstract Expressionism, defined by the *Dictionary of Art & Artists* as "little more than automatic painting–i.e., allowing the subconscious to express itself (a Surrealist idea) by the creation of involuntary shapes and dribbles of paint," made its debut at New York's Art of This Century Gallery. Jackson Pollack–"When I am in my painting I am not aware of what I am doing,"–delved into the exploration of an irrational subjectivity.

Harold Rosenberg, one of the chief theorists of Abstract Expressionism, described Abstract Expressionism as essentially a religious movement which sought "liberation from value–political, aesthetic, world." Rosenberg went on to say, "Most modern masterpieces are critical masterpieces. Joyce's writing is a criticism of literature, Pound's poetry a criticism of poetry, Picasso's painting a criticism of painting. Modern art criticizes the existing culture."

In one sense, the art scene increasingly became an expression of Picasso's comment about "rage" as the artistic style of an era. It was a far cry from the understanding of art and culture that had impelled Goethe, Arnold and Ruskin, as mentioned earlier.

In cinema, the "hero," represented by Jimmy Stewart or Gary Cooper, began to be replaced by the "antihero," as seen in James Dean and Marlon Brando. The 1950s saw Alan Ladd in *Shane* as the high-water mark of the Western as defining the American myth. Today that myth is more likely defined by Brando in *The Godfather.*

The birth of "rock" music in the 1950s was part of this cultural shift. Rock's underlying themes were exploitation of sex and rebellion. Neither of these were new themes, but to have them become the driving impulse of the culture was a clear break not only with the tradition of American music, but with the cultural tradition of most developed civilizations. One recalls Plato's comment from *The Republic:* "A change to a new type of music is something to beware of as a hazard of all our fortunes. For the modes of music are never disturbed without unsettling of the most fundamental political and social conventions."

At the same time, rock music reflected a change in the tempo of American life. The slower crooning of a Bing Crosby or a Doris Day was somehow out of sync with the emerging age of computers, instant global communication and potential nuclear devastation. And as blacks edged ever closer to the mainstream of American life, the tempo of black life became more apparent in popular music. It might be said that Elvis Presley's most significant effect on America was in making black rhythms acceptable to middle-class white teenagers.

In the political realm, what is most remembered about the 1950s is the wild rampage of Senator Joseph R. McCarthy of Wisconsin. A lawyer and controversial circuit court judge before the war, McCarthy had served in the marines during World War II. He was elected to the Senate in 1946 relying heavily on lies about his war record, falsely maintaining he had flown some 30 combat missions when in fact he had gone on none.

Casting about for an issue to boost his 1952 reelection campaign, McCarthy lighted on the issue of supposed communists in the government. His charges were wild and irresponsible, calling Secretary of State Dean Acheson, the "Red Dean," claiming he (McCarthy) had a list of 205 communists in the government (a list he never revealed or proved), and condemning General George C. Marshall, chief of staff of the army during World War II, for having "lost" China to the communists.

Nothing can justify McCarthy's behavior and tactics. That said, the 1990s declassification of both Soviet and U.S. Cold War intelligence files verifies the essence of McCarthy's charges. According to latest scholarship, Alger Hiss probably was a Soviet agent, and the U.S. government during the 1930s and 1940s did harbor scores of communist spies and even more fellow travelers. The copies of names, salary receipts, code names, sensitive messages on the Manhattan Project and American diplomatic strategy released after the breakup of the Soviet Union tell the story. In 1996, The *Observer* of London commented: "McCarthy has gone down as one of the most reviled men in U.S. history, but historians are now facing the unpleasant truth that he was right." Writing in *The Washington Post*, Nicholas von Hoffman concluded, "Point by point, Joe McCarthy got it all wrong, and yet he was still closer to the truth than those who ridiculed him." By 1954, however, McCarthy had overreached himself and crashed into popular disgrace.

All but unnoticed in this uproar at the time was the waning influence of the so-called Eastern Establishment. The John J. McCloys of life; the Wall Street bankers and lawyers; the captains of established industry, usually of Protestant origin; the graduates of Exeter, Andover, Harvard, Princeton and Yale; the Anglo-Saxon ethnic stock which had guided America since its founding, their time had now passed. While the Cyrus Vances of life would still make their contributions to public life, as a defined Establishment, the 1950s saw the fading of their influence.

Perhaps as a symbol of all this change, Sunday lost priority acceptance as a day of spiritual renewal and worship (something which all cultures throughout history have had in one form or another) and became just another day at the shopping mall. In fact, in 1954, America discovered the mall.

In sum, the 1950s were a watershed, the last decade when there was any semblance of cohesion in American life. As Daniel Bell describes the change in cultural attitude, "By the 1950s . . . the culture was no longer concerned with how to work and achieve, but rather with how to spend and enjoy . . . by the 1950s American culture had become primarily hedonistic, concerned with play, fun, display and pleasure . . ." It was such changes that gave substance to the concerns of Rollo May and others. As we shall see in the next chapter, the shift of tectonic plates that took place in the 1950s was responsible for much of the upheaval that characterized the 1960s.

Most Americans didn't realize how America was being reshaped in the '50s, and for good reason. Whatever was happening at home, America's attention was focused on Berlin, Quemoy, Matsu, Budapest, Kerela, Bandung, Guatemala, Lebanon, Peking, Suez and Tokyo. The struggle to rebuild war-ravaged Europe and Japan, to develop a world economic and trade structure, to contain Soviet imperialism and to assist newly independent nations absorbed the full energies of the nation. America was engaged in fulfilling her role as described by Walter Lippmann in 1945: "What Rome was to the ancient world, what Britain was to the modern world, America is to be to the world of tomorrow." This role of world leader was new for America, especially when one considers that, only a few years earlier, isolationism was deeply embedded in the American outlook. All but unnoticed, the seeds of America's eventual involvement in Vietnam were sown, as President Eisenhower failed to enforce the 1954 Geneva agreement calling for free elections in all of Vietnam.

In one sense, America did not choose her role after World War II nor during the 1950s; the role was thrust upon her. The acceptance of that role was not part of a considered plan for the development of the country. Rather, America was the only nation capable of responding to the mounting emergencies. And respond she did– as best she could–with the Marshall Plan ($13 billion; $88.5 billion in 1997 dollars), the Truman Doctrine, the formation of NATO, the defense of South Korea, the reconstruction of Japan and the creation of a world trade structure. As Edward R. Murrow, one of the founders of radio and TV journalism, noted at the time, America had come into its full inheritance. "We proclaim ourselves," he said, "as indeed we are, the defenders of freedom wherever it continues to exist in the world."

War on the Korean peninsula (June 1950-July 1953) exemplifies Morrow's statement. The Korean War was a direct outcome of World War II. At the end of the war in 1945, the Americans and Russians assumed responsibility for the surrender of Japanese forces in Korea. Korea was divided in half at the 38th parallel, with the Russians responsible for the North and the Americans the South. In June 1950, the North Korean army, trained and armed by the Russians, invaded the South believing that the Americans, who had withdrawn from Korea in 1949, would not intervene. As a Communist-controlled Korea would be a strategic threat to Japan, the United Nations Security Council called for an end to the fighting and the withdrawal of North Korean forces to the 38th parallel.

The North Koreans paid little attention to the UN demand, and thus President Truman made the decision historically dreaded by all American political and military leaders: to commit U.S. troops to fight on the land mass of Asia. As the Americans and South Koreans pushed north toward the Yalu River and the Chinese border, Mao Zedong sent the Chinese army into North Korea, and the United Nations forces were pushed south. Three years later, after 33,629 Americans were killed and 103,284 wounded, a cease-fire was arranged which left the boundaries as they are today, not greatly different than they had been at the start of the fighting in 1950.

It was just such global responsibilities as Korea that meant America did not have the time, or did not take the time, to evaluate her own growth path as a nation, to ponder the meaning of insights expressed by her most farsighted citizens, that America had arrived at a point where, in Adlai Steveson's words, "man must make another mighty choice."

So the choice, at least as related to any long-term direction, was not made. Instead, consumer demand, pent-up during the war, exploded, and a tidal wave of new technology–freezers, air-conditioning, malls, fast-food chains, dishwashers, copy machines, automatic transmissions, jet-powered planes–washed across America.

Wartime research and development had generated a cornucopia of technology which, America was told, would create the "affluent society" of leisure, plenty and, according to Madison Avenue, eternal happiness.

Chapter Sixteen

What, Really, Were the '60s All About?

SUMMARY: The largest, most educated, wealthiest cohort of youth in history. Escalation of the race issue. Collapse of the Establishment. Explosion of foreign policy flashpoints. Vietnam. Landing on the Moon and the emergence of a global civilization. New technology changes old perceptions. The Commission on the Year 2000.

When we think of the 1960s, dramatic images flood our minds–the Beatles on the "Ed Sullivan Show" in 1964, police dogs and water hoses pummeling blacks in Birmingham, helicopters swarming like bees over the rice paddies of Vietnam, thousands of war protesters at the Lincoln Memorial, Woodstock and a counterculture festival, Neil Armstrong walking on the moon.

It sometimes seems as if the '60s had a unique quality, a departure from patterns of the past and an opening up of new areas of exploration. The 1960s, one writer observes, marked "the definitive end of the Dark Ages, and the beginning of a more hopeful democratic period." Another writer sees the '60s as "a modern Great Awakening." Still another scholar believes the '60s "are likely to remain a permanent point of reference for the way we think and behave, just as the thirties were."

We tend to think of the '60s almost as a self-contained period of time, unrelated to the decades that preceded it. But no decade emerges full-blown out of thin air. Every decade is fulfillment of seeds planted at an earlier time. In this sense, all of the '60s grew from seeds planted at least in the 1950s, if not earlier. It might be said that the decade was the result of at least five developments:

(1) The arrival of the largest, most educated and wealthiest cohort of young people in the history of America or any nation; (2) The escalation of America's age-old race issue to a new dimension; (3) The collapse and demoralization of the Establishment that had sustained the great initiatives of the postwar period; (4) The explosion of foreign policy flashpoints; and (5) The end of the era of nation-states begun in 1648, and the emergence of a global civilization.

Let's look at each of these in turn.

The Baby Boomers have been a primary phenomenon in defining America for half a century. The origins of the Boomers obviously go back to 1946 and the end of the World War II. As a result, during the '60s the number of young people, those between the ages of 15 and 24, jumped 47 percent and accounted for 17.5 percent of America's total population. Never before or since have young people between those ages so dominated a decade.

From this cohort came the youth who launched Berkeley's "Free Speech" movement; who stormed the academic citadels at Yale, Columbia and Kent State, who threatened the Cornell University faculty with the use of firearms unless certain "reforms" were made (they were); who rioted at the Democratic National Convention in Chicago; whose sit-ins closed campuses from coast to coast (488 campuses in 1970 alone). These young people were being taught by professors raised on the '50s "Beat" culture of the nihilism of Sartre's "nothingness" and "abyss," of the meaninglessness of Camus's and Beckett's "school of the absurd," and of Allen Ginsberg's apocalyptic "Howl"–"I saw the best minds my generation destroyed by madness / starving hysterical naked / dragging themselves through the negro streets at dawn looking for an angry fix." They were reading Jack Kerouac's disoriented *On The Road*–"The only people for me are the mad ones, the ones who are mad to live, mad to talk, mad to be saved, desirous of everything at the same time, the ones who never yawn or say a commonplace thing, but burn, burn, burn like fabulous yellow roman candles exploding like spiders across the stars."

Perhaps the credo of this cohort was best expressed by Bob Dylan in his 1962 epic "Like a Rolling Stone": "How does it feel / to be on your own / with no direction home / like a complete unknown / like a rolling stone?" This song, about pain, loneliness and the emptiness of a world with no metaphysical anchors, was the song that sparked the impulse behind the counterculture and the alternative press.

Marching to this song, thousands of young people demanded "freedom" to live as they pleased in the dorms, with drugs when they wanted, with sexual restrictions removed, with exemption from military service, with an end to hierarchy or "elitism," and with almost no interference from the university authorities, to say nothing of civil authority. The new ethic instigated the belief that meaning is derived by group identity or personal preference. The study of history, philosophy and language yielded to consciousness-raising academic units known as Afro-American Studies and Women's Studies. Extensive grade inflation made it difficult to flunk anyone, and at many universities, the core curriculum gave way to "multicultural" studies.

With the end of the '60s and the eventual termination of the Vietnam War, many of the more radical students found positions on college campuses as administrators, lecturers and faculty. As a Middlebury College English professor, Jay Parini, said, "After the Vietnam War, a lot of us didn't just crawl back into our literary cubicles; we stepped into academic positions. With the war over, our visibility was lost, and it seemed for a while—to the unobservant—that we had disappeared. Now we have tenure, and the work of reshaping the universities has begun in earnest."

One of the most important facts about the kids of the '60s is that they constituted America's first TV generation, raised with habits, horizons and perceptions never before afforded any age group. During the 1960s television came into its own as a major force in American life. Indeed, the '60s would not have been the '60s as history has recorded it had television not existed. As Theodore H. "Teddy" White wrote in *In Search of History*, "Television belongs to that family of mechanical devices that change civilization, on the order of magnitude of the printed book." It has been one of the primary forces of the Interregnum.

Try to assess the impact of television on America in the 1960s. TV was a totally new mode of communication. It did more than simply transmit images and information; it extended awareness. An event happening on the other side of the country or the other side of the world suddenly became an event of the viewer's everyday life, usually shorn of context. In a sense, TV short-circuited what some like to think of as the innocence of childhood, as it brought worldly images and problems right into the living room for any age to see.

Television magnified events beyond their inherent value. Whether the event was good or bad, TV gave it a size and relevance that frequently was beyond its actual importance. In this sense, TV distorts reality; TV shows 600,000 anti-war protesters at the Lincoln Memorial, but it does not show the 6 million who may disagree with the protesters and actually support government policy. Thus the 600,000 take on a significance that is out of proportion to fact. This imbalance takes on its own reality; it becomes history. Dramatic images of rioting, police dogs, sit-ins and burning buildings become the *whole* story.

But the whole story was quite different. As James T. Patterson writes in *Grand Expectations,* a sweeping survey of America between 1945 and 1974, the "vast majority of Americans had little if anything to do with campus rebels, counter-culturalists, or anti-war protesters." In a 1986 public opinion survey by Yankelovich Clancy Shulman, 6 percent of those questioned about their political views in the 1960s said they were "radical," 31 percent said they had been "liberal" and 63 percent claimed to have been either "moderate" or "conservative." The same poll showed that 8 percent of those questioned "regularly" used drugs in the '60s, while 62 percent said they had never used drugs at all. Fifty-three percent said they were "mostly opposed" to the antiwar protests, while 34 percent said they were "mostly in favor" of the protests.

Similarly, a 1980 Harris public opinion survey showed that two-thirds of those who served in Vietnam were volunteers rather than draftees, that 77 percent of those who died in Vietnam were volunteers, and that 91 percent of those who served in Vietnam stated they were glad they had served their country.

In a 1970 briefing for President Nixon, Henry Kissinger assessed America's youth and the rioting then taking place on university campuses. Kissinger noted that the causes of America's domestic turmoil were much deeper than disagreement over Vietnam. The students rioting on American campuses were not alone. Students were also demonstrating in Berlin, Stockholm, Paris, Rome, Oxford and Amsterdam, demonstrations which had nothing to do with Vietnam or American domestic concerns. In other words, Kissinger said, "we are dealing with a problem of contemporary society, of how to give meaning to life for a generation, for a younger generation in states that are becoming increasingly bureaucratic and technological."

Kissinger understood that the rioting of the '60s was the consequence, not the cause, of America's self-doubt. His comments represent a range of awareness which few politicians seemed to understand, then or now.

Nothing exemplifies TV's revolutionary impact more than the 1960 presidential "debates" between Richard Nixon and John Kennedy. This was an event that triggered the transformation of American politics, including the presidency. As John Perry Barlow observes, from the Nixon-Kennedy debates on, "the president became more movie star than leader, more myth than manager, more affect than intellect." Barlow notes that the debates were "the first national instance in which what a politician said was less penetrating and prehensile [easily grasped] than his ability to look like he meant it." He concludes by saying it was at that point that TV assumed the role of "defining the national agenda." Writing in *The Public Interest* (Summer 1977), Michael J. Robinson, in discussing the relationship between TV and the political parties, writes that "network news has emerged as 'the loyal opposition,' more so than even the party out of office. *It is now the networks that act as the shadow cabinet.*"

Another major effect of television was to accelerate the shift of public appetite for the celebrity instead of the hero, a switch analyzed by Daniel Boorstin in *The Image: What Happened to the American Dream?*

(1961). The hero, Boorstin said, "was distinguished by his achievement; the celebrity by his image or trademark . . . The hero was a big man; the celebrity is a big name." It was Boorstin who first defined a celebrity as "a person who is well-known for his well-knownness." In a sense, this represented a shift from interest in the real to fascination with the imagined, for the hero represents something authentic, while the celebrity represents more semblance than substance.

So the '60s generation was the first to experience the final triumph of style over essence in America's discussion of public affairs.

A second development defining the '60s was the escalation of the question of race, which has bedeviled America for over two centuries.

The momentum for civil rights and equality in the '60s came on the heels of World War II and the realization that America could not ask African-Americans to die for their country and still deny them the full promise of liberty. Added to this was the effect of northern migration of African Americans during the Great Depression and the war. In 1940, 23 percent of America's black people lived outside the South, while by 1970 the figure had risen to 47 percent.

While the gains in racial equality during the '40s and '50s seemed significant in light of what prevailing attitudes had been, it took the 1960s, with the combination of mammoth demonstrations and the glaring focus of TV, to fundamentally move the conscience of the nation. Not since the Civil War had America seen such widespread, sustained and violent civil activity.

It started in 1960 in Greensboro, North Carolina where blacks staged a "sit-in" at a segregated lunch counter. Sit-ins soon brought to an end the segregation of lunch counters in over 100 Southern cities. In 1961, "Freedom Riders" met violence in Montgomery, Birmingham and Jackson as they sought to force integration of the bus terminals in the South. In 1962, 5,000 federal troops were sent to the University of Mississippi to quell the turmoil following the efforts of James Meredith to be the first black to attend "Ole Miss." Some of the worst violence took place in Birmingham in 1963 when police used dogs and fire hoses to confront demonstrators. Birmingham was the first protracted demonstration to be carried live on nationwide television. Perhaps more than any other event, the brutality of police reaction in Birmingham forced America to do more than pay lip-service to racial equality. In 1963, some 250,000 people stood at the Lincoln Memorial and heard Martin Luther King, Jr., set forth his dream in a rolling cadence that was his captivating style of oratory:

> I have a dream that one day this nation will rise up and live out the true meaning of its creed: "We hold these truths to be self-evident—that all men are created equal. . . .
>
> I have a dream that my four little children will one day live in a nation where they will not be judged by the color of their skin but by the content of their character . . .
>
> When we let freedom ring, when we let it ring from every village and every hamlet, from every state and every city, we will be able to speed up that day when all God's children, black men and white men, Jews and Gentiles, Protestants and Catholics, will be able to join hands and sing in the words of that old Negro spiritual, "Free at last! Thank God almighty, we are free at last!"

But despite King's ringing declaration, 1963 was the high water mark of his influence, for 1963 was the year that a significant number of blacks broke with King's advocacy of nonviolence. To some, the brutality of Birmingham needed to be met with more than the songs and marches of nonviolence.

In 1964, the 24th Amendment outlawing use of the poll tax as a means of preventing citizens from voting, and the passage of the Civil Rights Act of 1964 was adopted. In 1965, King led marchers on a 54-mile route from Selma to Montgomery, President Johnson signed the Voting Rights Act, and 35 people were killed in Watts before the National Guard quelled the riots.

In 1966, while Stokely Carmichael promoted "black power," the first black Cabinet officer was appointed Secretary of Housing and

Urban Development. The next year, Thurgood Marshall became the first black to serve as associate justice on the Supreme Court. The same year, the first blacks since Reconstruction were elected to state legislatures in Virginia, Mississippi and Louisiana.

The decade of the '60s, which had seen the most violent civil disorder of 20th century America, ended with the fury that characterized the time: Martin Luther King, Jr., recipient of the Nobel Peace Prize in 1964, was assassinated in Memphis in 1968. Not surprisingly, riots broke out in more than 100 American cities. But by this time, not only was the character of the civil rights struggle changing, but it had been melded to a significant degree into the anti war protests over Vietnam.

The third shaping force of the '60s was the collapse and demoralization of the Establishment, which had sustained the great initiatives of the postwar period.

What was the Establishment? Richard Rovere, writing in *The American Scholar*, once described the Establishment as "a more or less closed and self-sustaining institution that holds a preponderance of power in our more or less open society." David Halberstam sharpened the description by describing the Establishment as "an instrument of class propelled by certain traditions of loyalty and honor." Thus, until the 1960s, the Establishment was that group of influential men, linked together by manners, common values and vision, generally of a Protestant, Ivy League background, drawn from the financial houses and law firms of the east coast.

Nicholas Lemann writes that the first great achievement of the Establishment (1900-1940) was making the United States into a modern industrial welfare state, in which big corporations would coexist with government social and economic regulation. The next and even grander achievement was the winning of World War II and creation of a postwar order, most prominent features of which were the Cold War and the economic restoration of Western Europe and Japan. Men such as Dean Acheson, John J. McCloy, Robert Lovett and W. Averell Harriman were at the heart of the Establishment that defined the postwar world order that lasted for two decades.

By the '60s, the composition and cohesion of the Establishment were changing, for indeed, America was changing. Demographics revealed a shift to the south and west, and the concentrated influence of the Establishment begin to weaken. With the rise of the computer/ media/ telecommunications/entertainment component of the economy, the traditional centers of the old Establishment lost relative prestige. To a certain degree, the long ascent of Ronald Reagan in American politics symbolized the Establishment's loss of control over the nation. Where the Establishment tended to be moderate, Reagan's America was becoming more and more conservative. Where the Establishment had been of a certain breeding and outlook, the new power centers, as represented in such men as Henry Kissinger and Zbigniew Brzezinski, were increasingly run by the meritocracy.

Three other developments shook the Establishment's foundations. First, Vietnam. While the Establishment's main expertise had been in successfully directing America's foreign affairs, the defeat in Vietnam demoralized a whole phalanx of Establishmentarians who generally thought the world would bend to their better judgment. As Halberstam writes, "The Establishment's elite was made up of men who looked toward Europe. They had seen Vietnam as essentially peripheral, and they had made a fatal error in failing to understand not only the ineffectiveness of American technology there but also the revolutionary forces driving their opponents."

Second, the success of the civil rights movement gave African-Americans a voice in national affairs they had long been denied, especially in the foreign policy arena. It drew increased attention to the Establishment's essential WASPiness, the marked absence of women, Jews and other ethnic representations.

Third, the Establishment failed to comprehend what was happening to America. This was most glaringly reflected in the fact that it was the children of the Establishment who were storming the administration buildings of the prestigious Ivy League campuses. To a significant degree, the barons of wealth and power in America were out of touch with their own children, who were reacting to the collapse of the idealism that John Kennedy had represented for an entire generation. The leaders who had crafted America's foreign policy were particularly upset by the rage of the campus demonstrators. As Kissinger later noted, the "assault of these upper middle-class young men and women–who were, after all, their [the Establishment's] own children–was not simply on policies, but on life-styles and values heretofore considered sacrosanct." The insecurity of their elders, Kissinger, continued, "turned the normal grievances of maturing youth into an institutionalized rage and a national trauma." Kissinger's generation, he concludes, had failed the youth "by encouraging self-indulgence and neglecting to provide roots."

No one would suggest the Establishment has evaporated. It will continue to choose the presidents of the Ivy League universities, to gather at the Council on Foreign Relations and the Metropolitan Club, and to urge deficit reduction on Congress. And new recruits continue to swell Establishment ranks. But they no longer shape the global designs of a Marshall Plan or a Bretton Woods. Their influence is a far cry from the glory days of Stimson or McCloy. As Lemann writes, "If the Establishment is not a completely hollow shell, at the very least the suspicion is inescapable that today it runs only itself."

The fourth development shaping the 1960s was the explosion of foreign policy flashpoints.

When one looks at foreign policy crises throughout the 20th century, the number of dire crises that occupied Washington policy makers' attention in a given decade was relatively small, no matter how serious any particular crisis might have been. Throughout the 1920s, for example, the major foreign policy concerns were the 1921 Washington conference on naval disarmament and the Kellogg-Briand Pact outlawing war in 1928. Throughout the first half of the 1930s, America's attention was totally focused inward on the Great Depression. Even in the second half of the '30s, when Italy invaded Ethiopia, Hitler repudiated the Versailles Treaty, the Spanish Civil War erupted, and China and Japan went to war, such developments required little of America. Then, of course, came World War II, and America was totally involved in the fate of the world.

By the 1960s, both as part of the Cold War and quite aside from U.S.-Soviet relations, crises were exploding all around the globe which demanded America's attention, if not active involvement. The Bay of Pigs fiasco; an American U-2 is blasted out of the sky by the Russians; Greece and Turkey at war over Cyprus; election of Yasir Arafat as Chairman of the PLO and the continuing Arab-Israeli conflict; China exploding the H-bomb; Russian tanks invading Prague; the Berlin crisis and the building of the Berlin Wall; the Cuban Missile crisis–the closest the world has come to nuclear war; the Gulf of Tonkin resolution and the Vietnam War; Red Guards rampage in China; the constant threat of an India-Pakistan war; coup d'etats in the Congo and numerous other African countries; instability in Brazil, Chile and other South American nations; the Six-Day War in the Middle East; fighting between Protestants and Catholics in Northern Ireland; and on and on it went. Nightly television brought every crisis into the living room, with the result that people became at least aware of, if not concerned about, three or four potential crises at any given time. The increase in the number of crises that had implications for the nation, as well as the average person's awareness of these crises, was something completely new for Americans.

Part of the new foreign policy environment America faced was the perceived threat of communism in Asia, including Vietnam.

The stated purpose of U.S. involvement in Vietnam was to stem the spread of communism in Southeast Asia. This objective succeeded to a certain degree, as a country such as Indonesia might well have been saved from a communist coup as a result of America's Indochina commitment. The weakness of the final phase of our Vietnam commitment, however, failed to save Cambodia from a contemporary holocaust which took some 2 million lives; nor did it save thousands of Vietnamese "boat people" from risking their lives on the open seas rather than remain in Vietnam.

Stephen S. Rosenfeld notes in a 1999 *Washington Post* article that British journalist William Shawcross, a vehement critic of U.S. policy in Southeast Asia in the 1970s, wrote in 1994: "[T]hose of us who opposed the American war in Indochina should be extremely humble in the face of the appalling aftermath: a form of genocide in Cambodia and horrific tyranny in both Vietnam and Laos. Looking back on my own coverage for *The* [London] *Sunday Times* of the South Vietnamese war effort of 1970-75, I think I concentrated too easily on the corruption and incompetence of the South Vietnamese and their American allies, was too ignorant of the inhuman Hanoi regime, and far too willing to believe that a victory by the communists would provide a better future. But after the communist victory came the refugees to Thailand and the floods of boat people desperately seeking to escape the Cambodian killing fields and the Vietnamese gulags. Their eloquent testimony should have put paid to all illusions."

Rosenfeld further quotes Henry Kissinger as pointing out that a form of genocide in Cambodia included: "All former government employees and their families were executed . . . The 2 million citizens of Phnom Penh were ordered to evacuate the city for the countryside ravaged by war and incapable of supporting urban dwellers unused to fending for themselves. Between 1 and 2 million Khmer were murdered by the Khmer Rouge until Hanoi occupied the country at the end of 1978, after which a civil war raged for another decade."

As it was, a majority of Americans supported U.S. involvement in Vietnam up to the Tet offensive in 1968, an offensive which was a military disaster but a public relations victory for the Hanoi regime. It was then, when the war dragged on, when no decisive outcome appeared on the horizon, that public support faltered. It is hard to judge, but America's defeat in Vietnam probably had more repercussions at home than it did in the rest of the world. For our loss in Vietnam triggered over a decade of soul-searching, of debate over what might be called the "America in decline" syndrome. Despite our own misgivings, however, the rest of the world had no doubt about America's military capacity.

It may well be that we shall not fully evaluate the American venture in Vietnam until we have a fuller assessment of America's basic understanding of communism between 1945 and 1991, of how we responded to the threat posed by the Soviet Union. Nor shall we ever know what might have happened had President Kennedy not been killed, for some of his former aides assert that Kennedy had every intention of disengaging from Vietnam in late 1964. We may be still too close to some of these events to have an adequate perspective. One thing is certain: We cannot truly understand the tragedy of Vietnam if we judge it through today's perspectives and attitudes. We must go back to the perceptions and temperament of the late 1950s and early 1960s if we want to grasp both the valor and the blindness that shaped the Vietnam story. It could even be that historians a century from now will see the Vietnam war as the final conflagration of the era of nation-states.

The fifth development shaping the '60s was a palpable sense that a new phase of history, a global civilization (globalization), was emerging. Several factors contributed to this awareness.

John Kennedy's inauguration set the tone. After 32 years of the presidency represented by men of the age of Roosevelt, Truman and Eisenhower, John Kennedy, defeating Richard Nixon by a margin of 120,000 out of nearly 69 million votes cast (63.8 percent of all eligible voters) and becoming the first American born in the 20th century to assume the presidency, injected a sense of a new generation assuming command, of a new view of possibility, of the relevance of idealism. America frequently seems to want a dose of idealism after a decade of materialism. After junk bonds and the "Bonfire of the Vanities" of the '80s, the '90s has seen a refocusing on volunteering and helping the less fortunate. So it was that after the explosion of material wealth in the '50s, Americans rose to the sense of service reflected in the Peace Corps and Vista (the domestic Peace Corps).

While Kennedy's assassination in 1963 benumbed and bewildered America, it did not diminish the sense that the world had entered a new era. This was for a reason far larger than Kennedy or, indeed, than any individual human being: the images of Planet Earth and the moon sent back from space. With these pictures, the Interregnum was finding fulfillment.

Henry Luce, founder of the Time-Life publishing empire, wrote in *Life* in 1955 that when humans land on the moon, "that surely will radically change the whole outlook on the human adventure, which will have passed beyond any grasp I might have of its meaning and purpose." With the exploration of space, the human adventure did indeed pass into a new phase, and this is the vital significance of the 1960s. The dreams of poets and philosophers throughout the ages–the idea of the human race as just one human community–was given tangible form in the 1960s, and we are still adjusting to its implications.

It is almost impossible today to convey the sense of excitement of a new age aborning that was palpable in the '60s as images from space were flashed across the television screens of the world. The sequence of events is one of the most adventurous efforts in human history:

- 1961, Yuri Gagarin becomes the first human being to orbit earth;
- 1962, Mariner 2 becomes the first object made by humans to voyage to another planet when it reaches the vicinity of Venus;
- 1963, Syncom 2 is the first satellite to go into geosynchronous orbit;
- 1964, Ranger 7 takes 4,316 close-range pictures of the moon;
- 1965, Ed White becomes first American to conduct a "space walk," Mariner IV passes within 7,500 miles of Mars, Russian spaceprobe Zond III sends back first photographs of the back side of the moon, Gemini 6 and Gemini 7 perform the first space rendezvous;
- 1966, Soviet Union's Venera III is first object made by humans to land on another planet when it reaches Venus, Soviet Luna X is first spacecraft to land on the moon, U.S. Suveyor I lands in the Ocean of Storms on the moon and sends back pictures of the lunar surface, U.S. Lunar Orbiter I orbits the moon and sends back photographs, Soviet spaceprobe Luna XIII lands on the moon and sends back pictures and soil data;
- 1967, U.S. Surveyor VI lands on Central Bay on the moon;
- 1968, Surveyor VII lands on the moon and sends back 21,000 photographs, Frank Borman and James Lovell in Saturn V orbit the moon 10 times;
- 1969, Neil Armstrong becomes first human to stand on the moon, Charles Conrad and Richard Gordon spend 15 hours exploring the surface of the moon.

Today the pictures of men walking on the moon seem almost routine. The great "Earthrise" picture from the moon has become almost "ho-hum" to most people. Perhaps the only event today that could strike the American imagination with the same force as the space exploration did in the '60s would be if the president held a White House news conference and introduced several aliens from some other part of the universe.

In some ways, the most important aspect of the 1960s was the new view of ourselves the human race obtained from the moon. It was a new perspective, one that we had known in theory, but now experienced in reality. Our view of ourselves would be forever different. While the poets and philosophers throughout history had written about "the human family" or that "all men are brothers," here, for the first time, was the irrefutable demonstration that beyond the superficial definitions of nation, race or culture, all men and women live within one biosphere. Thus was the 1960s a defining moment in history. The global era was upon us.

Space technology, however, was only one aspect. The technological revolution was obliterating past certitudes and reordering America's sense of time, of space and of human possibility. Consider the following developments of the '60s:

- First industrial robot used.
- First artificial heart successfully implanted in a human being.
- Lasers developed.
- ESSA I launched, the first weather satellite capable of viewing the entire Earth.
- Telstar, the first active communications satellite launched.
- First circumnavigation of the globe underwater by a nuclear submarine.
- First linkup of two manned space vehicles.
- First satellite in orbit around the sun sending back radio data over 22 million miles.
- First heart transplant.
- Fermi National Accelerator Laboratory established.
- The scanning electron microscope reaches practical use.

- "Bubble memory" devices enable computers to remember even after the computer is turned off.
- Geothermal power produced in the U.S. for the first time.
- Lasers used in eye surgery for the first time.
- Internet and e-mail developed.
- First political TV debates in a presidential campaign, forever changing the character of American politics.
- Synthetic version of DNA produced.
- Quasars and pulsars discovered.
- Intel established and eventually becomes the world's leading maker of semiconductors.
- Penzias and Wilson detect radio waves of the Big Bang. Contact with the beginnings of time, space and matter possibly established.

These were some of the technologies which came on stream in the '60s, and that were changing Americans' perceptions of who we are, what attitudes govern our lives, and what, in fact, will shape our future.

In fact, these were the new technologies which, as Peter Drucker wrote in 1968, were engendering an "Age of Discontinuity," discontinuities which, he said, "are the continental drifts that form new continents, rather than the wars that form new boundaries."

Without elaborating, Drucker's four major discontinuities were: 1) Genuinely new technologies based on the science of the first 50 or 60 years of the 20th century; (2) The shift from an international economy in which separate nations are discrete units to a world economy in which common information generates the same demands regardless of national culture or boundaries; (3) The rapid change in the matrix of social and economic life—the dominance of large institutions, the increasing pluralism of American life, the emerging disenchantment with government, and a new sociopolitical reality which we didn't yet understand; and (4) The emergence of knowledge as the central capital and the crucial resource of the economy, a fact which would change labor forces, work, education, and the very meaning of knowledge and its politics.

These developments of the '60s, which gave Americans a tangible sense of having entered some new phase of human experience. These were some of the developments which caused *Time* to comment in 1965 that "technology has advanced more rapidly in the past 50 years than in the previous 5000."

Such new capacities spawned a plethora of predictions. Marshall McLuhan predicted that by 2000, the wheel and the highway would be obsolete, replaced by the hovercraft. Dr. Glenn T. Seaborg, chairman of the Atomic Energy Commission, told a women's meeting that by the year 2000 housewives would have a "robot maid" shaped like a box with several arms and hands and one large eye on the top. Isaac Asimov wrote in *The New York Post* that by the end of the century man would be exploring the limits of the solar system and living underground. *The New York Times* even went so far as to predict that in the year 2000, the "chic woman" might have "live butterflies fluttering around her hairdo, attracted by a special scented hair spray." Nothing, it seemed, was impossible.

But as the prospect of such new technical possibilities accelerating the tempo of life to a pace beyond human comprehension dangled visions of utopia, many felt the need to survey and understand the potential consequences. For what mattered most was not the new gadgets and conveniences technology would create, but the need for social and institutional arrangements that could deal with the attendant problems. What would be the relationship of the individual to ever-increasing bureaucratic structures? What new social forms could compensate for the increasing government centralization? How would institutions respond to the growth of the burgeoning educated professional and technical class, with its demand for greater autonomy at work? What would be the socializing agent for children, as families continued to lose their authority and social role? How would we deal with the increasing disjuncture between the culture and the social structure—the tendency for society to become more functionally organized around knowledge, while the culture becomes more hedonistic, permissive and distrustful of authority?

As the distinguished social psychologist Lawrence K. Frank noted, the America of 1965 faced a situation somewhat similar to that of 18th century Europe, when such inquiring thinkers as John Locke, Adam Smith and the French *philosophes* formulated the premises that underlie the democratic polity and market economy of the next 200 year–rationality, mobility and the transmission of public information and free exchange. Today, Frank argued, a new comprehensive political philosophy was needed that would formulate the assumptions of the pluralistic economy and the service society that was emerging.

To meet this need, Frank suggested the creation of what eventually became known as the Commission on the Year 2000, chaired by one of America's most eminent sociologists, Daniel Bell of Harvard University. The task of organizing the Commission and implementing Frank's proposal was taken up by the American Academy of Arts and Sciences, and selections from their eventual report, published in the summer 1967 issue of the Academy's journal *Daedalus*, was simply titled *Toward the Year 2000: Work in Progress*. The full report consisted of some 60 papers written by a roster of Academy members which reads like a *Who's Who* of America's more forward-reaching thinkers.

Perhaps the most significant contribution of the Commission on the Year 2000 was the conceptualization of the postindustrial society. Daniel Bell observed that during the industrial era, the key institutions were organizations for the production of goods. In the postindustrial era, Bell suggested, the primary institutions would be "intellectual institutions" such as research corporations, universities and scientific laboratories. Bell raised the critical question of the social role of work. Work, Bell stressed, has been the chief means of binding the individual to reality. What happens in a society where increasing amounts of work are assumed by technology, and where the required intellectual work becomes more concentrated in a relatively small minority of the population? Such reflections today may seem so obvious as to be irrelevant, but they were critical insights when first offered in the mid '60s.

Two books written as a result of the Commission on the Year 2000 were Daniel Bell's *The Coming of Post-Industrial Society* and *The Year 2000: A Framework for Speculation* by Herman Kahn and Anthony J.

Wiener. These two books became the defining documents of the emerging postindustrial era. Whereas in earlier times Jules Verne, H.G. Wells and others had written fictional accounts speculating about a distant future, Bell's and Kahn's books spelled out the contemporary dynamics of change that were accelerating so rapidly that the future was becoming indistinguishable from the present.

It was in this sense that the 1960s became the first decade of a new epoch of challenge and possibility for America and the world. It was as Rollo May writes: "We awake after a sleep of many centuries to find ourselves in a new and irrefutable sense in the myth of humankind. We find ourselves in a new world community; we cannot destroy the parts without destroying the whole. In this bright loveliness we know now that we are truly sisters and brothers, at last in the same family."

Chapter Seventeen

Future Shock and Millennial Neurosis—The '70s, '80s and '90s

SUMMARY: An overview of the developments in the areas of technology, economics, social/political and global affairs. The shock of "future shock." The major contexts of Toffler, Bell and Kahn, plus assessments of others. *The Late Great Planet Earth* as the best-selling nonfiction book of the 1970s. The Book of Revelation, Nostradamus and Cayce. Understanding the history and psychological meaning of the Apocalypse as a global phenomenon. Popular cultural expressions of Apocalypse in America.

By the last three decades of the 20th century, events of the Interregnum were moving at such velocity that it's impossible to look at these decades individually. Rather, a better way to obtain an overview of what has happened is by means of a matrix that divides the three decades into the categories of science and technology, economics, politics and social developments, and global developments. (See Appendix A.)

In 1970, two books swept America. From different perspectives, they heralded the arrival of something very new in the American experience, and they captured two of the themes that run through the final three decades of the century.

Future Shock, by Alvin Toffler, had its genesis in a phrase Toffler coined in 1965 describing the shattering stress and disorientation people experience when they are subjected to too much change in too short a time. Thus the subject of *Future Shock* is "the roaring current of change, a current so powerful today that it overturns institutions, shifts our values and shrivels our roots." *Future Shock* describes both the *rate* and *content* of change, and how both are reshaping the global landscape.

Toffler illustrates the accelerating pace of change by pointing out that in 6000 B.C. the fastest transportation available over long distances was the camel caravan, averaging 8 miles per hour. When the chariot was invented in 1600 B.C. the maximum speed of travel was raised to roughly 20 miles per hour. By the 1880s the steam locomotive reached a speed of 100 mph. Fifty-eight years later man was flying at speeds of 400 mph, and in another 20-year jump that had been doubled to 800 mph. By the 1960s man was traveling at 4,000 mph, and a few years later space capsules were circling the earth at 18,000 mph. In sum, it took man millions of years to reach a speed of 100 mph in 1880, and only 80 years to jump to 18,000 mph.

Elsewhere, it has been shown that the time for circumnavigating the globe decreased every 25 years by a factor of two between 1880 and 1928, and by a factor of 10 ever since 1928. This increase in speed of movement is a metaphor for the acceleration of the tempo of change humankind is experiencing.

As Toffler writes, "We are creating a new society. Not a changed society. Not an extended, larger-than-life version of our present society. But a new society."

Toffler quotes Sir George Thompson, the British physicist and Nobel prizewinner, who believed that the nearest historic parallel with today is not the industrial revolution but rather the "invention of agriculture in the neolithic age."

Toffler notes that as well as the cornucopia of new possibilities technological change is creating, it is also generating a crack-up of consensus, a fragmentation of values and belief, and an information overload that is contributing to increased mental illness. "By blindly stepping up the rate of change, the level of novelty, and the extent of choice," Toffler writes, "we are thoughtlessly tampering with [the] environmental preconditions of rationality."

Future Shock is probably one of the most influential books of the second half of the 20th century. While it built on the work done by The Commission on the Year 2000 and on Kenneth Boulding's writing, *Future Shock* became a best-seller, and it popularized the theme of radical technological change and its social, institutional and personal consequences. The book verbalized for a mass readership what people intuitively knew was taking place. The very words "future shock" entered the popular vocabulary as shorthand for a disorienting pace of change that seems out of control.

Future Shock

Propelled by the "future shock" of new technologies and the acceleration of events, including man's landing on the moon, a new discipline emerged through the late '60s and early '70–the study of the future. Human beings have always tried to divine tomorrow, some by charting the stars, others by consulting oracles or prophets, both methods surrounded by an air of the occult. It was only in 1902 that the first comprehensive survey of future possibilities was made by H.G. Wells in his *Anticipations of the Reaction of Mechanical and Scientific Progress upon Human Life and Thought*.

But by the mid-'70s, futures research, as a rational discipline, was an established profession. Hundreds of books and thousands of articles were written about a future that was hurtling toward us faster than we could absorb. In 1992, writing in *The Annals* published by the American Academy of Political and Social Science, Michael Marien published a list of over 100 books which, he said, served simply as an *introduction* to futures study.

Foremost among the books written during the '70s was Daniel Bell's *The Coming of Post-Industrial Society* (1973). With a rigor and scholarship that would be expected of one of America's premier sociologists, this was the book that became the most authorative reference on the emergence of postindustrial America. What Bell covers, as he says in his introduction, is "that the major source of structural change in society–the change in the modes of innovation in the relation of science to technology and in public policy–is the change in the character of knowledge: the exponential growth and branching of science, the rise of a new intellectual technology, the creation of systematic research through R&D budgets, and, as the calyx of all this, the codification of theoretical knowledge." In Bell's view, these were the defining characteristics of the epochal shift America was experiencing as the older industrial system gave way to a new order of affairs.

Bell offers graphic examples to describe what could be somewhat dry and abstruse phenomena. While discussing the change in the character of knowledge, for example, he notes that the editions of the *Encyclopaedia Britannica* published between 1745 and 1785 had been put together by one or two men who were "still able to take the whole of human knowledge for their province." But it was with the Third Edition (1788) that the need to draw on specialist learning was first adopted, as the relevant knowledge one individual needs had grown beyond the bounds one person could master. Thus Bell pinpoints 1788 as the watershed when "the unity of knowledge was fragmented." The 1967 edition, Bell notes, involved 10,000 "recognized experts" in its preparation. So from two people to 10,000 is a graphic measure of the explosion of knowledge that has taken place since the founding of America.

Along with Bell's *The Coming of Post-Industrial Society*, the second book defining the character of the emergent future was *The Year 2000: A Framework for Speculation on the Next Thirty-three Years* (1967) by Herman Kahn and Anthony J. Wiener. This book introduced a variety of methodological innovations to forecasting, especially the mixture of historical perspective with statistical technique.

After a 400-page survey of everything from differing historical epochs, to political cycles, to global economic growth patterns, to technology development, to the potential for nuclear holocaust, Kahn and Wiener offer a concluding note:

Man is developing enormous power to change his own environment–not only the outside world, but also his own physiological and intrapsychic situation . . . [T]his very power over nature threatens to become a force of nature that is itself out of control . . . In the final decades of this century, we shall have the technological and economic power to change the world radically, but probably not get very much ability to restrain our strivings, let alone understand or control the results of the changes we will be making.

For Kahn and Weiner, the only safeguard is to try to moderate our "Faustian impulses to overpower the environment," and to foster "an unflagging respect for the world as we find it."

In the following years a torrent of evaluations emerged describing the context of change that was reshaping the human condition. In 1972, John McHale described the last third of the 20th century as "the age of critical transition, revolution and discontinuity." McHale's analysis concerned "the explosive growth in man's actual and potential capacities to interfere on a large scale with the natural environmental processes." His second concern was the lag in our "conceptual orientation" in dealing with these new capacities, as well as our lack of a "social process" through which we may manage the changes reorienting human affairs.

Canada's Ruben Nelson saw "the world changing around us in ways which are too profound for us to easily understand." Japan's Taichi Sakaiya perceived a similarity between today's global situation and the dawn of the Middle Ages with its heightened emphasis on subjectivity. We are, said Sakaiya, "in the midst of the knowledge-value revolution." Alvin Toffler saw humanity experiencing the "third great tidal wave of history"–the information revolution.

Fritjof Capra believed that the planet as a whole had reached a "turning point," that we face "a crisis of perception," and that we must find a "new vision of reality." France's Jacques Attali saw economics as "the central organizing principle" for a future where "traditional notions of national sovereignty are increasingly irrelevant." Marilyn Ferguson described the "ascendance of a startling worldview" that has triggered "the most rapid cultural realignment in history."

Daniel Boorstin saw the emergence of the "Republic of Technology" where nations are no longer distinguished by their heritage or their culture, but by "their pace of change." Rapidly developing countries, he believed, "are those that are most speedily obsolescing their inheritance." Thus, for America at the dawn of the 21st century, Boorstin thought, the problem is "how to keep alive the sense of quest which brought our nation into being."

Jacob Bronowski told us that in every age, "there is a new way of seeing and asserting the coherence of the world . . ."

Given that the intellectual leadership of the 20th century rests with scientists, Bronowski told unnumbered Americans watching his immensely popular TV series *The Ascent of Man,* "No beliefs can be built up in this century that are not based on science as the recognition of the uniqueness of man . . ." For Bronowski, it "is not the business of science to inherit the earth, but to inherit the moral imagination; because without that, man and beliefs and science will perish together." Thus, he said, we "have to cure ourselves of the itch for absolute knowledge and power."

By the early '80s Daniel Bell saw "the cultural contradictions of capitalism" as "a watershed in Western society; we are witnessing the end of the bourgeois idea–that view of human action and social relations, particularly of economic exchange–which has molded the modern era for the last 200 years." Daniel Yankelovich described events in equally broad terms. What is required, he said, "is to accomplish the one great task that has eluded Western civilization since the age of science and technology began–breaking through the iron cage of rationalization and instrumentation in order to make industrial society a fit place for human life . . . we are obliged to find qualitative substitutes for the mindless pursuit of more of everything."

In the late '80s, George Gilder was telling us that in light of the advent of quantum theory, the "central event of the twentieth century is the overthrow of matter." This overthrow of matter, Gilder says, means we must stop thinking of the world as basically material and begin imagining it "as a manifestation of consciousness." In Gilder's view, the quantum era "takes the world from a technology of control to a technology of freedom." In this, we have come to the end of the "materialist superstition."

By the middle of the '90s, Kevin Kelly was defining our time as one in which "the realm of the *born*–all that is nature–and the realm of the *made*–all that is humanly constructed–are becoming one." Machines, he said, "are becoming biological and the biological is becoming engineered." Ken Wilber was describing the global transformation as being driven by "a new techno-economic base (informational), but it also brings with it a new worldview, with a new mode of self and new intentional and behavioral patterns, set in a new cultural worldspace with new social institutions as anchors." And by the late '90s, Jim Taylor and Watts Wacker were telling us that "we are experiencing a change so rapid and so massive that by century's end it will have swept away nearly the entire underpinning of modern life." We are, they asserted, in the midst of a "shift from reason-based to chaos-based logic."

These are the perceptions of "future shock." These are the views of a shift from one phase of human existence to a new and unknown stage. These are only a few of the perspectives of the global changes taking place that have been offered over the past three decades.

Millennial Neurosis

The second book that swept America in the '70s along with *Future Shock* was *The Late Great Planet Earth* by Hal Lindsey. Lindsey's book was a pre-millennial treatise that foresees nuclear destruction caused by the Antichrist, after which Jesus Christ returns to earth and saves mankind.

The Late Great Planet Earth was the best-selling nonfiction book of the 1970s, and by 1990 it had sold over 28 million copies. Thus Lindsey's book gave popular voice to the apocalyptic vision of St. John (author of at least the first two Epistles of John, and not to be confused with the Apostle John) written in Revelation about A.D. 95. St. John foretold of the end times, when, after rule of the Antichrist, Jesus Christ would return and reign for a thousand years. At the end of this 1,000 years, the Antichrist (Satan) will return and an ultimate battle will ensue between the forces of good and evil in which God will win, and a Last Judgment will condemn sinners to eternal torment.

Revelation doesn't specify any date for the Second Coming, and there has always been speculation as to whether John was encouraging the then besieged-Christians by suggesting Christ's return within the not too distant future. At no point has the Church ever attached any specific time for the prophecies of Revelation to come to pass, preferring instead to push it as far into the future as possible. As a matter of historical fact, the Christian dating system was only initiated roughly 500 years after Revelation was written, some time in the 6th century by the monk Dionysius Exiguus. And if the estimate that Christ was born in 6 B.C. is accurate, we are, in point of fact, already into the third millennium. Conveniently overlooked in most of the historical discussion about St. John's prophecies is St. Augustine's argument in *The City of God* that what Revelation was talking about was symbolic, not literal.

The concept of a thousand-year period of time after which judgment will ensue is not uniquely Christian. Indeed, there are a number of Jewish as well as Christian apocalyptic writings in the extra canonical literature. But certainly the most famous of that genre is Revelation, much of which is taken from Jewish apocalyptic writing, as well as from elements of Greek mythology. The main attribute of apocalyptic literature is the description of dreams or visions in which the seer is shown "otherworldly" secrets that climax in the end of the age. Most apocalyptic literature contains images of the last judgment, with the coming of a divinity or divine king who will impose his punishments and reconstitute life in a new order.

The concept of a final judgment expressed in Revelation is also found in Egyptian texts dating from 3000 B.C. Plato, writing in 434 B.C., entertains the idea of final judgment in the *Republic*. Vergil speaks of the Last Judgment in the *Aeneid*, written about 30 B.C. The notion of a Last Judgment is also found in ancient Chinese and Indian texts. Damian Thompson, author of *The End of Time*, writes that the existence of a divine plan for humanity, which can be glimpsed by arranging man's experience into epochs "has been taken for granted in every society which has recorded history." The most vivid–and horrifying–20th century example of the thousand-year concept was Hitler's Thousand Year Reich promulgated in 1933.

Given the pervasive presence of apocalyptic sentiment in America as the second millennium comes to a close, it is well to understand the *psychological* significance of what Revelation and the Apocalypse mean.(4)

The word "apocalypse" is the Greek word for revelation, or an uncovering of what has been hidden. There are four features to the image of the apocalypse: revelation, judgment, destruction and renewal. Revelation discloses new truth about life. Judgment assesses the state of contemporary conditions in light of this new truth. Destruction is the collapse of old forms which are no longer effective within the context of the new truth. Renewal is the recreation of civilization according to the requirements of the new truth.

In this sense, *from a psychological point of view*, the story of the 20th century can be seen as the working out of these four features of the meaning of apocalypse. In all areas of life, humanity has gained more new truth about the nature and workings of the universe in the 20th century than in all previous history combined. Against the background of this new scientific understanding of nature and the universe, we have judged the effectiveness of former beliefs and institutions. This assessment is at the heart of the spiritual search taking place in America today. It's the cause of our rethinking of the role of the nation-state or the status of past social relationships. Then has come the destruction or collapse of old forms of how we have organized our affairs, forms that are no longer effective in light of the implementation of our new discoveries. This collapse is seen in our need to reinvent all our institutions, from education to new modes of self-government. And finally comes the birth of some new pattern of civilization based on the laws of the new truth or understanding. This new birth is seen in the emerging global communications system and economy which are both largely based on quantum mechanics and Einstein's theory of relativity. The new birth is also seen in a greater openness and opportunity for the individual, whatever his or her background or social status.

To emphasize once again, from a psychological standpoint, we see this meaning of apocalypse manifesting itself through most of the 20th century. We can now see that the "end time" which has been referred to in past descriptions of the apocalypse does not mean the end of the world. Rather, it means the end of a particular view of the meaning of human existence, while some new dispensation comes into fulfillment. It is literally world-shattering, as we are talking about the end of one *Zeitgeist*, and the birth of a new world view. Revelation "lays out the final scenario of the end of the Christian eon, and describes symbolically the concluding events of the Judeo-Christian myth, the myth that has been the womb and metaphysical container of Western civilization." (5) This imagery of world destruction and consequent regeneration is basic to the revitalization movements in countless cultures throughout history. This is the deeper meaning of the apocalypse, and it is a meaning that is only now becoming apparent. With this wider understanding, we can now evaluate the writings of Lindsay and others who gave us one particular interpretation of the apocalypse.

Lindsay's 1970 book was only the latest in a long line of apocalyptic writings. Perhaps best known of earlier manuscripts was that of the 16th century French doctor and seer, Nostradamus, who is said to have predicted any number of events, from the Great Fire of London in 1666 to Hitler and World War II. Nostradamus's most quoted book, *Centuries*–the title designating 100 forecasts–told us that a "great King of terror" would come from heaven in July 1999, after which there would be a thousand-year peace starting somewhere near the middle of the 21st century.

In the 20th century, support for St. John's Revelation predictions was given a boost when Pope Pius X taught in 1910 that the Antichrist had already arrived. At one point he is even said to have had a public vision of the destruction of the Vatican. In 1914, Pope Benedict XV issued an encyclical declaring World War I to be the beginning of the "Last Age." In 1922, Pope Pius XI issued an encyclical "Miserimus Redemptor" stating: "These are really the signs of the last age as was announced by Our Lord."

Even Pope John Paul II, shortly before he became pope, told an audience in Cracow, Poland: "We find ourselves in the presence of the greatest confrontation in history, the greatest mankind has ever had to confront. We are facing the final confrontation between the Church and the Anti-Church, between the Gospel and the Anti-Gospel." As

Damian Thompson commented, Pope John Paul II's statement "is an apocalyptic statement about the course of human history."

Probably the best known American so-called prophet was Edgar Cayce (1877-1945). Cayce predicted sudden shifts in Earth's polar axis in 1998, with northern Europe and Japan destroyed, World War III erupting in 1999, and civilization demolished in 2000. Cayce has been a significant source of truth and inspiration for many people who believe a literal interpretation of Revelation.

In terms of the effect of millennial theories on America's psyche, Liesl Schillinger wrote in *The Washington Post* in 1999 that as the millennium nears, "thoughts of eternity and death joust in the collective unconscious, emerging in art, politics, religion, music, dress, and social behavior. In other words, people start believing in psychics, joining cults, dressing in black, piercing their flesh, killing themselves and writing songs about Heaven, Hell, Satan, and the Madonna."

Thus we've seen apocalyptic cultural images gain momentum throughout the last three decades. Images of the end of the world, of nuclear catastrophe, of a new holocaust, of secret machinations of government, of an epidemic of the Ebola virus, of environmental destruction, of Los Angeles destroyed by fire and volcano lava and much more pervade the culture. Survivalists and self-styled "militia" give practical expression to many of these images.

In 1985 Colleen McCullough's novel *A Creed for the Third Millennium* described the "Millennial Neurosis" abroad in America, a mood which expresses itself in the loss of hope in the future and faith in the present. It is, she says, a perpetual feeling of futility and lack of purpose. "It is a dull and utterly unproductive fury turned in upon itself." It is believing in nothing. Such a tone pervades contemporary culture, from Beavis and Butt-head, to "Dilbert," to movies such as *Bladerunner, Terminator, Demolition Man, Strange Days, Seven,* and *Face/Off.*

In *Face/Off,* a movie about good and evil exchanging places, the opening scenes show a massive choral group singing the "Hallelujah Chorus" while a demonic drug lord, disguised in priestly garb, activates the timer on a biological time-bomb that will kill everyone in Los Angeles. A final scene takes place in a Catholic Church where the deranged drug lord–the Antichrist–arms stretched out, is superimposed on a crucifix where the crucified Christ, arms stretched out, is nailed to the Cross. Intended or not, it is powerful symbolism for the final face-off between good and evil.

In popular music, David Browne reports in *The New York Times*, "From the mosh pit to 'death metal' rock to the urban brawls of gangster rap, pop music has never sounded so aggressive and intense. Its clattering noise, using samples of grinding guitars, is the sound of civilization falling apart. The electronic dance music known as techno is nothing but a series of disconnected, computerized bleeps and groans–the soundtrack for a world in which phone sex is taking the place of human interaction."

Thus it would seem we've gone from Paul Simon singing in the '70s, "And so you see I have come to doubt / All that I once held as true; / I stand alone without belief, / The only truth I know is you," to the Smashing Pumpkins singing in the '90s, "welcome to nowhere fast / nothing here ever lasts . . . living makes me sick / so sick i wish i could die / down in the belly of the beast."

In the words of Canada's Michael Posner, "[W]atching the decline of Western culture, the steady erosion of its social norms and values, one feels an impending sense that Yeats' rough beast is getting mighty close to Jerusalem. We're nearing the end of something, not just the century, and the pace is quickening." *The Economist* reports that some sociologists of religion sum all this up as PMT, "pre-millennial tension." The common symptoms of PMT, they say, are disorientation, loss of faith in institutions, a rising sense of unfocused excitement, and visions of an apocalyptic or utopian future.

"A utopian future." This is as much an expression of the apocalypse mentality as is the expectation of destruction. Perhaps the most dominant statement of such present-day utopianism is represented by those who see technology–especially computers–as evolution itself producing something beyond the human species. In this view, CD-ROMs, the telephone, television and computers are equated with chemicals, cells, multicelluar organisms and neural structures as specialized structures allowing evolution to take place in microseconds. As Danny Hillis writes,

"We're at that point analogous to when single-celled organisms were turning into multicelled organisms." Hillis believes we're "now using programs to make much faster computers so the process [of evolution] can run much faster." We're "taking off" he exudes. Such belief would appear to be the latest manifestation of the apocalypse archetype, which has expressed itself in different forms throughout the 20th century.

Inasmuch as Christianity has, over the past century, ceased to be the inner dynamic of Western culture, widespread spiritual fragmentation takes place as people seek spiritual refuge wherever they can find it, according to their individual inclination. And so we see Americans reaching for a smorgasbord of spiritual or psychological experiences.

Such experiences include–but are not limited to–resurgent fundamentalism which accepts a literal interpretation of Revelation; increased dependence on astrology; the spread of various cults such as the Branch Davidians and Heaven's Gate; exploration of the paranormal as in the TV show *Millennium*; the search for a higher consciousness; belief in the intervention of angels; the New Age phenomenon; the search for some ancient wisdom a la *The Celestine Prophecy*; TV shows such as *Touched by an Angel* or *The X-Files* with its mantra, "I want to believe"; increased interest in mysticism, occultism, Buddhism, and Eastern thought; visitation to such supposed religious sites as the Egyptian pyramids, Stonehenge, the Mayan temples and Machu Picchu; the belief that extraterrestrial life has come to save us from ourselves; the emergence of countless new schools of psychology; science and rationalism elevated to a religious status; and even despair and nihilism given philosophical garb.

The Internet assumes a spiritual dimension as it sprouts everything from the First Cyberchurch of the Scientific God, to the Aquarian Concepts Community Divine New Order Government, to Ecunet–an online network of virtual prayer chapels and prayer meetings. The Internet, we are told, could even change our ideas about God. Says MIT psychologist Sherry Turkel, "People see the Internet as a new metaphor for God."

From the standpoint of depth psychology, all of these phenomena are displays of that archetype that expresses the apocalypse; for the apocalypse is not simply some abstract notion floating out of the ether; it is a universal motif embedded in the human psyche, and, increasingly, it seems to be manifesting itself in symbolic and collective form.

And so *Future Shock* and *The Late Great Planet Earth* express two of the Interregnum's threads of temperament that weave together to form the mental fabric of early 21st-century America.

Chapter Eighteen

Quo Vadis, America?

SUMMARY: Robert Nisbet on the fraying of civil society. Expressions of the "American Decline" syndrome. Reagan and "America is back!" Fall of the Berlin Wall and the Soviet Union.

A primary characteristic of an Interregnum is a sense of subjectivity, an inward-looking orientation. Throughout the '70s, '80s and '90s, America was in the midst of possibly the most intensive self-searching she had ever known. For 16 years, from the fall of Saigon in 1975 to the fall of the Soviet Union in 1991, *Quo vadis, America?* gripped the national psyche. America's defeat in Vietnam, the energy crisis, the perceived declining competitiveness with its "Japan is No. 1" syndrome, the after shocks of Watergate, the obvious dysfunction of our institutions, the increasing ethnic fragmentation, the seemingly intractable problems of rising drug use and its associated crime—these and many more issues gave rise to a profound disquiet in the American spirit.

This disquiet was given voice in 1975 by Robert Nisbet, one of America's foremost scholars and sociologists. Nisbet saw America experiencing a retreat "from the major to the minor, from the noble to the trivial, the communal to the personal, and from the objective to the subjective."

Nisbet's concerns went to the very essence of whether or not

America still possesses the elements without which even an elemental form of civil society can exist:

> [W]hat was present in very substantial measure in the basic works of the founders of political democracy was a respect for such social institutions as property, family, local community, religion, and voluntary association, and for such cultural and social values as objective reason, the discipline of language, self-restraint, the work ethic, and, far from the least, the culture that had taken root in classical civilization and grown, with rare interruptions, ever since . . . The architects of Western democracy were all students of history, and they had every intellectual right to suppose that moral values and social structures which had survived as many vicissitudes and environmental changes as these had over the two and a half millennia of their existence in Western society would go on for at least a few more centuries
>
> *But in fact they have not.* [Emphasis added.]

If Nisbet's appraisal is valid–and mounting evidence would appear to support him–then America is faced with a challenge for which there is no precedent in the history of Western civilization. Thus his statement merits considerable reflection. He is suggesting that the elements which historically have constituted the foundation and fabric not only of civil society, but of *civilized life*, no longer exercise enough intensity to control events and to shape the framework of contemporary existence. If this is correct, it is a new departure point in the long story not only of America, but of Western society.

Nisbet was far from alone in his alarm. Just as President Reagan was proclaiming, "America is back," Lance Morrow wrote in *Time*–the original voice of the "American Century,"–"For some time, a suspicion had taken hold that the trajectory of history is descendent, that the world moves from disorder to greater disorder, toward darkness–or else toward the terminal global flash." Thomas Griffith argued in the pages of *Fortune* that a "persuasive case can be made that if the American dream is dead, or dormant, it is because the dream of the fathers has been mostly realized, while the dream of the sons has not yet been successfully formulated." *U.S. News & World Report* decried "the decline of old certitudes . . . that once bred faith in leaders, institutions and the U.S. future." Angst even entered the comics, as Garry Trudeau had a "Doonesbury" character blather to a friend, "The American dream is over, Mac. It's been shattered into a million jagged pieces. All that's left is a nation of middle-class hustlers."

Even the conservative *Wall Street Journal* sensed the significance of the moment. Comparing America with the end of the great age of Greece, an editorial noted that our century is "a similar time of flux, an interstice between eras. Old beliefs have decayed and new beliefs have not sprung forward to replace them." The *Journal* noted that it was "not only religious belief that has declined; so has the powerful secular faith that sprang from the Enlightenment. The power of reason, the power of science, the belief in progress—all are coming under increasing doubt."

Such doubt was manifesting itself in our concept of the "good life." As Paul Samuelson, the first American Nobel prizewinner in economics, points out, "'[M]ore' isn't enough. People are better housed, fed, and educated than twenty-five years ago, but that isn't producing satisfaction. There's a spiritual element missing . . ." Another noted economist and author, Robert Heilbroner, sees this spiritual vacuum as common to both capitalism and socialism. "Economic growth and technical advancement, the greatest triumphs of our epoch of history," says Heilbroner, "have shown themselves inadequate sources for collective contentment and hope. Material advance, the most profoundly distinguishing attribute of industrial capitalism and socialism alike, has proved unable to satisfy the human spirit."

By the end of the '80s, Allan Bloom, a University of Chicago classical educator of world renown, assessed America's higher education during the '60s, '70s and '80s. America's universities, Bloom thought, are no longer providing the knowledge of the great tradition of philosophy and literature which alone equips students with an awareness of the order of nature and the human place within it. Bloom decried the assembly-line production of students who lack an understanding of the past and a vision of the future. "What each generation is," Bloom wrote, "can best be discovered in its relation to the permanent concerns of mankind." Academe is no longer training students to understand such fundamental concerns.

As if to validate Bloom's critique, the student speaker at a Stanford University graduation described his class as not knowing how it "relates to the past or the future, having little sense of the present, no life-sustaining beliefs, secular or religious," and as consequently having "no goal and no path of effective action."

As has often been the case, America's foreign admirers provided insights during the '80s that went to the heart of what was becoming seen as the American malaise. France's Michel Crozier, educator and author of worldwide acclaim and long a friend of America, asked, "When all is said and done, what is missing in American culture? I venture to say, it is evil, or more precisely the acknowledgment that evil exists." In Crozier's view, "When a people suppose that evil does not exist, choice does not exist for them anymore, and freedom loses its balance." Crozier acknowledged America's past role as "mankind's main laboratory." Other countries, he thought, "were observers," and they basically implemented in their own way the promises of history that were being worked out in America. America is still the world leader, Crozier believed, not only because of its size, but because "history still holds them in this role."

Time magazine's Robert Hughes was only one of those who saw in the America of the late '80s and early '90s a similarity with Rome in her decline. In a biting cultural criticism, Hughes wrote of an American polity "obsessed with therapies and filled with distrust of formal politics; skeptical of authority and prey to superstition; its political language corroded by fake pity and euphemism. Like late Rome," Hughes continued, "in its long imperial reach, in the corruption and verbosity of its senators, in its reliance on sacred geese (those feathered ancestors of our own pollsters and spin-doctors) and in its submission to senile, deified emperors controlled by astrologers and extravagant wives.

A culture which has replaced gladiatorial games, as a means of pacifying the mob, with hi-tech wars on television that cause immense slaughter and yet leave the Mesopotamian satraps in full power over their wretched subjects." Those who crave a return of the Delphic sibyl, Hughes concludes, "get Shirley MacLaine, and a 35,000-year-old Cro-Magnon warrior named Ramtha takes up residence inside a blonde housewife on the West Coast, generating millions upon millions of cult dollars in seminars, tapes and books."

The climax of the *Quo vadis, America?* search may have been signaled by Paul Kennedy's book, *The Rise and Fall of the Great Powers*. An Englishman who moved to America in 1983, Kennedy is a widely respected Yale University professor of history, and his book became a focal point of national debate. Kennedy surveyed the decline of several nations as a result of what he described as "imperial overreach." Applying this same analysis to America, the "America in decline" syndrome fueled heated debate for several years. Whether or not such debate actually resulted in offering a sense of a future compelling enough to focus and energize the national will, or to deal with a fragmenting America, is open to question.

Such absence of a coherent expression of national purpose, such a collapse in any underlying agreement as to both content and direction of the American experiment, was reflected in mounting social disarray, especially in education. The Carnegie Foundation for the Advancement of Teaching, in a report based on 13,000 interviews with faculty, undergraduate students and administrators, found that America's colleges and universities are "[F]ailing to give students a coherent larger view—a way to think about and understand deeper ethical, historical and civic issues." The American Council on Education reported a 1985 survey showing that "[D]eveloping a meaningful philosophy of life" declined as a main goal among college freshmen by almost 50 percent between 1967 and 1983. Derek Bok, then president of Harvard University, reported that the stated goals of the student applications of incoming freshmen were first, money, second, power and third, making a reputation.

What the pollsters found in education reflected a broader social confusion. Patrick Cadell, head of the opinion research company Cambridge Reports, wrote in 1984: "We are finding substantial numbers of people who believe that the future is slipping away . . . we have lost our sense of control . . . we feel poorer not because we are, but because tranquility is part of our standard of living—and it is on the wane . . . we have been learning that the gross national tranquility will not rise in step with the Gross National Product." The general tenor of Cadell's comments was echoed in a University of Louisville study on illness, which concluded, "Our mode of life itself, the way we live, is emerging as today's principle cause of illness."

By the beginning of the '90s, however, the "decline" debate had given way to sweeping calls for the renewal of America's "civil society"—those private, spontaneous, grass-roots efforts, Nisbet had seen disappearing, and that Tocqueville had said characterize the uniqueness of American democracy. The National Commission on Civic Renewal, the National Commission on Philanthropy and Civic Renewal, the National Commission on Society, Culture, and Community, and the Council on Civil Society were some of the responses to the concern over the condition of civil society in America.

Equally important in ending the "decline" debate was the 1989 collapse of the Berlin Wall and the 1991 dissolution of the Soviet Union, and with it the end of the Cold War. These liberating events were celebrated around the world, and Americans took just pride in the role we had played in bringing them about. We enjoyed a respite from the doubt and soul-searching that had marked the decade just past, and we indulged in the "victory" that made us feel better about ourselves. We seemed to need psychic reassurance, and our chest-thumping over the end of the Cold War served the purpose. Democracy and free markets, we assured ourselves, would now somehow bloom in the ashes of communism.

And in our enthusiasm over the apparent spread of free markets and democratic elections, the question of "*Quo vadis, America?*" was left unanswered. Or rather it was answered by an America which became mesmerized by faster computers, the Internet, glitzy entertainment and a whole new world of information technology.

Chapter Nineteen

The 21st Century and the Crisis of Meaning

SUMMARY: We come now to the heart of the Interregnum–the "crisis of meaning" so prevalent in the Western world, and even visible in such countries as Japan and China. Compared to earlier periods of history, the world appears to be moving into a time of "mythlessness."

To help consider this new epoch, this final chapter will be written in a different style. We shall move from the third person narrative and return to the first person informal tone employed in the Introduction. I hope this will provide both energy and intelligibility as we consider this most critical of issues.

I offer this chapter in two parts–"The Contemporary Crisis" and "New Meaning for the Human Venture."

Part I – The Contemporary Crisis

The Hypothesis

At least two profound developments emerged in the world that began to find coherent expression in the 1,000-year period roughly between 800 B.C and 700 A.D. First, a great swath of humanity left the earlier stage of "animism"–projections of psychic content into trees, rocks, brooks and sacred places–and moved forward to the stage when the great culture-forming spiritual dispensations of the world took shape. The human relationship to the "other" (God) began to be expressed in new symbols and metaphors. The spiritual and ethical framework these myths provided–whether those of Confucius, Buddha, Zoroaster, Greek gods, Israel's Yahweh, Mithras, Christianity, or Islam–endowed the individual, whatever his or her ethnic identity or stage of development, with delineated values, and they offered answers to the ultimate questions of existence.

Second, consciousness became apparent. Not consciousness as we know it today, but an earlier manifestation of consciousness as exemplified, say, by the archetypal symbolism of the Old Testament or early Greek mythology.

Both these developments represented milestones in human psychological development.

With this in mind, I offer a hypothesis to consider, a hypothesis that suggests we are in the midst of another seminal psychological development. This hypothesis is twofold: First, we may be in the midst of the long term weakening of the various spiritual myths just referred to. Such a statement may seem to fly in the face of the various spreading fundamentalisms, but fundamentalism may actually be a symptom of this demise. Second, despite appearances and conventional wisdom, we've been experiencing a contraction of consciousness.

If these suggestions are fact, then we're likely in the midst of the most significant reorientation of human affairs to take place at least since the Greco-Roman world gave way to Christianity and the early beginnings of modern Europe. It's a reorientation of which the most dramatic expression is the crisis of meaning so apparent in the Western world and gradually spreading in Asia.

This is the hypothesis we'll explore. It is not my intent to try to "prove" this hypothesis. It can't be proven. Rather, my aim is simply to suggest an explanation for *some* of the trauma the world is experiencing today.

But first, a word about the word "psychology." Simply to use the word "spooks" a lot of people. They immediately think of neurosis or mental illness of some sort. Indeed, contemporary psychology primarily deals with such problems.

The older meaning of the word psychology, however, is "the study of the soul." It's in that sense I will refer to psychology and psychological reorientation; in reference to the totality of the *psyche*, the Greek word for soul.

Finally, given the fact I'm not a psychologist, one might ask by what authority I venture into such uncertain territory. It's a fair question.

My understanding of psychology is drawn heavily–but not exclusively–from C.G. Jung and Edward Edinger, Jung's most authoritative American interpreter over the past four decades.(6)

It's necessary to say a word about C.G. Jung as I will be referring to him, and the significance of his work is simply not in focus for most Americans. In 1980, Marilyn Ferguson published *Aquarian Conspiracy*. In researching the book, Ferguson sent out a questionnaire to several hundred so-called "thought leaders" around the world. Included in the questionnaire was the query "Who has most influenced your thinking in life?" Jung was second only to Teilhard de Chardin. Assessing Jung's impact on the 20th century, London's *Sunday Telegraph* said: "Jung was on a giant scale . . . one of Western Civilization's great liberators."

Throughout the 20th century, Jung's insights influenced such diverse disciplines as atomic physics, anthropology, philosophy, history, art, and theology, as well as psychotherapy. Arnold Toynbee, Lewis Mumford and Joseph Campbell are only three of the giants in various fields who were significantly influenced by Jung. During World War II, Allen Dulles, head of the OSS in Europe, sought Jung's advice in order to better understand the psychology of the German leadership and people. Whenever Jung was in America, he was interviewed by *The New York Times* and other media. His last major article for a U.S. publication was a 1957 article written for *The Atlantic Monthly*. Countless major corporations today test new applicants based on Jung's analysis of personality types. Finally, and perhaps most importantly, Jung's concept of the *collective unconscious* takes the theory and practice of psychotherapy and relates it to the whole history of the evolution of the human psyche in its various manifestations of art, myth, culture and religion.

The Setting

Jung was the first to articulate the "crisis of meaning" as the central crisis of the 20th century. "Man positively needs general ideas and convictions that will give a meaning to his life and enable him to find his place in the universe . . . Meaninglessness inhibits fullness of life and is therefore equivalent to illness."

Today all we have to do is look in any bookstore or cinema to see the full extent of the crisis of meaning. Dilbert announces from a calendar cover, "I'm scheduling more meetings in order to fill the emptiness in my life." *The Simpsons* is TV's hymn to irony and the crisis of meaning. Tom Wolfe's book *A Man in Full* is a brilliant description of an entire city and culture whose inner emptiness belies the superficial wealth that substitutes for civilized life. *American Beauty* certainly wins the "Oscar" when it comes to portraying de-centered people living meaningless lives that, inevitably, create dysfunctional relationships and a dysfunctional family. In this sense, the movie–which could well have been titled *American Shadow*–was an accurate reflection of much of American life. Each person in the story was alienated from the center of his or her own personality. No one was a "whole" person. And this lack of wholeness is what has happened to America as we've moved deeper into the crisis of meaning that is engulfing the Western world.

I first became aware of this "crisis of meaning" in 1956 when I was working in South Africa. I was 26, had fought in the Korean War and had viewed America from the Asian perspective, and now was looking at America from the vantage point of Africa, as well as delving into de Tocqueville, and I began asking myself, "Is America in decline?"

Hindsight tells me that was the wrong question to be asking. But the symptoms that made me ask it were valid, for, in my view, the 1950s were the hinge of the 20th century for America. It was in the 1950s when meaninglessness became the primary American cultural expression.

The most popular play of the '50s–*Death of A Salesman*. The most popular novel, *Catcher in the Rye,* made the alienated adolescent a staple of American literature. It was only in the 1950s that *The Great Gatsby*, the archetypal American story of alienation, became the classic it is today. It was in the '50s that the anti-hero–Marlon Brando and James Dean–became movie icons. Camus, Beckett, Sartre, existentialism and the "School of the Absurd" were all the rage on campuses from Princeton to Berkeley.

What happened with the culture in the '50s was, in the view of Archibald MacLeish, "truth stopped being the criterion of culture" because "life had suddenly been discovered to be absurd."

This was the 1950s, the supposed quiet, uneventful, "Leave It to Beaver" decade. Little did Beaver realize that meaninglessness was becoming institutionalized in America's culture and higher education. Against this background, the 1960s to a certain extent can be seen as a revolt against the emptiness and hypocrisy of the '50s and as an attempt to find some greater idealism.

If We Are Passing Through a Major Psychological Reorientation, How is it Expressing Itself?

Several examples come to mind.

The roles of religion and psychology have been radically changing. One of the arresting facts of the last century is the rise of psychology and the corresponding demise of the Judeo-Christian tradition as the inner dynamic of Western culture. There seems to be a correlation between these two developments. It was especially noticeable in the first half of the century, when people with personal problems stopped seeking counsel from the priest and instead started going to the psychotherapist. Between 1918 and 1981, the population of the U.S. increased by 122 percent while the membership of the American Psychological Association grew over 14,000 percent. This shift in the relative roles of the priest and psychotherapist tells us much about 20th century America.

At the same time, as the initial dynamic of the Judeo-Christian tradition has lost its resonance for many people, religion has been "privatized" or "decentralized." There are now some 1,600 religions and denominations in America, 800 of which were founded in the past 30 years. In Los Angeles alone, 600 distinct religious traditions have been identified, including hybrid contradictions such as Catholic-Buddhists.

Another indication of this reorientation is the breakup of our collective inner images of wholeness. For example, we used to talk of Mother Earth with all its vital emotional connotation. Now we speak of "matter," which is totally devoid of emotional meaning. We once talked of "Heaven," which denoted the transcendent realm, eternity, the dwelling place of the gods. Now we just speak of "space." In this sense, the symbols and vocabulary that our culture was based on and that give it a structure of meaning, which in turn yielded values by which people could live, have disintegrated. The function of symbolic language is to link consciousness to the roots of our being, and when that link is devalued or snapped, there is little left to unconsciously sustain the inner life of the individual.

Thus the individual who lacks the support of a compensatory psychological development inside him drops out of the ordered fabric of the collective ethos holding civilized life together. For him, this means a breakdown of transpersonal experience, and the loss of certainty and meaning in life. One reaction this produces is, say, for the creative person, the submersion into the unconscious in search of fresh symbols of meaning. This is what modern art is all about. Thus Jackson Pollack's celebrated remark: "When I am in my painting I am not aware of what I am doing."

Part of the cause of the breakup of inner images has been *the profound way in which our material environment changed during the 20th century.* In 1900, one in 10 children died before age one. Today, it's one in 150. During the century, death from infectious disease dropped from 700 to 50 per 100,000 people. Over the same period, the real Gross Domestic Product (GDP) increased by $48 trillion in constant dollars.

The average annual per-person economic output grew from $5,000 to $30,000. Since 1950 alone, more financial wealth has been generated in the U.S. than was created in all the rest of the world in all the centuries before 1950. This rapid growth contrasts with the economic performance of the world over the last 1,000 years, when, according to the late Harvard economic historian Simon Kuznets, economic growth was "virtually stagnant." Today, the percentage of Americans graduating from college (28%) is higher than the percentage graduating from high school in 1920 (22%). In 1900, all the greatest mathematicians in the world together did not have the problem-solving resources of today's fourth grader with a $19.95 pocket calculator. An $800 Pentium-chip laptop computer has more computing power than was contained in all the computers in the world during World War II. In other words, generally speaking, the context in which most Americans live has changed more radically in the past 100 years than in the previous 1,000 years.

Reason has been in retreat. When Pope John Paul II feels compelled to issue an encyclical defending reason (*Faith and Reason*), or when more Americans say they believe in astrology than in logic,(7) you know reason is in trouble. Reason is one of the supreme achievements of Western development. The conscious mind must have reason to establish order out of the chaos of disorderly personal affairs and world events. But in author Alvin Kernan's view, reason is yielding ground to "the growing irrationality" of the academy. As John Leo notes in *U.S. News & World Report*, reason, in fact, "is now a villain on campus. Feelings, identity, and personal opinion are kings." Frederic Jameson and other postmodern scholars announce this as the triumph of the unconscious. Leo suggests that by undercutting the validity of language, deconstructionists announced that words "were empty, grounded in no reality, thus discrediting all the word-built value systems that make the world real and stable." The result, according to Leo: "The intellectual climate of meaninglessness and breakdown pervades our colleges."

The move from an agricultural to an urban society over the past century has shifted people from the natural environment of the land to a synthetic environment of the city, thus decreasing our contact with nature, which had been the normal context for humans since humans first appeared.

We no longer live in the realm of natural experience, but of artificial and illusory experience. Such a shift has fostered the creation of a "mass mind" as opposed to an "individual mind," which, historically, an agricultural environment produced. The urban setting emphasizes the collective over the individual.

We have been losing the boundaries that, psychologically, have defined people. For millennia, tribal, ethnic, national and cultural boundaries gave an individual or a group identity. Now these boundaries are falling, and they constitute the defining source of a people's identity less and less. We even see the boundary–and thus the very structure–of the family falling, which Daniel Patrick Moynihan tells us, is the first time in human history such a collapse has taken place.

The cascading inundation of raw information has outrun our capacity for assimilation and our ability to find the underlying significance of the data that engulf us. If one were to read the entire Sunday edition of *The New York Times*, one would be exposed to more information in that one reading than was absorbed *in a lifetime* by the average American living in Jefferson's day. "We are drowning in information," declares *Interactions*, the journal of the Association for Computing Machinery, "while precious little is in drinkable form." We have even reached the point of what some experts call "negative information"–so much information that, in some cases, the quality of decisions made by managers actually decreases.

I once attended a dinner given for Alvin Toffler, and I asked him what is to be the end result of everyone having instant access to all information, philosophies, religions, politics and ideologies through the Internet. Toffler replied quite simply, "The end of truth." That's a thought so immense that it's hard to absorb. At least since the ancient Jews and Greeks–let's say the past 4,000 years–the search for truth, whether spiritual or philosophical, has been life's highest pursuit. Some collective truth has always been at the core of every civilized society. As we continue to make ever-faster computers that are making the Internet increasingly ubiquitous, however, it's hard not to think Toffler may be right.

The changing roles of men and women are only one indication that the feminine impulse may be emerging as the defining impulse of the ascending period of history. This would, obviously, represent a profound psychological shift. But such a possibility is seen in various ways. Cooperation, rather than confrontation, is seen as becoming essential for further development, essential, in fact, for our very survival. One might even say that globalization–the impetus toward wholeness–is a manifestation of the feminine impulse.

If this is an accurate understanding of what's happening, then it could be said that, in terms of the Western experience, we may be entering the third great age of the feminine impulse. The first period was Athenian Greece, with its emphasis on philosophy, mythology, form and beauty. It was followed by the Roman period, with the predominance of conquest, law, order and construction, which are primarily masculine attributes.

The second feminine era was the medieval period, epitomized by the veneration of the Virgin Mary, by towering Gothic cathedrals reaching heavenward and by Dante's *Divine Comedy*. It was followed by another masculine era, the Modern Age, lasting some 500 years. The hallmarks of this era were exploration, conquest, rationalism, the scientific method and the Industrial Revolution.

Now we may be entering the third great feminine era. It is exemplified by the collapse of hierarchical structures and the search for more cooperative modes of organizing life; by an increased emphasis on intuition and relational awareness; by a renewed focus on *being* rather than *having*; by the redefinition of feminine and masculine roles in society and in the home with its resulting reformation of the family; and by the end of patriarchal dominance, an attribute characteristic of most cultures throughout most of history. Perhaps most significantly, we see a possible new feminine era in the action of the Catholic Church (1950) in making the Assumption of Mary official Catholic dogma, which, in theological terms, changes the Trinity into a quaternity. From a psychological point of view, a quaternity is the symbol of spiritual wholeness.

This may be another watershed in history, for the feminine impulse, as expressed in both men and women, is shaping the coming decades. It may even be that a new epoch is emerging in which the feminine and masculine join together in the creation of a compensatory whole.

The *changing character of 20th century culture* has been a dramatic suggestion of a psychological reorientation taking place. In fact, *during the past century, the very concept of culture has been changed.* No longer does culture have its historic connotation of cultivating the realm of the mind and spirit in order to elevate oneself to a higher plane of under-standing and sensitivity, or to encourage wholeness of personality, or to link the individual with some transcendent vitality. Culture has now come to mean whatever one wants it to mean, whether talking about "Levis," "Beavis and Butthead," "Coke," "Baywatch" or "corporate cul-ture."

From a psychological standpoint, culture is the continuity and con-servation of what is highest and most sublime about human experience. Cultural artifacts are psychic products that preserve the past and show the maturation of the psyche over long stretches of time. Civilized life does not consist of mindless destruction of old cultural—and, ultimately, psychic—values, but in developing and refining the good that has been won over millennia of human struggle. When a culture, which is a living organism, is cut off from its roots, its tradition, it loses connection with the foundations of its existence. A living culture is a unity; its technical, political, cultural and spiritual parts are united with one an-other. But when a society is in a state of psychological reorientation, as today, this unity is dissolved, and novelty becomes all the rage.

It's within this context we can evaluate the two primary cultural expressions of the last 100 years—Modernism and postmodernism, which have illustrated a clear—and indeed, intended—break with the historic roots of Western civilization. This is not to comment on the *aesthetic* quality of contemporary Western culture, only on its psychological implications.

I repeat the observation made in an earlier chapter by English cultural historian Christopher Dawson. In his 1947 prestigious *Gifford Lectures,* noted: "Throughout the greater part of mankind's history, in all ages and states of society, religion has been the great central unifying force in culture." T.S. Eliot shared Dawson's view writing, "No culture can appear except in relation to a religion."

If we go back to the creative giants of Western culture, Goethe went so far as to say that "man is only creative when he is truly religious; without religion he merely becomes repetitive and imitative." Bach said his purpose in life was, "to write well-ordered music to the glory of God." In *The Divine Comedy*, Dante specifically invoked divine assistance: "Make strong my tongue / that in its words may burn / one spark of all Thy glory's light / for future generations to discern."

This is a different psychological mind-set than that of 19th-20th century modernism, which told us that life had lost its mystery; that rational mind, not gods, can rule the world; that reason could unlock the secrets of nature and formulate the scheme of an immutable objective reality; that custom and tradition must yield to experimentation in every area of life; and that at the core of existence there is only the void of nihilism. The thrust of modernism was to substitute the aesthetic taste for the prevailing moral and spiritual order. Accordingly, modernism demanded liberation from all inner restraint and the destruction of all prevailing forms. The aesthetic expression of this view required the attempt to eclipse distances, whether aesthetic, social or psychological. Modernism, wrote literary critic Irving Howe, is "an unyielding rage against the existing order."

The inevitable extension of modernism is postmodernism. The word "postmodern" was first used in 1917 in Germany to describe the nihilism of 20th century culture. This feeling of a void at the core of existence has characterized postmodernism ever since. A distinctive feature of postmodernism is its acceptance of reality as unordered in any objective way the human mind can discern. As author Huston Smith notes, this acceptance "separates the Postmodern mind from the Modern Mind, which assumed that reality is objectively ordered, and the Christian mind, which assumed it to be ordered by an inscrutable but beneficent will."

According to Lawrence Cahoone, professor of philosophy at Boston University and editor of a compendium on postmodernism,(8) postmodernism announces "the end of rational inquiry into truth, the illusory nature of any unified self, the impossibility of clear and un-equivocal meaning, the illegitimacy of Western civilization, and the op-pressive nature of all modern institutions." Daniel Bell tells us that for postmodernists, impulse and pleasure alone are real and life affirming. Reason is the enemy, and the desires of the body constitute truth. Referring to postmodernism and academia, Roger Shattuck writes in *The Atlantic Monthly*, "Our culture, in particular the institution of the university, has contrived over the past few decades to transform sin and evil into a positive term: 'transgression.' As used by postmodern critics, 'transgression' aspires . . . to an implied form of greatness in evil. On an intellectual level . . . evil can become supremely cool."

Jeremy Rifkin notes that if people in the modern world sought purpose, postmodernists seek playfulness. "Order of any kind is consid-ered restraining, even stilting. Creative anarchy, on the other hand, is tolerated." Everything is less serious, Rifkin says. In the postmodern environment, "Irony, paradox, and skepticism are rampant. There is no great concern with making history, but only making up interesting stories to live by." Concludes Rifkin, because there is no overarching historical frame governing nature or society, history "is less a reference for understanding the past and projecting ourselves into the future, and more loose story fragments that can be recycled and made part of contemporary social scripts."

In sum, America has had almost a century of literature, art, cinema and higher education expressing first the supremacy and then the nega-tion of rationality, the denial of any God, freedom as unfettered expres-sion of ego desires, the impossibility of absolute truth, nihilism at the core of existence, the absence of any transcendent meaning, the irratio-nality of any degree of self-discipline, and the arrival of the multiple de-centered self.

Such a culture, according to Christopher Lasch, writing in the aus-picious year 1984, has prompted people "to prepare for the worst" by executing a kind of emotional retreat from long-term commitments that presuppose a stable, secure, and orderly world." This has resulted, Lasch suggested, in a "minimal selfhood"; the "replacement of a reliable world of durable objects by a world of flickering images that make it harder and harder to distinguish reality from fantasy." Four years later, Dr. Martin E.P. Seligman reported to the American Psychological Association that, taking population growth into account, psychological depression in America was at a rate "ten times as high as before World War II."

Commenting on America's postmodernist culture, Zbigniew Brzezinski, National Security Advisor to President Carter, remarked, "Precisely the values that have been considered throughout civilized history by all societies and all religions to be destructive and disintegrative—greed, debauchery, violence, unlimited self-gratification, absence of restraint—are the daily fare glamorously dished up to our children." It's hard to think of any nation in history that has consciously fed its children on a cultural diet known to be destructive of its children's character and healthy psychological development—and done it intentionally for financial gain.

Brzezinski relates such a culture to America's world leadership role. "I don't think Western secularism in its present shape is the best standard bearer for human rights," he says. "It [Western secularism] is essentially a cultural wave in which hedonism, self-gratification and consumption are the essential definitions of the meaning of the 'good life.' The human condition is about more than that. The defense of the political individual doesn't mean a whole lot in such a spiritual and moral vacuum." In this respect, Brzezinski concludes, America's culture has become a major threat to our national security.

I have emphasized culture for a particular reason. Public opinion polls tell us that a huge percentage of the population says it believes in God, and any number of commentators point to this fact to say what a "religious" nation America is. But in assessing the spiritual condition of a people, public opinion polls are, quite frankly, of limited value. What really tells the story is the character of a nation's culture. Culture is to a nation what dreams are to an individual—an indication of what is going on in the inner life.

Finally, consider a few phrases from *a report issued by The United States Commission on National Security/21st Century,*(9) headed by former U.S. senators Warren Rudman and Gary Hart. Its interim report addresses a broad range of conventional security issues, but then it gives an unconventional description of *some* of the changes reshaping our existence that they're considering as a result of accelerating technology.

"The upshot of the changes ahead is that Americans are now, and increasingly will become, less secure than they believe themselves to be. The reason is that we may not recognize many of the threats in our future . . . they may consist, too, of an unraveling of the fabric of national identity itself . . . Compared to the present, everything will be hurled into relative motion . . . a considerably more stressful cognitive environment . . . democracy may be hollowed out from inside . . . The growing sense of power that will accrue to many individuals could corrupt moral balances and erode moral discipline . . . threaten the balances of healthy civic habits that have long sustained democratic communities . . ."

The report discusses potential consequences of biotechnology such as altering the human genome, mixing the organic with the non organic, and changing the very composition of a human being. It then offers this paragraph: "The implications of such developments should not be underestimated. Our understanding of all human social arrangements is based, ultimately, on an understanding of human nature. If that nature becomes subject to significant alteration through human artifice, then all such arrangements are thrown into doubt. It almost goes without saying, too, that to delve into such matters raises the deepest of ethical questions: Can humanity trust itself with such capabilities? Should it? How can it know before the fact? Who gets to decide?" The report concludes by saying that "there is a growing unease that we are upping the ante to the point that a single mistake or a single act of sheer evil could leave a potentially fatal wound."

To be actively considering such issues represents not only a technological, but also a psychological change on a scale that could not have been conceived of before the 19th century. I say that for this reason: It may be that we do not accurately understand what's happening to the world. We think technology is the driving force that's changing the world. But could it be that the driving force is a change in human psychological orientation that has resulted in our creating technology capable of redefining what it means to be a human being, and, indeed, attempting to redesign nature itself?

Technology–Are People Superfluous?

I preface my comments on technology by emphasizing I'm not a Luddite. I appreciate the marvels of technology as much as the next person–perhaps more than the next person, as in 1997 I had a quadruple heart bypass using state-of-the-art medical technology. So I'm a believer. But I nonetheless have serious concerns.

Technology is actually older than *homo sapiens,* the first known technological instrument–a stone for scraping and cutting–being some 2.5 millions years old. Since then, until fairly recently, technology was considered to be an extension of human capability, whether it was the wheel, the stirrup or the steam engine.

The question now is whether certain technologies exist in their own right, under their own laws, and for purposes that have little to do with extending human capability. Rather, their purpose is *to supplant human effort and meaning altogether.*

To illustrate, consider some thoughts of America's foremost technological visionaries:

James Watson, Nobel Prize winner and director of the National Center for Human Genome Research: "Evolution can be just damn cruel, and to say that we've got a perfect genome and there's some sanctity to it, I'd just like to know where that idea comes from. It's utter silliness. If we could make better human beings by knowing how to add genes, why shouldn't we do it?"

Marvin Minsky, cofounder of MIT's Artificial Intelligence Laboratory: "Suppose that the robot had all of the virtues of people and was smarter and understood things better. Then why would we want to prefer those grubby, old people? I don't see anything wrong with human life being devalued if we have something better."

Stephen Pinker, author of *How the Mind Works*: "[B]rain science has shown that the mind is what the brain does. The supposedly immaterial soul can be bisected with a knife, altered by chemicals, turned on or off by electricity, and extinguished by a sharp blow or a lack of oxygen."

Sherry Turkel, a psychologist at MIT: She tells us that computer scientists see the future in terms of "the reconfiguration of machines as psychological objects and the reconfiguration of people as living machines."

Richard Dawkins, E.O. Wilson, Francis Crick and other members of the International Academy of Humanism: "Humanity's rich repertoire of thoughts, feelings, aspirations, and hopes seems to arise from electrochemical brain processes, not from an immaterial soul that operates in ways no instrument can discover."

Bentley Glass, as president of the American Association for the Advancement of Science, enunciated "the right of every child to be born with a sound physical and mental constitution based on a sound genotype." Looking to future reproductive technologies, Glass continued, "No parents in that future time will have a right to burden society with a malformed or a mentally incompetent child."

Robert Jastrow, director of the Mount Wilson Observatory: He speculates that eventually scientists will "tap the contents of my mind and transfer them into the metallic lattices of a computer." Emancipating our minds from "the weaknesses of mortal flesh" will transform us into a race of "disembodied intellects, as evolutionarily suited for life in the future as man is designed for life on the African savanna."

John McCarthy, cofounder of MIT's Artificial Intelligence Laboratory, coined the term "artificial intelligence" in 1955: "What do judges know that we cannot tell a computer?"

Ray Kurzweil, a computer scientist, inventor, award-winning author, recipient of nine honorary doctorates and honors from two U.S. presidents: "When we can determine the neurological correlates of the variety of spiritual experiences that our species is capable of, we are likely to be able to enhance these experiences in the same way that we will enhance other human experiences. With the next stage of evolution creating a new generation of humans that will be trillions of times more capable and complex than humans today, our ability for spiritual experience and insight is also likely to gain in power and depth.

"Just being–experiencing, being conscious–is spiritual, and reflects the essence of spirituality. Machines, derived from human thinking and surpassing humans in their capacity for experience, will claim to be conscious, and thus to be spiritual. They will believe that they are conscious. They will believe that they have spiritual experiences.

"Twenty-first century machines–based on the design of human thinking–will do as their human progenitors have done–going to real and virtual houses of worship, meditating, praying, and transcending– to connect with their spiritual dimension."

Kevin Kelly, editor of *Wired* magazine: "In the great vacuum of meaning, in the silence of unspoken values, in the vacancy of something large to stand for, something bigger than oneself, technology–for better or worse–will shape our society. Because values and meaning are scarce today, technology will make our decisions for us."

Jaron Lanier, who coined the term "virtual reality" and founded the world's first virtual reality company: "In the computer science community there's a perspective that things are going to change at such a rapid rate that at some point something very dramatic will change about the fundamental situation of people in the universe. In the mythology of computer science, the limits for the speed and capacity of computers are so distant that they effectively don't exist. And it is believed that as we hurtle toward more and more powerful computers, eventually there will be some sort of dramatic Omega Point at which everything changes– not just in terms of our technology but in terms of our basic nature. This is something you run across again and again in the fantasy writings of computer scientists: this notion that we're about to zoom into a transformative moment of progress that we cannot even comprehend."

"Medical science, neuroscience, computer science, genetics, biology – separately and together, seem to be on the verge of abandoning the human realm altogether . . . it grows harder to imagine human beings remaining at the center of the process of science. Instead, science appears to be in charge of its own process, probing and changing people in order to further its own course, independent of human agency."

Bill Joy, chief scientist and cofounder of Sun Microsystems, puts it all in a needed perspective. Discussing the potential effects of GNR technologies (genetics, nanotechnology and robotics, which will all eventually be able to self-replicate) combined with computers a million times as powerful as today's PCs, Joy says, "I think it no exaggeration to say we are on the cusp of the further perfection of extreme evil, an evil whose possibility spreads well beyond that which weapons of mass destruction bequeathed to the nation-states, on to a surprising and terrible empowerment of extreme individuals." Joy says philosopher John Leslie has studied the potential effects of the GNR technologies and has "concluded that the risk of human extinction is at least 30 percent, while Ray Kurzweil believes we have 'a better than even chance of making it through.'" Joy suggests that the only way to guard against the potentially destructive effects of GNR technologies is "relinquishment: to limit development of the technologies that are too dangerous, by limiting our pursuit of certain kinds of knowledge."

Joy acknowledges the pursuit of knowledge as one of the primary human goals at least since Aristotle, and then says, "If open access to and unlimited development of knowledge henceforth puts us all in clear danger of extinction, then common sense demands that we reexamine even these basic, long-held beliefs." Only a person of Joy's scientific stature could put in the pages of *Wired* magazine a proposal that is so idealistic that it's the only realistic proposal that can avert the human extinction he foresees. "If we could agree, as a species," he writes, "what we wanted, where we were headed, and why, then we would make our future much less dangerous–then we might understand what we can and should relinquish."

These people are not evil madmen. They're brilliant human beings on the outer edges of scientific inquiry. In my view, however, some of them exemplify a most profound psychological change that conceivably could radically alter human existence in the next few decades. What some of these people are talking about has little to do with bettering the human condition, which has been the justification for scientific research going back at least to Francis Bacon, who believed the "true and lawful end of the sciences is that *human life* be enriched by new discoveries and powers." Indeed, it would seem that some of this effort has little to do with the human condition at all. It's about displacing the human being and creating something that, in their minds, is superior. It's about *self-destruction*–destruction of the self that is at the core of the human personality.

In fact, it's about how human humans will be in the future. Dr. Philip Tobias is a world-renowned anthropologist who worked with Louis Leakey in East Africa. Says Dr. Tobias: "I regard [the computer] as the most significant leap since humans first acquired the capacity for spoken language some two million years ago. Many of us have seen in the birth of spoken language the most monumental piece of humanization since the family of mankind appeared on earth between five and seven million years ago

"Against this background, it's pertinent to inquire what is the computer age doing to the development, cultivation and use of the faculty of speech? Already, when we've scarcely entered upon the computer age, educational psychologists and sociologists have begun to raise such questions. With ever-increasing dependence on the computer, they ask, will the capacity for spoken language fall into disuse atrophy? If the very qualities and capacities that have made humans human are attenuated and even brought to the verge of extinction, how human will the humans of the day be?"

But I want to return to Kevin Kelly's comment. He said, "Because values and meaning are scarce today, technology will make our decisions for us." I'm not sure that's an accurate picture of what's happening. Kelly's remark suggests that technology is some purified, abstract instrument, free from the contamination of human meaning and value. But I don't think that's the case. Technology is the manifestation of the meaning and value we humans have attached to life at this particular point in history. It's not technology that's making our decisions; it's the meaning and values of computer scientists and business people who produce the technology that make the decisions. It's the values of we who use–and become addicted to–the technology that make the decisions. The root issue here is not technology; it's us as human beings and what meaning and values we choose.

The question of meaning and values raises the question of what motivates contemporary scientists–such as those quoted above–to abandon the historic implicit role of science, which has been the investigation of nature in order to better the human condition, and to have taken off on their own course that appears to have little to do with bettering the human condition. Perhaps one answer is found in a story reported in *The Washington Post*. A brilliant Carnegie Mellon University computer science professor was hired by Microsoft as a researcher. The story quoted the professor as saying, "To me, this corporation is my power tool. It's the tool I wield to allow my ideas to shape the world."

My power tool. Such a statement is a classic expression of the power drive, of an ego inflated beyond what most people would consider proper human limits. We need to seriously ask whether such ego-inflation isn't what's driving the effort by *some* scientists to redesign or replace humans and human meaning altogether. Freeman Dyson made the same point in the documentary *The Day After Trinity*, quoted by Bill Joy in his *Wired* manifesto. Said Dyson, "The glitter of nuclear weapons. It is irresistible if you come to them as a scientist. To feel it's there in your hands, to release this energy that fuels the stars, to let it do your bidding. To perform these miracles, to lift a million tons of rock into the sky. It is something that gives people an illusion of illimitable power, and it is, in some ways, responsible for all our troubles—this, what you might call technical arrogance, that overcomes people when they see what they can do with their minds."

It's a thin line between research designed to alleviate human need and research driven by the arrogance of power, ego power. The potential implications—what Bill Joy terms "something like extinction"—of some areas of research have reached a point where public accountability must come at the start of the research process, not after the fact. As C. S. Lewis has written, "Man's conquest of Nature, if the dreams of some scientific planners are realized, means the rule of a few hundreds of men over billions upon billions of men. Each new power won *by* man is a power *over* man as well."

Consider this possibility. Does the effort to create an intelligence greater than human intelligence, something that can supersede the human being, need to be seen in the context of the 20th century psychic breakdown that produced two world wars with close to 80 million people killed (greater than the population of France); the triumph and then dethronement of rationalism; the psychologically disintegrative effects of modernism and postmodernism; and the breakdown of the social structures of civilized life, i.e., marriage, the family, education as development of the whole person, and collective belief in some supreme transcendent authority? If God is dead, then is the scientist Nietzsche's "Superman," and the super intelligent robot is the result?

In any event, is there an antidote for the individual who is now enmeshed in an inescapable web of technology, and who tries to make sense out of his or her life in these disorienting times? Indeed there is!

The first part of the antidote is to understand what has happened– and what is happening–that has resulted in the loss of life's "highest value," and the emergence of a culture of meaninglessness.

Daniel Bell, who coined the term "post-industrial," was and has been one of America's foremost sociologists for the past 50 years. He wrote in his book *The Winding Passage*: "From the end of the nineteenth century to the middle of the twentieth century, almost every sociological thinker . . . expected religion to disappear by the onset of the twenty-first century. If the belief no longer lay in Reason . . . it now lay in the idea of Rationalization. Reason is the uncovering–the underlying structure–of the natural order. Rationalization is the substitution of a technical order for a natural order–in the rhythms of work; in the functional adoption of means to end; in the criteria for use of objects, the principle criterion being efficiency–and the imposition of bureaucratic structures of organization to replace the ties of kinship and primordial relations. It is a world of technical rules and bureaucratic roles."

Three points in Bell's quote stand out. First, every sociological thinker expected religion would disappear by now. That is an astonishing statement, as it suggests that America's "best and brightest" totally failed to appreciate the *psychological* function of religion.

Second, rationalization as the substitution of a technical order for a natural order. From the dawn of human existence up until the 19th century–a span of around 6 million years, as Tobias said–man lived in a natural order. His very being, his psyche, was formed in relationship to that order. Even his religions were born out of this man-nature relationship.

In the 20th century, this has all been changed—at least as far as America goes. We now live in a technical order. We have cut our bond with nature to a large extent. We're so divorced from the natural order that we go to "nature stores" to buy recordings of natural phenomena such as rushing streams, waves breaking on the shore, wind blowing through the trees, the music of the songbird, or the haunting call of the whale. We have alienated ourselves from our natural habitat.

Third, Bell talks of the principle criterion being efficiency. Efficiency, it would seem, has become America's "highest value," our god. We worship at the alter of efficiency, whether of the computer, the Net, the financial markets, or the production process. Obviously, efficiency is certainly better than the alternative. But when it becomes a god, then abstract quantification comes before human qualities and need, and we end up with the people at the MIT Lab proclaiming the virtue of devaluing human beings.

What's the result of de-linking ourselves from the natural order and establishing a technical order whose god is efficiency? It was well stated by Max Weber, an earlier and even greater sociologist than Bell:

> With the progress of science and technology, man has . . .
> lost his sense of the sacred. Reality has become dreary, flat
> and utilitarian, leaving a great void in the souls of men
> which they seek to fill by furious activity and through
> various devices and substitutes.

So this is the context—we're living in a technical order where the god is efficiency. Such an order has its obvious benefits. From a material standpoint, no society in history has enabled such a high proportion of its people to live as well as do those Americans even at the lower end of the income scale.

The computer and Internet, of course, are increasing the shift to an order that is not only technical, but also primarily conceptual. Kids are growing up with a minimal soul-feeding relationship with land, trees,

rivers, clouds and animals, and instead are developing an abstract relationship with what is, in the words of Stephen Talbott, author of *The
Future Does Not Compute,* a "disembodied rationality." Many kids delve
into their on-line vicarious life simply because they do not know how to
handle the relationships involved in their off-line real life. Pretense and
simulation become their reality. For the computer represents, in Talbott's
words, a "kind of perfection of our one-sided tendencies" over the past
300 years–rational, theoretical, symbolic–purified, or so we think, of
human emotion, complexes or "superstition." The computer tends to be
abstracted form with little depth of humanly felt content. In this sense,
the computer is not "neutral." It expresses primarily one side of the
human character. It tends to express "surface," but not "interior." And
yet, just as quantum mechanics teaches us that the psyche of the observer affects the outcome of a particle experiment, so, too, the psyche
of the computer programmer enters the program.

Another aspect of understanding the loss of life's highest value is
revealed as we consider the most ancient story on which the religions
born in the Near East–Christianity, Judaism and Islam–were founded:
the tale of Adam and Eve in the Garden of Eden. Before we dismiss the
story as a naïve relic of the past–there was no Garden of Eden, Adam
and Eve never existed, etc.–we would do well to consider that while the
story may not be literally true, it may be symbolically true. It may be
psychologically true. For the story originated from the human psyche
(soul), and it may refer back to the psyche, as do most myths and
symbolic stories. Indeed, that is the function of myth–to bring to light
deeper truths of existence that are not readily apparent to ego-consciousness, to keep our consciousness linked to the roots of our deeper
being. So the tale of the Garden of Eden may not be simply a fanciful
fable left over from the childhood of man. It may represent an underlying truth of life that is valid for all time.

In the legend, there were two trees in the Garden, the tree of the
knowledge of good and evil, and the tree of immortal life. The serpent
in the garden enticed Adam and Eve to eat the fruit of the tree of the
knowledge of good and evil. When God saw what had happened, he
expelled Adam and Eve from the garden in order to prevent them from

eating the fruit of the second tree, the tree of immortal life. God did this for fear that if Adam and Eve ate the fruit of the tree of immortal life, "They would become like us, they would become as gods."

Why is this story relevant? It's relevant because with our deciphering of the human genome, with our entry into the secrets of genetics, we are on the verge of being able to give humans something very close to immortal life. Some geneticists talk of enabling people to live to be 120, 150 or even 200, while others say there is no reason why eventually we'll not be able to enable a person to live for as long as he wishes. At the same time, we are not only on the verge of being able to cure heretofore incurable diseases, we are on the brink of making genetic changes that are transmissible to succeeding generations. We will be able to alter, in advance, specific future individuals, and to create new human capacities. It is one thing to cure disease, which has been the focus of the human genome public relations efforts. It's quite another to alter the genetic composition of future generations. Thus in terms of the Biblical story, we are on the threshold of becoming as gods.

What does it mean to become as gods? One thing it means is that the scientists (who comprise an extremely small minority of earth's 6 billion people) will assume the role of creator-judge-savior, and the rest of humanity will assume the role of creatures judged and manipulated. As gods, we become all-powerful; we can do anything we like. Indeed, today we're not only able to destroy all life on the planet–certainly a god-like capacity–but we're close to creating elemental forms of life or to determine genetic inheritance for generations to come. We are very close to being able to determine who shall live and who shall die–on the basis of genetic merit, which is surely a god-like power.

Becoming as gods also means is that we are free of all restraints. As gods, we are free of any external authority. We are beholden to no one but ourselves, and we believe we can set the rules. We dismiss our temporal fallibility and assume a certain eternal omnipotence. No limits are recognized, no human inadequacies acknowledged. We replace what heretofore has been divine prerogative with human will and capability.

Finally, there is an area of the human composition about which the geneticists know next to nothing, and that is the area of the unconscious.

Science is extremely interested in consciousness, but ever since Jung died in 1961, science has left the collective unconscious outside its boundaries of exploration. And that's for an understandable, if not necessarily valid, reason. The unconscious is not susceptible to the rational, reductionist methods of contemporary science. As Crick, Wilson and others acknowledge, the "immaterial soul" operates in ways "no instrument can discover."

Nevertheless, the unconscious may have as much to do with our daily functioning as does our ego-consciousness. There is clear evidence that the unconscious operates across time and space. Physicists acknowledge that the presence of a human observer affects the outcome of an experiment with sub-atomic particles. As Freeman Dyson wrote in *Infinite in all Directions*, "The old vision which Einstein maintained until the end of his life, of an objective world of space and time and matter independent of human thought and observation, is no longer ours." This raises the question of the relationship between psyche and matter, something about which we know very little. How is our inner psychology also part of the outer physical world, and vice-versa? This may be part of the ultimate question of life–what is the relationship between matter and spirit. Are they simply two aspects of some larger reality? Is man related to something infinite and transcendent or not? The unconscious may be the realm where the answers to these questions are most likely to be found. Beyond that, some psychologists hypothesize (as did Hegel with his suggestion of a "World Spirit") that, on a certain basic level of the unconscious, everything is connected to everything else.

So to tamper with the man's basic genetic constitution would seem foolhardy until we understand these larger questions more fully. In light of our utter ignorance not only of consciousness, but especially of unconsciousness, one can only marvel at the arrogance of scientists who propose to "download" consciousness onto a silicon chip.

Yet here we are, ready to experiment with genetic engineering in a manner that could potentially alter future generations, and we're about to do it without the slightest understanding of how it might affect the unconscious, that area of the human being which is still our greatest mystery.

As Craig Holdrege and Stephen Talbott write, "The fundamental problem with genetic engineering from the very beginning has been the absence of anything like an ecological approach. Genes are not the unilateral 'controllers' of the cell's 'mechanisms.' Rather, genes enter into a vast and as yet scarcely monitored conversation with each other and with all the other parts of the cell. Who is that speaks through the whole of this conversation–what unity expresses itself through the entire organism–is a question the genetic engineers have not yet even raised, let alone begun to answer . . . What we need is to overcome an epidemic of abstract, technological thought that conceives solutions in the absence of organic contexts."

As far as the Biblical story goes, there was good reason why God did not want man to become as the gods. Every culture in the world has myths that underline this reason–because then man is consumed by what the Greeks called *hubris*, pride and arrogance, and inevitably man destroys himself. This, of course, is not only mythology; it's history. Preventing man from becoming as gods is for man's own protection, for, as our experience with modern technology demonstrates, man simply lacks the necessary wisdom and judgment to prudently handle the power that resides in the hands of the gods.

So where does this leave us? It leaves us realizing, in the words of the great scientist and author Jacob Bronowski, "We have to cure ourselves of the itch for absolute knowledge and power . . . It is not the business of science to inherit the earth, but to inherit the moral imagination . . . what we are as ethical creatures." It leaves us realizing that technology, and particularly genetics, robotics, the computer and the Net, raise the question of human meaning as it has never before been consciously raised. It leaves us realizing that the computer and the Net fragment life unless there is a commensurate growth of the human personality and spirit, which alone unify life. It leaves us realizing that the issue is not where is technology taking us, but where do we want to go? It leaves us realizing that technology is a great enabler, not a great goal. The greatness of a people is expressed in the unifying power of their beliefs, in the quality of their culture and in their social arrangements, not simply in their tools. It leaves us realizing that for the first time, Americans now must consciously, independently, grapple with our own individuality and inner wholeness.

Should we fail to do this, the predictions of the technological visionaries mentioned above will not bring the technical nirvana they suppose; more likely such developments will bring social collapse on a scale we've not known before. (The indicators already abound.) For what the technologists fail to consider is people, the individual human being, and how much hyper-change, acceleration and experimentation the human nervous system can take before losing emotional and mental balance. Life, not technology, will ultimately prevail. But life's creative impulse may have moved to some other part of the world, some part that still recognizes the primacy of the human over the technological. As Philip Tobias asks about the future, "Will the increasingly technologized minority have become dehumanized, while the pre-technologized or under-technologized peoples [80 percent of the world's population] will still be there to remind the world of the earlier meaning, or meanings, of human?" Or as Bronowski writes, "The ascent of man will go on. But do not assume it will go on carried by western civilization as we know it. We are being weighed in the balance at this moment . . . If we do not take the next step in the ascent of man, it will be taken by people elsewhere, in Africa, in China." Thus in the contradiction of technological wonder and spiritual alienation, we must find new meaning for the human venture.

A (Very) Short History of Consciousness

On February 23, 2000, Francesca DelaRosa Clemente first saw the light of day. Francesca is my granddaughter. For me, it's always an awesome experience to see a baby 45 minutes after she was born. Life is such a miracle. One of the things that interest me is that the newborn baby has absolutely no consciousness, no ego, and no sense of "I am." Her ego-consciousness is only a potentiality completely subsumed in the unconscious. The development of ego-consciousness, of a sense of identity, of course, is what the first few years of life are all about. Francesca has a two-year old brother, Dominick, whose cry, "That's my toy!" is not an expression of incipient selfishness; it's an assertion of self-identity.

As I've marveled at this process of emerging consciousness, I've realized that the whole human race went through the exact same process as Francesca. Millennia ago, humans had little or no ego-consciousness. It was contained as potentiality in the unconscious. There was no discriminating ego, and man identified himself with his surroundings. Hence the gods were seen in rocks, trees, brooks and mountains. Inanimate objects were endowed with a healing, magical power, through which they participated in us and we in them. Man did not live in time, only in eternity. It was the age of "animism," when the gods were manifestations of psychic projections. To a limited degree, this same phenomenon can be seen today in so-called indigenous people in the jungles of Brazil, Indonesia or Africa. They have a minimal sense of self, of ego, as we in the West experience it, which tells us that there are many different stages of consciousness.

Somewhere along the line ego-consciousness began to appear–"Let there be light." Light is a universal symbol for the birth of consciousness in most religions and origin stories of world culture.

In our Western tradition, many similarities exist between the myths of the Garden of Eden and the Greek fable of Prometheus, both of which can be interpreted as the birth of an elementary consciousness. God told Adam and Eve not to eat of the fruit of the tree of the knowledge of good and evil. Knowledge of good and evil clearly suggests awareness of the opposites, which is the distinctive feature of consciousness. Eating the forbidden fruit marks the transition from a state of unconsciousness to a real, conscious life in space and time. In short, the myth symbolizes the birth of the ego. Joseph Campbell tells us that while Genesis was first written in the eighth century B.C., the symbolism of the story of the Garden of Eden–including the garden, the trees and fruit, the serpent and the divinity–is expressed in Sumerian texts, and on Sumerian seals and artifacts dating back to 2000 B.C.

Similar Greek mythology tells us how Prometheus stole fire (consciousness) from the gods and gave it to man. As Prometheus says in Aeschylus' timeless words, "At first, mindless, I gave them mind and reason . . . In those days [pre-conscious] they had eyes, but sight was meaningless; heard sounds, but could not listen; all their length of life they passed like shapes in dreams, confused and purposeless . . . Their every act was without knowledge, till I came." While Aeschylus' play was written in the fifth century B.C., it was Hesiod, writing three centuries earlier—roughly the same time as Genesis was recorded—who gives us the first written record of the Promethean myth.

In both stories, God(s) withholds consciousness—symbolized by the fruit and the fire; in both stories Adam, Eve and Prometheus steal the forbidden treasure from God(s); and in both stories the transgressors are punished by God(s). The parallels in these stories have always amazed me, as they clearly indicate the emergence of ego-consciousness in the two regions that represent the foundation of the Western psyche—Israel and Greece. With the evolution of consciousness came the birth of freedom and conscious choice.

Still, by the time of the *Iliad*, also in the eighth century B.C., consciousness, as we know it today clearly had not yet emerged. One doesn't get any sense of subjectivity, reflection, introspection, assimilation or willing in the *Iliad*. They didn't think as we do; thoughts just appeared. People heard internal voices of the gods saying, "Do this, do that." There are indigenous people in different parts of the world today who still reflect this stage of consciousness; and, quite frankly, it would be a tragic loss to humanity if ever those people were unable to survive.

For us in the West, early Greek mythology and philosophy, as well as the Old Testament are self-revelations of the early Western psyche as it emerged out of the mists of the preconscious stage. The early Greek philosophers were visionaries, quite similar to the great Hebrew prophets. Indeed, early Greek philosophy lacks the dry intellectualism we associate with later Western philosophy, but has much the same tone and spiritual feel, as does the Old Testament. As Richard Tarnas tell us, the "immortal [Greek] deities" were an archetypal expression of "certain primordial essences or transcendent first principles . . ."

We see distinct differences in psychology between the Old and the New Testament. The Old Testament is collective; it's all about God's relation with Israel. It's not until we get to the Book of Job that man encounters Yahweh as an individual and not as a function of the collective psyche. The Book of Job marks the beginning of the transition from collective psychology to individual psychology. By the New Testament era, Christ's message is highly individual–about how the individual finds inward peace and wholeness, as well as about the individual's responsibility to his fellow man.

The New Testament marks a further change from the Old Testament psychology. In the Old Testament, Yahweh embodied both good and evil, for he continually exhibits his vengeful and angry side as he instructs Israel to slaughter women and children and commit all sorts of immoral acts. But he also represented the God of justice, the Torah and the Covenant. He thus symbolized the opposites of good and evil that are at the heart of life.

But by the time of the New Testament, God had become uniquely the God of love, and the dark side of Yahweh had been suppressed. As the ancient gods of Olympus crumbled, as Rome moved from being a republic to an empire, Christ offered love and humility as the new spiritual dispensation for the individual and as the social bonding force of nations. With Christ comes the primacy of the individual person. As Lewis Mumford wrote, Christ "sought to bring the inner and the outer aspects of the personality into organic balance by throwing off compulsions, constraints, automatisms. No one else has spoken of the moral life with fewer negations or with so many positive expressions of power and joy." This represents one of the great psychological dividing lines of Western history, even though it would take centuries for Christ's message to reach its fullest expression.

The Bible and early Greek philosophy represent Western consciousness in its earliest expressions. They embody the archetypes that have dominated Western myth, religion and culture ever since.

During the Roman Empire, we continue to see a mind at work that's still quite different from our mind today. For centuries after Caesar, the College of Augurs was consulted before the government would make major decisions. The particular augurs, maybe 12 or 16 men, would sit on a certain hill, face the south, and ask the gods for a sign. They then watched the movements of various birds. Different movements at different times in different directions had particular significance. The augurs reported to the government that their reading of the birds was or was not "auspicious" for a particular course of action. We may smile at such an undertaking, but "taking the auspices" was as real to the Roman consciousness as is any activity associated with our consciousness today.

Over the next millennium there were significant psychological developments, as represented by the emergence of monasticism in the sixth century, numerous spiritual movements–such as the Holy Ghost movement, Joachim of Flora, and the Cathars–around 1000 (give or take a century), and, eventually in the 13th century, Thomas Aquinas's *Summa Theologica*, which sought to unite Aristotle's philosophy with Church doctrine.

One of the most significant developments came in 14th century Florence, where *individuality* as we know it today was born. As the great Swiss historian of the Renaissance, Jacob Burkhardt, wrote: "In the Middle Ages both sides of human consciousness–that which was turned within as that which was turned without–lay dreaming or half awake beneath a common veil . . . Man was conscious of himself only as a member of a race, people, party, family or corporation–only through some general category. In Italy this veil first melted into air; an *objective* treatment and consideration of the State and of all things of this world became possible. The *subjective* side at the same time asserted itself with corresponding emphasis; man became a spiritual *individual*, and recognized himself as such."

One can see this change exemplified in the difference between the magnificent cathedral of Chartres, where no sculptors' names adorn the different statues and no one knows who was responsible for this or that portion of the great church, and the subsequent advent of men such as Giotto and Pico della Mirandola, who represent a new mood of the human individual self. Even religion was reshaped to this new sense of individual consciousness as Martin Luther translated the Bible into the common vernacular of Germany so that each person could follow the dictates of his own conscience.

At the same time, a new development took place in the 1500s, and that was the birth of the Faust legend. There actually was a John Faustus who died in the 1540s, and within a century of his death there were over 50 versions of the Faust legend circulating throughout Europe. The one we know best, of course, is Goethe's *Faust*. In its conventional summation, the Faust legend is about a man who sold his soul to the devil to gain the knowledge and pleasures of the world. But that may be an incomplete interpretation. Another way of viewing the Faust legend might be: Between the time of Christ and the late Middle Ages, Western man's psyche was contained in a symbol-system that gave priority to the spiritual side of life, to that experience where man's ego is subordinate to the transpersonal (eternal) dimension of the psyche. Some time in the late Middle Ages this began to change, and Western man's energies began to focus on the material side of life. It was a shift from the vertical (heavenly) to the horizontal (earthly). In a psychological sense, Western man's psychic energies "fell out" of heaven and into the earthly realm. This shift was exemplified by such giants as Columbus, Leonardo de Vinci, Galileo and Copernicus. As Edward Edinger sums it up, in the past 500 years, "There has been a vast expansion of conscious human energies and initiatives in all the areas of human enterprise. This has been accompanied by progressive ego inflation. It is a characteristic of our times that has reached such proportions that scarcely anyone can disregard it."

So one summary of the Faust legend might be that man's psychological orientation began undergoing a change that refocused human energies to a "this-worldly" focus rather than the "other-worldly" orientation which had dominated Western man's psychological attitude for the previous millennium. Whereas the Gospel of St. John begins, "In the beginning was the Word [Logos or Mind of God]," Goethe's Faust proclaims, "In the beginning was the act." This shift from the eternal to the temporal, from the "other-worldly" to the "this-worldly" ultimately gave us the Renaissance, the Enlightenment, the scientific method, rationalism, individualism, democracy and the modern technological state.

With Rene Descartes comes a further development of consciousness. "I think, therefore I am."–which Edinger suggests is better translated as, "I am conscious, therefore I am."–becomes the foundation of Western individualism and rationalism, the two principles, according to Rollo May, on which modern philosophy, and to a large extent culture, were based. In a very real sense, Descartes represents the emergence of psychological man, as can be seen in Descartes' resolution "to study within myself . . . those modes of consciousness which I call perceptions and imaginations." This detached speculation about the workings of the psyche is totally new in history.

Descartes, however, represents a further psychological shift for the West in the arrival of the "scientific method." Whereas before the scientific revolution, qualities were felt to reside *both* in nature and in man, the science of Descartes saw reality solely in those quantitative qualities that could be measured, reduced to their constituent parts and verified by repeated experiment. Thus when the Royal Academy was established in London in 1660 for the study of science, all the human qualities incapable of measurement by physical means (subsequently given a lesser status as the "humanities") were deemed unfit for study. Thus also it was that years later Owen Barfield would note how "the qualities formerly treated as inherent in nature have, as far as any scientific theory is concerned, disappeared from it, and how they have reappeared on the hither side of the line between subject and object, within the experiencing human psyche. We perceive ourselves as 'projecting' qualities onto nature rather than receiving them from her."

How the Scientific Revolution of the 17th century affected the Enlightenment is difficult to say, but despite both Descartes's and Newton's professions of religious belief, some process was at work that ultimately flowered into one of the decisive developments in the history of Western consciousness–the Enlightenment's rejection of Christianity. For over 1,500 years, Christ on the cross had been the spiritual, cultural and psychological symbol of Western civilization. But with the Enlightenment, Christ's love as the *Summum Bonum* gave way to the Goddess of Reason as the source of Western man's highest meaning, while Diderot and the *philosophes* became the precursors of Comte, positivism and the 19th and 20th century modernists.

An event of equal importance during the Enlightenment came in the person of Immanuel Kant. Kant is of such significance that I'm going to quote directly from Edward Edinger, whose concise description of Kant clarifies an otherwise obscure achievement. Kant's basic discovery, Edinger says, "Is that of the *a priori* forms and categories. According to Kant, perceptions of outer reality are structured and ordered by means of innate, built-in forms of perception. These forms of perception are space and time. Space and time do not exist in the outer world. They are forms of perception that the human mind imposes on the flux of sensory data to order it. Furthermore, our understanding of what we perceive, our ability to grasp and conceptualize what we perceive, is brought about by a number of innate categories of understanding–categories such as quantity, quality, cause and effect, and relation. His [Kant's] discovery, then, is that the human mind, the human psyche, pours into sensory data the forms of perception and the categories of understanding which create our total view of the world." (10) In other words, the thing-in-itself, ultimate reality, is unknowable because each of us–as the knower–inevitably views reality from within innate categories of understanding that are intrinsic to the psyche. This insight was one of the seminal advances in understanding consciousness. Jung called it a threshold that divides "two epochs."

Finally, in the early part of the 20th century, Freud discovered the personal unconscious and Jung discovered the collective unconscious *as empirical realities* and as the source of consciousness. In the long-hidden story of consciousness, a new epoch had begun.

Is Consciousness Contracting?

But the question has to be asked whether or not Western consciousness has become so detached from its moorings that it's begun to contract, and thus lose its life-creating relationship with the deeper reaches of the soul, which is essential for balanced personal and social health. We must ask whether we see such detachment in 20th-century consciousness reflected in the suicidal insanity of history's two most destructive wars, in the ascendancy of materialism, positivism, nihilism, and existentialism; in modernism's denial of man's need for a deity and in its worship of rationality and efficiency; in postmodernism's schizophrenic angst; in de-centered individuals destroying, or at least severely weakening, civilized life's most essential institution–the family; and, eventually, reflected in the hubris that seeks to become as God himself, i.e., to develop artificial life. We must ask what such a disorienting record represents in terms of contemporary consciousness.

The contraction of consciousness? The thought almost seems ludicrous. Man's awareness of the world, of the primary elements of nature, of the universe, of the micro and the macro has never expanded as it has during the past 150 years. So how can the suggestion of the contraction of consciousness be seriously considered?

The starting point for such consideration is a look at the etymology of the word "consciousness." It's interesting to note that "consciousness" and "science" stem from the same Latin root, *scire*, "to know." But while science derives solely from the word meaning "knowing," consciousness comes from both knowing and the added word *con*, meaning "with." "Knowing with,"–there's an added dimension. So consciousness is the experience of "knowing" in the presence of an "other." Consciousness is the ego's cognizance of itself and the external world, but it's a recognition that's subordinate to the archetype of wholeness and completeness. In spiritual terms, the "other" is God; psychologically, the "other" is the Self. In this sense, the task of life is the creation of more and more consciousness. Consciousness is the supreme value of life.

It's the melding of "knowing in the presence of an other" that has produced wisdom throughout the ages. Wisdom, as distinct from knowledge, is marked by a certain inner breadth and depth, it resonates at the soul level.

So back to our original question: How can we talk about the contraction of consciousness at a time when man's awareness is expanding exponentially? Part of the explanation may be that consciousness exists in terms of both time and space. It is spatially that our consciousness has expanded so remarkably. But in terms of time, that is, history, tradition, legend and the sense of the sacred continuity of the past—indeed, any connection to the past, our consciousness has been substantially diminished. We define progress by how quickly we can erase the past and live only in the present moment. Information technologies tend to reinforce this inclination. Moreover, the 20th century has seen consciousness increasingly subordinated to a purely rational, technological and commercial outlook, which, on the whole, expresses collective, not individual, values.

Part of this process has been fostered by the transformation of the "seven deadly sins" into "seven worldly virtues." Throughout history, every civilization employed some means of tempering the more avaricious aspects of man's nature. In the Western Judeo-Christian tradition, such characteristics were enumerated under the seven deadly sins of pride, wrath, envy, lust, gluttony, avarice and sloth.

Most of these attributes have now been converted into virtues. Avarice is celebrated as the national hallmark of a "successful" person, and magazines annually list the net (financial) worth of such people. The literature on how to get rich quickly probably outsells every other genre of literature, and the financial news cable TV channels' in-your-face ads telling how to make millions are inescapable. Pride and self-promotion are essential ingredients to success—if not necessarily happiness. Lust has become the single most prominent feature of what passes for our culture. Indeed, lust in "high places" is perhaps America's most popular form of entertainment. And on and on it goes, aided and abetted by Madison Avenue, which, in reality, reflects, feeds and magnifies America's appetites.

Such a shift is not simply a minor change of moral attitude, a "preference," as contemporary jargon has it. It represents an underlying erosion of consciousness, a devaluation of proportion, a corrosion of those protections consciousness has built up over centuries in order to protect man from the inflating and destructive effects of his nature. Such attributes are what constitute civilized life. Indeed, minus such restraints, there is no civilized life. Protection against these eroding aspects of our nature had been achieved by labeling such attributes as "sins" which required confession and penance, thus keeping man's ego within the bounds of propriety.

It' clearly possible that our educational curriculum has contributed to this contraction of consciousness–especially in K-12, where the curriculum is so weighted toward science and technology. We don't even pretend to educate the whole person. Literature, poetry, history, music, memorization and now even physical education class–all the subjects that expand and deepen the inner person–are increasingly dropped from the curriculum. So we're left with an education that teaches our children how to make a living, but not how to live a life. They end up with minimal relationship to the past and no understanding of the present or sense of the times in which they live. And despite the emphasis on science and technology, the kids end up with no comprehension of the human-technology relationship and how it shapes their attitudes, character and very being.

So it's little wonder T.S. Eliot could ask in 1934, "Where is the Life we have lost in living? / Where is the wisdom we have lost in knowledge? / Where is the knowledge we have lost in information?" Or Sven Birkerts could write in *The Gutenberg Elegies,* "My core fear is that we are, as a culture, as a species, becoming shallower; that we have turned from depth–from the Judeo-Christian premise of unfathomable mystery–and are adapting ourselves to the ersatz security of a vast lateral connectedness." Or that Lord William Rees-Mogg, former editor of *The Times* of London could argue in an editorial, "mankind has somehow lost touch with the spiritual forces that guide our species."

While Rees-Mogg was writing about the disappearance of the inner daemon that has fostered individual greatness from Socrates to Churchill, his comments apply equally to the various manifestations of consciousness: "By the standards of Rembrandt or Picasso there is no visual artist of genius; by the standards of Aeschylus or Shakespeare no poet of genius; by the standards of Mozart or Wagner no composer of genius; by the standards of Charlemagne or Abraham Lincoln no statesman of genius, not in the whole wide world." He might have added that although the population of America has increased over 6,000 percent since Thomas Jefferson's day, is there even one person in America today who could begin to equal the depth and majesty of Jefferson's gift to the world?

In his book *The Age of Access*, Jeremy Rifkin refers to "the fall of historical consciousness and the rise of therapeutic consciousness." Throughout the 18th, 19th and early 20th centuries, Rifkin notes, the bourgeoisie "viewed themselves in historical terms." But by the middle of the 20th century, Rifkin suggests, "historical consciousness was giving way to a new therapeutic consciousness . . . while 'historical man' sacrifices in the present and lives for the future, 'therapeutic man' lives for the present and gives up any pretense of a grand historical mission."

Pondering the contraction of consciousness, Stephen Talbott writes, "History suggests a progressive contraction of consciousness into the skull of the detached, self-contained, and isolated observer, so that we come to know the world as set apart from ourselves. More and more of our experience," he concludes, "becomes a chronicling of 'world' or 'other,' until we stand finally as detached observers even of our own subjectivity."

Christopher Lasch, one of the most perceptive observers of the second half of the 20th century, noted in 1979, "We are fast losing the sense of historical continuity, the sense of belonging to a succession of generations originating in the past and stretching into the future. It is a waning of the sense of historical time." (In a 1999 survey, only one-third of the seniors from top-rated colleges and universities could name George Washington as the American general at Yorktown. Most named Ulysses S. Grant. Only 22 percent could identify the Gettysburg Address as the source of the phrase "government of the people, by the people, for the people." Most thought it came from the Declaration of Independence or the Constitution. None of America's 55 "elite" colleges and universities requires a course in American history before graduation.)

Vaclav Havel, president of the Czech Republic, echoes Lasch when he says, "Humanity appears to be irrevocably losing what various civilizations previously have had—a link with the eternal and infinite, and a resultant sense of humility and responsibility, a relationship to the world as a whole, to its metaphysical order, to the miracle of creation."

Sir Laurens van der Post, South Africa's eminent author and naturalist, sums up what has happened: "What has been happening not only historically but psychologically, is that the basis of consciousness for modern man has been narrowed, has been narrowed so much that it will not admit all the material that is coming from the collective unconscious, that it cannot admit all the energies that would give us new meaning, that would give us the power to renew ourselves, that would expand our consciousness . . . the assumption of consciousness on which modern man operates is too narrow." van der Post sees the contraction of consciousness as "one of the great sources of our loss of meaning."

Finally, psychiatrist Erich Neumann says the "overvaluation of the ego" has gone to such an extent that the modern mind "is no longer capable of seeing anything that transcends the personal sphere of ego consciousness."(11)

What the above-mentioned people are suggesting is almost beyond our capacity to comprehend: The loss of historical consciousness and continuity; a truncated link with the eternal and infinite dimension of existence; loss of tradition which is the expression of the psychic history of humanity; and a disintegration of the social and psychic structures and values which have been the architecture of the collective psyche and of social cohesion. Taken together, this could portend the interruption of the normal process of human development and the introduction of a period of cultural and psychic retardation.

There is little question that Western consciousness is one of the great achievements of humankind. Ever since the Greeks and the Hebrews, the whole meaning of Western history has led toward the creation of an individual who would walk freely in his own consciousness; an individual who would make all the great universal truths of life individual and specific; a person who would make the collective psychology of humankind individual in his own time, and therefore give a heightened purpose and enrichment to society. To say this is not a judgment on the consciousness of other people and nations. It's to say that Western consciousness has been something unique in human history, something that if we debase or lose it, could have catastrophic consequences.

Globalization

And now consciousness faces possibly the greatest test it has ever confronted–the test of globalization.

Sir Fred Holye was an eminent British mathematician and astronomer. He made a remark in the 1940s that was prophetic: "Once a photograph of Earth, taken from the outside, is available, a new idea as powerful as any in history will be let loose." That photograph was taken in 1969 from the moon, and it provided a visual symbol of globalization for humanity. Globalization–the long-term effort to integrate the global dimensions of life into each nation's economics, politics and culture. In my judgment, this is the most ambitious collective experiment in history. If it succeeds, humanity may enter an epoch of opportunity and prosperity for a greater proportion of the earth's inhabitants than ever before. If it fails, it could retard progress in some nations for generations.

For globalization to fulfill its potential, it must be more than just a technical process. It must be a human process, a process of increasing sensitivity to other people and cultures, a spiritual and psychological process. At heart, it must be a process of deepening consciousness.

Our comments about globalization and consciousness thus far have been about Western consciousness. But just as today's Western consciousness is vastly different from that of Homer's Greece, so is Western consciousness different from the consciousness of the rest of the world. This is not a value judgment. It's not to say one is better or worse. It's simply to acknowledge that over the eons, consciousness has evolved differently in different parts of the world, and it has produced different cultures, values and attitudes about life.

Take some basic differences between Eastern and Western civilizations. The West prizes individuality, while the East emphasizes relationships and community. The West highlights rationality, while the East stresses intuition. The West sees man dominating Nature, while the East sees man as a part of Nature. In the West, God ordains the separation of man from Nature, while in the East the Tao relates man to Nature. The West sees a dichotomy between Mind and Body, while for the East, Mind and Body are simply the Yin and the Yang–the harmony and interconnectedness between opposites. The West tends to be absolutist–"Thou shalt not," while in the East the Tao–literally, the Way of Nature–is relative and even refuses definition. While the West tends to be extroverted, the East is inclined to be introverted. The West is apt to emphasize discrete parts, while the East looks for the wholeness of pattern. The West prizes knowledge, the East seeks wisdom.

Up until a few decades ago, the East had produced nothing equivalent to what the West calls psychology. Rather, countries such as India and China lived in the realm of philosophy and metaphysics. The word "mind" as used in the East has the connotation of something metaphysical, a conception of mind not seen in the West since the Middle Ages. Western psychology knows the mind as the mental functioning of the psyche, as the mentality of an individual. In Asia, mind is a cosmic factor, the very essence of existence.

In Asia there is no conflict between science and religion because no science there is based upon the passion for facts, and no religion simply upon faith. The East believes in the self-liberating power of the introverted mind, while nothing in the mainstream of Western history encourages such a view. While the ego is at the center of the Western concept of mind, the Eastern mind has no difficulty of conceiving of a consciousness without an ego. Consciousness is deemed capable of transcending its ego conditions; indeed, in its "higher" forms, the ego disappears altogether. The ego simply does not play the same role in Eastern thought as it does in the West (and therein may be a primary reason why the West has developed scientifically and technologically ahead of the East). The Christian West considers man to be wholly dependent upon the "grace of God," whereas the East insists that man is the sole cause of his higher development. While the East believes in identification with the divine, the West shuns such identification and seeks relatedness to the divine. The Eastern attitude stultifies the Western, and vice versa. You cannot be a good Christian and redeem yourself, nor can you be a Buddhist and worship God.

True, change has been taking place in Asia. Psychology, for example, has now been introduced into certain parts of Asia. Wimal

Dissanayake of the East/West Center in Hawaii (1989) notes that with increased technology and modernization, "the loss of self is an acute problem in Eastern societies." He points to the atrophy of authority, historically the basis of civil stability; and he also notes the decline of family and religion, which had been the unifying forces of Asian societies. Ironically, as Westerners increasingly dip into Eastern religion and philosophy, Dissanayake offers this comment: "[Eastern] Religion no longer is the binding force in society; it lacks the power or authority to provide individuals with systems of meaning and symbols that would enable them to impose a unity on the diverse activities associated with living." Dissanayake seems to be suggesting that Asia is experiencing something akin to Western secularization. In like manner, Joseph Campbell expressed concern over his Hindu, Buddhist and Islamic students, who all were having the same kind of "doubts" about their religions that Western students have had about Christianity for over a century. If what Dissanayake and Campbell report is an accurate picture, Asia may be undergoing a similar psychological reorientation to the one that has affected the West over the past few centuries, albeit at a somewhat slower pace.

So the question arises, what's going to happen to Asian consciousness as globalization spreads–a globalization, it must be recognized, based almost entirely on Western rationalized, secular, materialistic concepts of technology, economics and administration? Not to be alarmist, but one sees the potential for a vast psychic dislocation as Asian nations seek to incorporate the techniques of globalization into their affairs. For globalization is not just about harmonizing financial reporting systems, or opening up markets, or controlling capital flows, etc. It's also about tradition, culture, historic relationships and modes of human interaction; it's about existing institutions and why and how they evolved. In short, globalization goes to the psychic foundation of a people.

Already the Japanese government is considering change in Japan's centuries-old cultural traditions so that the Japanese become more independent as individuals, less preoccupied with convention, more open to ethnic diversity and immigrants, less insistent on the compulsory academic school week, and more knowledgeable of the English language. In the words of the executive director of the commission appointed to consider such changes, "We are really advocating a fundamental reorientation of society. The 21st century will be the era of individuals." In other words, globalization is causing the Japanese to force changes in behavior patterns that stem from psychological and cultural foundations that go back centuries. The Japanese engineered major social reorientations in 1868 and 1945, but neither were of the depth and scale they are now contemplating. It's a bold and uncertain gamble.

We sometimes forget that free markets in the West were the outgrowth of a unique historical experience, a specific religious orientation and a psychology characteristic of Europeans and their descendents. It took centuries to develop the attitudes, conditions and mechanisms supportive of free markets in the West. Globalization is forcing other parts of the world to achieve these conditions as fast as possible, to graft an alien economic system onto an indigenous social structure, the roots of which go back millennia. The question now is whether globalization is proceeding at a pace beyond the human capacity to digest it psychologically.

If globalization is posing such challenges for Asia–as well as for Islam–just think of what the implications are for Africa, which has a basic consciousness that is of a different order altogether. It is little wonder that the World Health Organization warns that "psychic distress" will be an increasing health concern worldwide over the coming two decades.

The above comments about the possible contraction of consciousness in the West are not intended as an indictment, and much less as a glorification of the some supposed "golden age." It's an attempt to understand the reality of our condition today, for such understanding is essential for any hope of globalization to fulfill its potential. For globalization can only succeed if it expresses the wholeness of the human psyche, the unity of what is in the soul of both East and West. And as globalization matures and expresses something new for humanity, the consciousness that is to come will be immensely broadened. A global civilization will be a human civilization in a far higher sense than any that has ever been before, as it will have overcome the constricting social, ethnic and national limitations of the past. The birth pangs of such a new consciousness will bring infinite suffering as familiar attitudes and institutions fall away, causing some people to resist change. But economically, politically and, eventually spiritually and psychologically, our world is an indivisible whole. This can only be made reality if, individually and collectively, we address the question of meaning and its relevance for the human venture.

Part II – New Meaning for the Human Venture

The Question of Meaning

The question "What is the meaning of life?" is a question probably not too much on the popular mind throughout most of Western history. In any event, the Church had a ready answer: "The chief end of man is to glorify God and enjoy him forever," as the Presbyterian catechism says. For those contained within the Christian myth–which was mostly everyone up to the end of the 18th and the beginning of the 19th centuries–that was a satisfying answer.

But the new myth of Enlightenment, rationalism and positivism, as Isaiah Berlin reminds us, told us that "everything in the world moved by mechanical means, that all evils could be cured by appropriate technological steps, that there could exist *engineers both of human souls and of human bodies.*"

Surveying the results of two hundred years of rationalism's myth, Rollo May wrote only a decade ago: "We have driven away the ghosts of superstition and authoritarianism in religion, but instead of having purified beliefs, most people have few beliefs left to be purified . . . We are open-minded about philosophy, but where are the philosophers who have anything to tell us about the meaning of life?"

I suggest, however, that "the meaning of life" is not a product of philosophy or the intellect. It comes from a deeper level. The only way the "What's the meaning of life?" question can be answered is by asking it differently: "What is the meaning of *my* life?" This shifts the question from a philosophical abstraction, to a human question relating to that area in the personality where meaning is created. For transcendent meaning–which has been at the core of every civilization in history– has not vanished. It's simply that it must find fresh expressions for a new epoch of the human experience.

It's against this background of meaninglessness that we come to the relevance of Jung for the contemporary world. While Jung was a psychiatrist, psychiatry was only a base for his larger work. What was that work? As van der Post described it, "Jung's work was to restore to modern man his capacity for religious experience, to renew the relationship of modern man with his highest meaning, to renew his relationship with the source of that meaning, with his Creator, with God." Or as Edward Edinger wrote, Jung "wanted to preserve the meaning that previously had been embedded in theological and metaphysical concepts [but which have lost their root connection with natural experience], by uncovering the psychic realities which had formerly been projected into them."

This raises the question of the relationship between religion and psychology, and here we get into some of the heart of what Jung discovered. This has always been controversial, as comparatively few in the religious community have considered the *psychological* function of religion. I repeat what I said at the outset about psychology: that I refer to it in its original meaning of "the study of the soul."

That said, let me suggest that the next pages contain highly concentrated material, and if you're anything like me, you may require several readings to comprehend and assimilate the import of what is written. The psyche is not something to be understood by speed-reading, and Jung is certainly one of the most profound writers of the 20th century. But I suggest it may be some of the most rewarding work you have ever done.

As we pursue these questions, I emphasize that when I refer to "God," I'm not talking about God per se; rather, I'm talking about the *God-image* that resides in the psyche. In my view, what we humans have done is to take something that may actually be beyond human comprehension, i.e., the immense, mysterious, numinous power that created the universe, and we've reduced it to a size we can intellectually encompass and given it the name of "God." We know all about God; we've even given this transcendent might human attributes such as "just," "benevolent" or "forgiving." But this immeasurable force may actually be unencompassable by the human mind. This may be why the Bible and early Greek mythology and philosophy are expressed in archetypal images rather than in rational intellectual discourse. Our ability to comprehend God may be akin to a snail's ability to understand nuclear physics.

So in point of fact, when we speak of God, it may be that what we're actually talking about is the *God-image* embedded in the psyche. That's understandable, for all experience is, to a certain degree, psychic experience simply because the psyche is the only mechanism we have through which to view reality and the world we live in. As Jung once put it, "Psychic experience is the only category of existence of which we have *immediate* knowledge, since nothing can be known unless it first appears as a psychic image." This is not to say that God is "nothing but" a psychic projection. Far from it. As Jung once said, "It is my practical experience that psychological understanding immediately revivifies the essential Christian ideas and fills them with the breath of life." But humans being human and the psyche being limited in its capacity, it may be that our reference to God is more in terms of a "God-image" than in terms of the actual unencompassable magnitude of the Creator.

With this as a preface, let's look at a small sampling of Jung's experience with the dynamics of the psyche. For the psyche–the soul– is the crucible of transcendent meaning; and keep in mind that what we're considering is the question "What is the meaning of *my* life?" That's the point of what we're talking about.

Jung's work shows that the psyche–the totality of the conscious and unconscious–is an active phenomenon in determining the course of human affairs. It exists as an empirical reality.(12) One could even say that the relation of the ego to the unconscious–and of the personal to the transpersonal–decides the fate not only of us as individuals, but also of humanity.

Contemporary psychology, however, deals primarily with consciousness and its various forms of neurosis, and it tends to dismiss Jung's pragmatic experience with the unconscious–which may tell us more about our times than about Jung. Any so-called model offered in these pages is simply a *suggestion of relationships*, for we're dealing with insubstantial attributes. Jung would be the first to say that the psyche, in its fullest dimension, is, like God, unencompassable by the human mind, for we have no Archimedean point outside the psyche from which to view the psyche.(13) Jung would also be the first to say no one psychological theory explains everything about the psyche. Indeed, he never attempted to establish a psychological theory, which is one of the many points that distinguish him from Freud. Jung once said, "Thank God I'm not a Jungian." With this in mind, my suggestions about Jung's work will be an extremely simplified version.

Figure A on page 270 shows the psyche illustrated as a sphere with a bright field (A) on its surface representing consciousness. The field's center is the *ego*. What Jung called the Self (B), which we'll elaborate on in a moment, is at the same time the nucleus of the psyche as well as the whole sphere itself. This is a paradox that must be kept in mind. Also, remember, that this diagram symbolizes relationships.

This visualization shows that there are *two* autonomous centers of psychic being–the ego and the Self. The ego is the center of the conscious personality, the seat of subjective identity, while the Self is the seat of objective identity. The Self is the supreme psychic authority and subordinates the ego to it. So we'll start with the Self. Jung's concept of the Self is quite different from what is thought of in usual reference to the self, which generally means the ego's awareness of itself and its surroundings.

As Edinger reminds us, and throughout the following discussion, I draw heavily on his book, *Ego and Archetype* (14), Jung's most far-reaching discovery is the *collective unconscious,* or what he sometimes called the *archetypal psyche*. Because of Jung's work, we know that the individual psyche is not simply a product of personal experience. It also has a *transpersonal dimension*, which is manifested in universal patterns and images–archetypes–such as have been seen in all the world's cultures, religions and mythologies throughout all time. It's obvious that contemporary psychology tends to adopt Freud's view of the unconscious as a receptacle for repressed complexes or discarded memories. Sort of a psychic trash can. Nonetheless, Jung's work provides evidence of the psyche operating on a broader dimension, namely that the psyche reaches across time and space. Jung also discovered that the collective unconscious has *a structuring* or *ordering principle*, which unifies the psyche's archetypal contents, and it *functions as a regulating center of the psyche*. This ordering principle is the central archetype of wholeness, which Jung called the Self.

In other words, *the Self is the ordering and unifying center of the total psyche*–conscious and unconscious–much as the ego is the center of the conscious personality. From an empirical psychological standpoint, the Self is identical to the God-image, which also acts as a supreme ordering principle.

The second autonomous center of the psyche is, of course, the ego, which is the center of consciousness and the seat of the individual's experience of subjective identity. The ego's relation to the Self is extremely important. It's a relationship that is reflected in our day-to-day life in countless ways that we're generally unaware of. From a psychological viewpoint, for example, one could say the ego-Self relationship is reflected externally in such phenomena as the science versus religion debate.

Figures 1-4 on page 271 illustrate Jung's view of the different stages of development of the ego-Self relationship. The shaded portions illustrate where the ego and Self have not yet separated and are still identified with each other. The line connecting the center of the ego with the center of the Self represents the ego-Self axis–the vital connecting link between ego and Self that ensures the integrity of the ego. I reemphasize that there's a certain paradox in this, as the Self is defined as the center as well as the totality of the psyche, which, obviously includes the ego. So it should be understood that these diagrams are also paradoxical in order to illustrate the ego-Self relationship.

According to this, when a child such as my granddaughter Francesca is born, the ego and Self are one. The ego is present only as a potentiality. Francesca, obviously, has no sense of "I am."

Figure 2 shows an emerging ego which is beginning to separate from the Self, but which still has its center and greater area in primary identity with the Self.

Figure 3 shows a more advanced state of development. However, a certain degree of ego-Self identity remains. The ego-Self axis, which in the first two diagrams was completely unconscious and therefore indistinguishable from ego-Self identity, has now partially moved into the individual's realm of consciousness.

Figure 4 is an ideal theoretical limit that probably does not exist in reality. It represents a total separation of the ego and Self and a complete consciousness of the ego-Self axis.

These diagrams are designed to illustrate the thesis that psychological development is characterized by two processes occurring simultaneously, namely, progressive separation of the ego from the Self, as well as the individual's increasing consciousness of the ego-Self axis.

The point to be made here is that normal psychic development brings about a growing differentiation of the ego and the Self. In the first half of life, the ego assumes greater independence from the Self as the individual defines himself in the external world. The ego wants to disengage far enough from the Self in order to find independence and its own place in the world; but it doesn't want to move so far away from the Self that it loses touch with its source of transpersonal meaning. Keep in mind that the ultimate objective over time is to reach a creative relationship between the ego and the Self, and for the individual to be conscious of the relationship between the ego and the Self.

Thus the ego-Self axis becomes extremely important. Jung discovered that as the ego and Self–what he called the "I" and the "Thou"–engage in a dialogue, consciousness is transformed into *a new kind of awareness* which draws, as it were, a translucent light out of the darkness of the collective unconscious. He believed the future of humanity depends on people knowing themselves so well that they can move into this area of their psyche so this dialogue can take place.

This relationship between the ego and Self may seem complicated, but it's basic to assessing the cause of America's crisis of meaning. If we understand this, we at least begin to have an inkling of the origins of the twin phenomena of alienation and psychic inflation, which are such hallmarks of our time. For as Jung's lifelong experience with hundreds—if not thousands—of people indicates, it's somewhere in the area of the ego-Self relationship that our capacity for spiritual experience is either nurtured or diminished.

The evidence from Jung's work with people led him to believe that in the collective unconscious, a pattern exists that defines the area from which man draws his capability for spiritual experience; a blueprint that appears to be man's link with the infinite. It is a pattern that gives man his highest sense of meaning, which, through all time and in most civilizations has been called God. In a letter Jung wrote to van der Post shortly before Jung died, he said, "I cannot define for you what God is. I can only tell you that with my work, I have empirically proved that the pattern of God exists in every human being, and that this pattern has at its disposal the greatest transforming energies of which the human spirit is possible." Jung's lifelong work was to link people with that pattern inside themselves, for it is not only capable of providing psychic healing, but also an energizing sense of meaning.

Religion, Alienation and Psychic Inflation

Spiritual experience—which we codify into a religion—is not a matter of opinion, taste or preference. The historical record shows that virtually all peoples through all time have expressed some sort of collective spiritual life. And for good reason. Religion has served distinct functions in all civilizations. Joseph Campbell offers four functions served by the religious myths of all civilizations. (By "myth" I mean a story reveling some deeper, unseen truth about life; quite the opposite of the contemporary use of myth as falsehood.)

First, a religious myth gives the individual a sense of awe and wonder before the mystery of life. It gives the individual a living relationship to that omnipotent and transcendent Creator who represents what is most sublime and all-powerful about existence. A religious myth affirms life; it affirms a sense of gratitude to be part of the unfathomable mystery of being. Second, a religious myth renders an image of the universe and man's place therein which will maintain and enhance that sense of awe and wonder. The third role of a religious myth is to relate the individual to his group, to give him a sense of participation in society, a society that has a "holy" origin. A true myth validates a certain collective moral order, and human societies cannot exist without a commonly accepted moral structure. Finally, a religious myth links a person's conscious life with his unconscious life, with the deepest roots of his being, with his instinct system. In this way, a religious myth provides the individual with psychological coherence, anchorage and meaning to the individual personality.

The historical record also shows that when the containing religious myth disintegrates for whatever reason, a people fall apart both psychologically and socially. All we have to do is look at what's happened to indigenous people in North and South America, Asia and Africa as Western rationalism, positivism and secular technology have increasingly reshaped their life and culture. Two common manifestations of this loss of collective spiritual meaning are alienation (an ego turning its back on God) and psychic inflation (an ego identified with God), two phenomena clearly prevalent in today's America.

Edward Edinger suggests that, understood psychologically, the central aim of all religious practice is to keep the individual (ego) related to the deity (Self). All religions are repositories of transpersonal experience and archetypal images. The intrinsic psychological purpose of religious ceremonies of all kinds seems to be to provide the individual with the experience of being related meaningfully to these transpersonal categories of life. That is true of the Mass and of the Catholic confessional in a more personal way, where the individual has the chance to unburden himself of whatever events brought about a sense of alienation from God.

All religious practices hold up to view the transpersonal dimensions of existence and attempt to relate them to the individual. Thus religion is the best collective protection available against both psychic inflation and alienation. So far as we know, every society has had such suprapersonal categories in its collective ritual of life. It may be that collective human life cannot survive for any extended period without some common shared sense of awareness of these transpersonal categories.

Jung comments on the origin of religious practices. It should never be forgotten, he writes, "that morality was not brought down on tablets of stone from Sinai and imposed on the people, but is a function of the human soul, as old as humanity itself." Morality, Jung continues, "is not imposed from outside; we have it in ourselves from the start—not the law, but our moral nature without which the collective life of human society would be impossible."

Religious practices and folk wisdom of all races and ages have always recognized the psychic dangers of inflation and alienation, under different names. In the Christian tradition, for example, the basic psychological message of the Beatitudes—Christ's Sermon on the Mount—is that God's blessing will come to the non inflated personality. By labeling the "seven deadly sins"—pride, wrath, envy, lust, gluttony, avarice and sloth—as sins that require confession and penance, the individual is protected against what, from a psychological viewpoint, are recognized symptoms of potential inflation.

In Zen Buddhism subtle techniques have been developed for undermining intellectual inflation, the illusion that one *knows*. One such technique is the use of koans, or enigmatic sayings. The Zen master asks the novice, "Who discovered water?" The novice ponders the question, and the master says, "I don't know who discovered water, but I can tell you who didn't discover it—the fish." (Think about that one, for therein lies the story of the psyche.)

The taboos encountered in so-called primitive societies have had much the same purpose—protecting the individual from the inflated psychic state, from contact with powers that would be too strong for the limited ego to keep in bounds. For example, isolating victorious warriors when they returned from battle tended to temper any psychic inflation that may have taken place as a result of victory.

When the collective psyche is in a stable state, the majority of people share a common living myth or deity (Figure 6 on page 272). Each person projects his inner God-image (the Self) to his or her chosen religion. The collective religion then serves as the container of the Self for a large number of people. The reality of the individual's transpersonal life forces is mirrored in the imagery the church embodies in its symbolism, mythology, rites and dogma. As long as it is functioning adequately, the church protects the society against any widespread inflation or alienation.

Alienation and Inflation

If a people lose their belief in God, or, from the psychological standpoint, if the established religion no longer expresses what is welling up from the collective unconscious, which is the fountainhead of spiritual experience, we have the condition that Nietzsche announced for the modern world, "God is dead." Commenting on Nietzsche's remark, Marie von Franz, perhaps Jung's most able collaborator and an accomplished psychiatrist in her own right, noted, "Instead of saying with Nietzsche 'God is dead,' it would have been more clear to the truth to say, 'The highest value, which gives life its meaning, has got lost.' It is by no means rare for a cultural community to lose its god and to fall thereby into severe social and psychological crisis."

While Nietzsche's "God is dead" pronouncement was written in 1883, at least 25 years earlier Victor Hugo had used the phrase in *Les Miserables* as a description of the intellectual temper of the times, and indeed, in 1843 Thomas Carlyle had written that the moderns "have closed our eyes to the eternal Substance of things and opened them to the Shews and Shams of things . . . There is no longer any God for us!" And had not the great Hegel himself written in 1827, "*God has died–God is dead*–this is the most frightful of all thoughts, that everything eternal and true is *not*, that negation itself is found in God." So some deep denial of a deity, some loss of life's highest value, was taking place long before Nietzsche.

Interestingly, this exact same process of alienation–even the same phrase–appeared at the end of the Greco-Roman age with the cry, "Great Pan is dead." Thus Lucretius could write of the "aching hearts in every home, racked incessantly by pangs the mind was powerless to assuage." Sounds familiar.

What happens when life's "highest value" becomes "lost" is that the psychic energy and values that had been contained in the religion now flow back to the individual, activating that portion of his or her psyche that had been quietly contained in religion. Figure 7 on page 273 illustrates this.

Two of Western literature's most famous 20th-century poems describe this condition. T.S. Eliot, in *The Waste Land,* speaks of a "heap of broken images," while W.B. Yeats, in *The Second Coming,* says, "the falcon cannot hear the falconer." From a psychological standpoint, these two phrases characterize much of the Western world's "creative minority"–the writers, artists, academics, intellectuals, technologists–throughout most of the past century.

As a result of this loss of life's "highest value," we now have a language of dysfunction that has entered the vocabulary only since the beginning of the 20th century. "Stressed," "paranoid," "repressed," "burned out," "mid-life crisis," "identity crisis"–they're all terms we think of as individual problems, but in fact they may represent a deeper condition of our times.(15) Such a condition suggests that, despite our knowledge and "enlightenment," psychic disintegration steadily "corrodes the thin veneer of civilization from below," as Steve Talbott puts it. Such psychic disintegration has created a culture of dysfunction with its own media, music, codes of existence and style of life.

What happens now? We see examples of several possibilities. One is that with the loss of the God-projection into religion, the individual ego becomes disconnected from the Self. Such disengagement is the essence of the alienation that expresses the empty meaninglessness that is such a common theme of today's culture. Alienation suggests that the ego has lost the essential connection with the Self that gives the ego foundation, structure, and security, and also provides energy, interest, and meaning to life. The Biblical Cain is an archetypal figure representing alienation, a story retold in contemporary terms in John Steinbeck's *East of Eden.* Herman Melville's *Moby Dick* offers an image of alienation in its very first line–"Call me Ishmael." Ishmael was the illegitimate son of Abraham whom Abraham cast out into the desert when Isaac, the legitimate son, was born. The ever-growing therapeutic "self-help" literature is another result of burgeoning alienation. Alienation is almost the staple of contemporary rock lyrics. The "Smashing Pumpkins" are an example: "welcome to nowhere fast / nothing here ever lasts . . . living makes me sick / so sick I wish I could die / down in the belly of the beast." And we've already mentioned the alienation that typified every character in the movie, *American Beauty.*

A second possible reaction to the loss of life's "highest value" is that the individual takes on himself, on his own ego, all the psychic energy previously attached to the deity. Such a person succumbs to psychic inflation. Inflation is a psychological phenomenon that involves an extension of the personality (ego) beyond normal human limits. The power motive mentioned earlier is one example. Such an attitude is held by many of America's scientists and technologists. They sincerely believe they're taking evolution to its next stage—an attitude that unconsciously identifies them with God. Such an attitude is the essence of psychological inflation (the ego becomes identified with the Self). The Greeks called it *hubris.* St. Paul, writing to the Corinthians, simply said, "Knowledge puffeth up." Jung's view was that an "inflated consciousnesses is always egocentric and conscious of nothing but its own existence."

Such psychic inflation is obviously not limited to scientists thinking they're in charge of evolution. One has to ask how many of the corporate mega.-mergers that have taken place in recent years were driven more by inflated egos than by economic rationality.

There is another expression of psychic inflation which is causing America and the world no end of harm but which is little understood—and that is the phenomenon of terrorism. Edinger describes this phenomenon clearly and simply in his book *Archetype of the Apocalypse.*(16)

According to Edinger, the psychological root of terrorism is a "fanatical resentment—a—quasi-psychotic hatred originating in the depths of the archetypal psyche and therefore carried by religious (archetypal) energies." Articulate terrorists generally express themselves in religious (archetypal) terminology. The enemy is seen as the Principle of Objective Evil (Devil), and the terrorist perceives himself as the "heroic" agent of divine or Objective Justice (God). In other words, in the psyche of the terrorist, his ego has not maintained the necessary independence from the Self, but instead has become identified with the Self (with the God-image). This is a condition in which the human ego has been overrun by the collective unconscious. The primitive energies of the collective unconscious take possession of the individual who, in turn, loses his humanity. Such possession may partially explain the massacres that have taken place in Central Africa and, to a certain degree, even the Holocaust.

Edinger suggests such people are not criminals or madmen, although they have some qualities of both. But he prefers to call them "zealots" who are possessed by transpersonal, archetypal dynamism coming from the collective unconscious. Their goal is always a collective, not a personal one. In the name of a transpersonal, collective value– a religion, an ethnic or national identity, a "patriotic" vision, etc.–they sacrifice their personal life in the service of their "god." Although individual and perverse, this is fundamentally a religious phenomenon that derives from the archetypal, collective unconscious.

Edinger's case study of David Koresh, leader of the Branch Davidians who died in Waco, Texas, in 1993, illustrates the point. Koresh's real name was Vernon Howell. Without going into the background of Howell's upbringing–which is essential for a full understanding of the mentality and actions of any terrorist–Howell went to Israel in 1985, where he had a vision in which "God told him" he was none other than the reincarnation of Cyrus the Great, the Persian king who had rescued the Israelites from Babylonian captivity. Thus Howell changed his name to "David Koresh," David being the archetypal king of Israel and Koresh meaning Cyrus in Hebrew. It is, in psychiatrist Erich Neumann's words, "a spirituality that has lost touch with reality."

Edinger concludes his study of Koresh noting that Koresh "represents a new phenomenon that is quasi-criminal, and quasi-psychotic due to possession by the Apocalypse archetype. That means that since the human ego has been bypassed, the possessed individual is functioning 'inhumanly.' It is by that very fact a psychological state that generates charisma with tremendous energy to it!" Edinger suggests Herman

Melville gives us an extraordinarily accurate picture of this phenomenon in the figure of Captain Ahab in *Moby Dick*. In our own times, Edinger concludes, "Hitler is the outstanding example of the same psychological phenomenon writ really large. He was simultaneously 'beast and savior,' a savior to his friends and a beast for his enemies; and he, too, thought of himself in religious terms."(17)

I have commented on the phenomenon of psychic inflation as it relates to terrorism simply because I believe it to be a threat the whole world will increasingly be dealing with in the coming two decades.

The third possible reaction to the loss of life's "highest value" is that the projected supra personal value which has been withdrawn from its religious container will be reprojected onto some secular or political movement, even though secular purposes are never an adequate container for religious meaning. The two major examples of this in recent times have been communism and Nazism, which attempted to channel religious energies into secular ends. But even with the fall of communism, we see this same phenomenon today. Increasingly, secular causes are being pursued with a religious, almost fanatic, fervor. This will likely increase over the coming years. Again, see Figure 7.

There's a fourth possible way of dealing with the loss of a religious projection. If the individual is able to face the ultimate questions that are at the heart of his personal crisis of meaning, he may be able to use the opportunity for significant growth in his consciousness and personality, and he may find a fresh expression of life's "highest meaning." If he is able to work consciously with the psychic contents that are activated by his unconscious as a result of the loss of collective transpersonal meaning (God), he may discover the lost value, the God-image, within the psyche. It's a law of psychology, expressed throughout Western literature going back to the Greeks, that significant increases in consciousness derive from a creative encounter with darkness. As chaos prevails, the law of compensating opposites is engaged and, eventually, new projections of light and life, of the God-image, emanate from the psyche.

What this suggests is *the need to become more conscious of our unconscious life*. Consciousness and unconsciousness–the two great forces that shape us as individuals and as societies. When we think about ourselves, obviously, we're reflecting on our conscious life. But the unconscious area exerts at least as great–and possibly a greater–influence on the course of our personal lives as on the direction of history in general. Psychic wholeness can never be achieved in the realm of the conscious mind alone. As Jung says, it must include the "indefinite and indefinable extent of the unconscious" as well. So the issue is how to discover more about our unconscious, about the Self, how to achieve the ego-Self dialogue so we're more aware of it as a creative factor in life.

Unfortunately, there is no formula, no 12-step program. What we're talking about is the most individualized activity in life. There are highly effective approaches such as working with therapists skilled in understanding the collective unconscious and the archetypal significance of dreams. A process called "active imagination" is also a proven approach.

But I've not tried such methods, and all I can do is to speak from my own experience. I'd mention two points that have helped me. First, to achieve a greater awareness of my shadow–those less attractive aspects of my personality which I tend to suppress and are thus kept in the unconscious–and integrate as much of my shadow as possible into my conscious personality. Only then do we achieve greater wholeness. As Edinger puts it, "The process of coming into awareness of one's wholeness involves the acceptance and assimilation of all those shadow aspects that one has previously considered the most despicable." Only then do we become conscious of our own dark side and stop projecting it on to other people (and other nations), which only generates human conflict. Then the qualities seen as "negative" actually have valuable strengths. There is nothing in our unconscious that can't become useful and good when it is brought to the right level and made conscious. The result is a new integration, which, over time, brings an enlargement of personality.

The main way I look at my shadow is to study my reactions to people. Looking at my reactions to how I am treated has two components. One is the objective assessment of the other person's actions and character. The second component is the emotional intensity with which I react. It's this second component that can teach me about myself. The emotional content of my reactions usually has a negative shadow projection of some degree attached to it. If, for example, I strongly react to being manipulated by someone else, the emotional intensity of my reaction may suggest the degree to which I actually want to control my circumstances, or even manipulate others. As I confront the truth of my reactions, my shadow side comes to the light and becomes integrated with my conscious personality. Thus the negative qualities we don't like about ourselves can be integrated with the positive qualities to make us more complete personalities, as what has been unconscious becomes conscious. In a sense, it's the working out of the ultimate paradox Henry Miller captured when he wrote: "The full and joyful acceptance of the worst in oneself may be the only sure way of transforming it."

Parenthetically, this is one of the great benefits of marriage. My wife and I react to each other all the time. But by studying the emotional content of my reactions, I learn more about myself and, hopefully, grow to be more complete.

The second way to discover more about our unconscious is to study those who have explored this area and learn from their experience. People such as Jung, Edinger and von Franz are goldmines of understanding not only of ourselves personally, but also of how individual human behavior relates to the larger social, political and geopolitical issues we face. For the great problems of the age are, at root, personal human problems. Such study is not accomplished with a quick reading of a couple of books. Understanding the human personality is one of life's greatest–and most rewarding–challenges, and it requires work and persistence.

The possibility of establishing a dialogue between the conscious and unconscious, and gaining a greater wholeness of spirit, is represented in the diagram–Figure 7.4 on page 273–by the circle that now has a larger section of itself outside the arc of unconsciousness. The dialogue between ego and Self of which we spoke earlier is now consciously realized. The ego-Self axis suddenly breaks into conscious view, and the condition represented by Figure 3 is achieved. In this case, the ego becomes aware, experientially, of a transpersonal center to which the ego is subordinate, and life again finds its "highest value." The individual experiences a fresh oneness with life, a new degree of wholeness.

In this case, the loss of a religious projection, rather than ending in either alienation or inflation, has been the stimulus that leads to the development of greater individuality and an enlarged personality. This, of course, is the desired outcome when loss of life's "highest value" takes place, and it is an outcome that is available to everyone.

Final Thoughts

A new millennium is a time for a new hope for the world, a new vision of the human enterprise. Despite all the marvels of our amazing technology, we need something larger and more inwardly satisfying than our current impersonal scientific and technological concept of truth. We need an expression of truth that will encompass the truth that science is teaching us, but also the truth of the meaning of the human journey—a truth that relates us to the sacred continuity of life. We need a truth that links a deeper understanding of both consciousness and unconsciousness with the potential of our scientific knowledge, as well as with fresh interpretations of the world's spiritual experience. We need a contemporary synthesis of the two great sources of Western development—religion and science—which can offer a new meaning to our presence in the universe. We need Truth in all its awesome wholeness.

Possibly such a new expression of truth can be found in the implications of the heightened role we have been given as human beings— the role of *participant*—that is, "junior partner"—in the evolutionary process. We've been taught to think of creation as something which happened millions of years ago and that is now essentially complete. But what if creation, far from being complete, is only in an early stage of development? What if creation is a profound on going process that is happening every minute of every day? Certainly as we peer through the Hubble telescope at the far side of the universe, as we see galaxies and nebulae take shape, we see the indescribably beautiful process of creation.

It's clear that in some manner, at least for now, humans have been made partners in this process of creation; perhaps not on the far side of the universe, but certainly here on earth, where daily we alter earth's geological structure, its chemical composition and its living forms on land and sea. We employ genetic engineering to alter nature's products and augment human capacities and characteristics. Most fundamentally, we have come to realize that, as far as we know, human consciousness is the only agent that gives our earth, indeed the universe, consciousness of their existence. It's as if a new partnership between humans and our Creator has emerged, a partnership, which, in Erich Neumann's words, can "create a new spiritual world of human culture in the likeness of the divine."

It is not at all clear whether this is a trial experiment by Nature, which depends on how we humans conduct ourselves. If conscious humanity can conduct ourselves in such a manner as to enhance the total natural process, perhaps Nature will permit the experiment to continue. But if we humans, in the flush of hubris, conduct ourselves in a manner so as to substantially degrade or possibly destroy nature's efforts, it is not impossible that Nature will bring to a close—at least for the time being—the historic experiment with consciousness as an independent instrument of human intention.

Is this not part of the meaning of a new millennium? If so, it suggests we must raise our comprehension of moral maturity and responsibility to a totally new level—to a plane that's commensurate with the seriousness of our new role. We must come to know ourselves as individuals in a new and deeper way. The challenge is to know the opposites—the good and evil, the heights and depths—that dwell within each of us, that constitute the totality of the personality. The task is to strengthen the dialogue between consciousness and the limitless creative powers of the collective unconscious, wherein resides life's "highest meaning" (God). Each one of us must become an integrated personality, for common sense suggests that it takes integrated personalities to create an integrated world. In fact, it's not too much to suggest that integration of the personality, its integrity and wholeness, becomes the supreme imperative on which the fate of humanity depends. For both the human family as a species and each individual face a common task, namely, to become whole people who can create a unified world.

For myself, what I've been expressing is a dimension of life I've explored for over 40 years. Personally, it's a most profound source of inner peace and endless wonder. Some eternal, infinite power is at work in each of us and in the universe, and this power is the source of renewal of all man's most vital and creative energies. With all our problems and possibilities, the future depends on how we–each in his own unique way–tap into that Eternal Element that resides in the deepest reaches of the human soul.

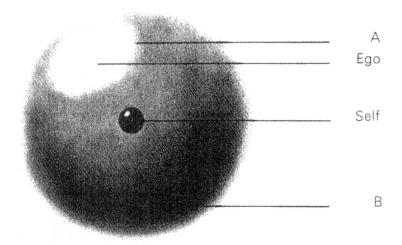

A
Ego

Self

B

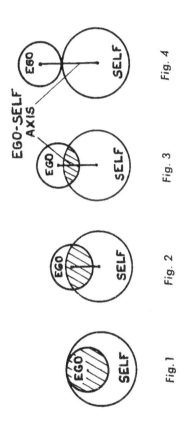

EGO-SELF
AXIS

EGO

SELF

Fig. 4

EGO

SELF

Fig. 3

EGO

SELF

Fig. 2

EGO

SELF

Fig. 1

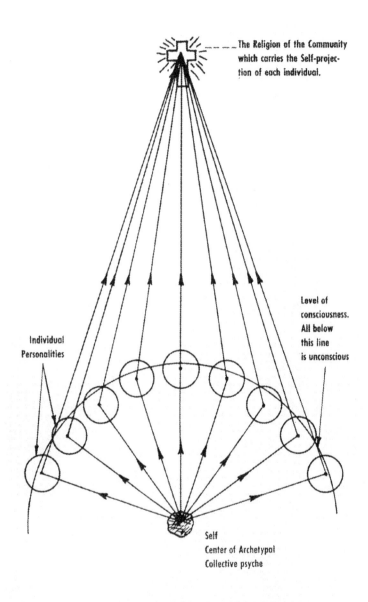

The Religion of the Community which carries the Self-projection of each individual.

Level of consciousness. All below this line is unconscious

Individual Personalities

Self
Center of Archetypal
Collective psyche

Figure 6. Stable State of a community of Religious believers.

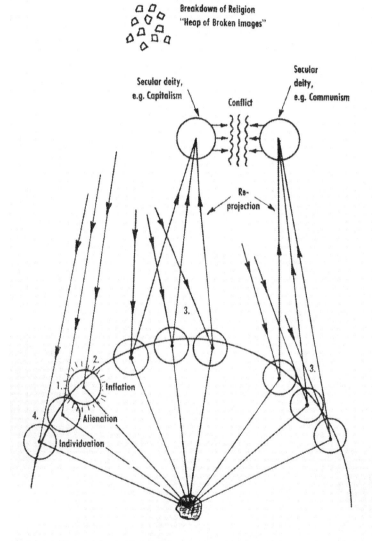

Breakdown of Religion
"Heap of Broken Images"

Secular deity,
e.g. Capitalism

Conflict

Secular
deity,
e.g. Communism

Re-
projection

3.

2.

1.

Inflation

3.

4.

Alienation

Individuation

Figure 7. Breakdown of a Religious Projection

EPILOGUE

As the Interregnum will be the context of life for America and the world for the foreseeable future, we end this survey with an imagined televised speech by the president of the United States to the American people.

Good evening, my fellow Americans. I want to speak to you tonight about the future of our country, and I speak not only as your president, but also as a father, a grandfather and a citizen.

We Americans have been blessed by Providence as have no other people in human history. We live in a land overflowing with the riches of nature. Our founders comprised one of the wisest groups of statesmen ever to establish and guide a nation. We have incorporated the richness of most of the world's heritage and cultures into the fabric of our cultural and social life. While we have shed our blood four times in the past century for the defense of freedom and human dignity on this planet, we were the only major industrial nation to have been spared the devastation of our cities and industrial plants in times of war. Today we stand unequalled in our inventiveness, our material well being and our worldwide influence.

And yet, we all know that something disturbs the depths of the American spirit. Even as our freedom and prosperity continue, apprehension about the future invades the fabric of our life. I shall not recite the litany of social and cultural indicators that reflect such apprehension, for they are all too familiar. Indeed, they are the stuff of national discourse and political debate.

Instead, I want to speak to the larger context in which we find ourselves at the start of this new century.

Let me put it to you as straight as I know how. We Americans face the most difficult challenge that ever faced any generation of Americans. Our challenge is more testing than the challenge confronting Washington at Valley Forge; more complex than the challenge bedeviling Lincoln during the Civil War; deeper and wider than the task thrust on Roosevelt during the Great Depression and World War II.

Why do I say that? I say it because America and the world are passing through one of the most dynamic and disruptive periods of technological and cultural change ever to engulf the world. Times of change in the life of nations are not new. But in the past, change has taken place relatively slowly, allowing people time to adjust their mode of life to new conditions. Change was gradual, and it would be years, even generations, before change in one part of the world affected people in other lands.

The world is now experiencing change of a totally different character and order. For the first time in the history of humanity, economic, technological, social, cultural and even spiritual change is uprooting the foundations and social structures of every nation simultaneously. No people are immune to the tidal wave of change rolling across the globe. Also for the first time in history, all people are redesigning their modes of administration and production, and are seeking fresh expressions of the core beliefs that have informed their collective association as nations.

We all live with the causes of these changes. When Lincoln was assassinated, it took 12 days for the news to reach London. Today, time has been eliminated, and the whole world instantly knows, indeed even watches, the critical events of the moment. We fly from Washington to Paris for a conference and return to Washington all in the same day. The computer, which cultural anthropologists describe as one of the two or three most significant developments since the creation of language many millennia ago, gives everyone access to all information.

Our communication technologies mean that someone can stand on the top of Mt. Everest and speak instantly with someone else rafting down the Colorado River in the Grand Canyon. Space technology means that, for the first time since the dawn of time itself, humans can view the earth from another celestial body. Our genetic research means we can alter the very essence of what it means to be a human being. These are only a few of the forces that are altering life as we've known it.

Such developments are opening up productive opportunities as well as unknown dangers, not just for America, but also for the human race. Throughout history, great changes in technology have created change in human institutions as well. All America's institutions–education, government, law, medicine, business and the economy, even the family and our religions, were developed before the modern technological era.

So what we are experiencing today is the clash of new technological modes of production, of organization and of communication–the clash of these new possibilities with the institutions that were formed before such technical possibilities existed. And in most instances there is a disconnect. The older way of doing things doesn't work as well in light of the speed, ubiquity and totality of the new technology.

It's not possible to have such drastic change in the external material world without at the same time having equally significant change in the subjective internal world–change in how we perceive reality, and the way we understand and see the world. Such change is creating uncertainty at a very deep level in all of us. That is inevitable. It is forcing us to rethink what we believe, who we are, why we're here, how to use our power, what our destiny is on planet Earth and even in the universe. Indeed, with more and more technology taking over our daily work, we're even having to rethink what is the very purpose of human beings in a world of total technological possibility.

When you put all these changes together, this is the most profound degree of change to take place since man became a conscious human being some three to four thousand years ago. So this is what I mean when I say, as I did a few moments ago, that we face the most difficult challenge ever to confront any generations of Americans.

How do we meet such challenges? What does it all mean for us? What do we do? In the coming weeks I shall lay out my vision of what we need to do in specific areas of life–education, the economy, international relations–to successfully engage the technological and global changes we face. But tonight I want to address more general issues.

We must meet the demands of change on at least two levels. There's the practical level of redefining and restructuring all our institutions, a work well under way. Corporations are redefining their mission, structure and modus operandi. In education, we're trying countless new experiments. Alternative Dispute Resolution (ADR) is helping lift the burden off the back of our legal system. Civic and charitable organizations are assuming functions formerly undertaken by local governments. Some local functions, such as firefighting and sanitation, are being privatized. More people are involved in efforts to preserve the environment or to help the elderly and those in poverty. In fact, it's estimated that well over 50 percent of all adult Americans donate a portion of their time to non profit social efforts.

This is good. But we can do more. I especially want to mention two items.

Given the all-pervasive role of information technology in our lives, one of the most important actions we can take is for each one of us to study the relationship between human beings and our technologies. The computer and television especially affect each of us in ways we generally are unaware of. Let me offer a simple example. It used to be that a five year-old child's closest friend was an animal of some sort–a dog, a cat, a rabbit or maybe a gerbil. Now that child's closest friend is a computerized toy or a character in an animated TV cartoon. From its earliest years, that child lives in a fabricated, technological or mediated world rather than in the world of natural experience. This change implies profound psychological effects of which we are only dimly aware.

I believe our comprehension of this human-technology relationship is so essential to our future that I will make recommendations urging education in technology to be part of the curriculum, starting in primary school. Our children must understand that technologies such as television and computers are not toys; they are powerful mind-shaping, character-forming instruments. It's critical for young people to know how best to use technology in a manner that enhances their own humanity.

Other technologies such as genetic engineering, nanotechnology and robots can have even more far-reaching results. Some scientists tell us that these technologies conceivably could alter life as we've known it on this planet. Consequently, I am directing the National Security Council to establish a blue-ribbon commission to examine these technologies, and to recommend whether there are some technical capacities that should not be developed, or at least for which research should be substantially slowed. I realize such a step could constitute a limited reversal of the age-old search for knowledge; but it is my view that the uninterrupted continuation of the human quest for life itself takes precedence over all other considerations. This is an investigation of such import that it must be undertaken in cooperation with other nations.

I want to turn now to the need for every American to understand what it means that America is moving into a global epoch. To put it simply, every major issue America faces–the environment, immigration, natural resources, culture, economic growth, drugs, national security, AIDS and much more–is part of a global process. The world has moved into an era in which it's no longer possible for any nation to solve such problems on its own or to develop in isolation. All nations are now part of an evolving global system.

This is not to suggest that nations are going to disappear and we'll all be under the rule of some world government. That is *not* going to happen! The nation-state will be the primary unit of human organization for the foreseeable future. But it does mean that, as I said, the nation-state is now part of a worldwide system.

Thus I urge every American to take the time to learn about the peoples, history and culture of other nations. We cannot fulfill our role in a global era–indeed we probably cannot maintain our present standard of living–if we are ignorant about the rest of the world. Certainly the availability of information on the Internet ought to be a significant help in familiarizing ourselves with other nations. For those who are able to travel to other lands, I say go and make friends, learn, appreciate the contributions of other peoples and cultures. Equally important is to meet visitors from other nations who come to our country; welcome them into your homes.

The second level we must work on to meet the test of change is the individual level, each of us. In the end, it's the individual who is the carrier of civilization—not the state, not institutions, not technology. Each of us needs to understand the character and depth of the change we're experiencing, and what the implications are for us and our children.

Take globalization, for example. People somehow think computers, the Internet, easy plane travel and global TV will create a global civilization. Such technologies, however, are only the physical infrastructure of globalization.

If we're going to have a workable global age, it cannot be simply a mechanical process. It must also be a human process, a psychological process, a spiritual process, a process of deepening consciousness and increasing sensitivity to other people and cultures. For common sense suggests that a unified world must be built on the solid foundation of a unified self in us as individuals. For each of us, this means we must take the time to deepen our inner life so that we are anchored in stabilizing realities as the storms of change blow ever more forcefully. There's no one way to achieve this, and each person must confront this need for himself or herself.

Finally, I would mention what I believe to be perhaps the most vital aspect of America's world role as we enter a new phase of the human experience. There was a period of our history when America was emulated around the world, not because of the material goods we produced, but because of the compelling power of our ideas. Many a nation has incorporated various aspects of the Declaration of Independence and the Bill of Rights into its own legal system. Lincoln's Gettysburg Address is held as a standard to support by parliamentarians and schoolchildren across the globe.

In one sense, America is a laboratory for the world. No other nation has the mixture of races and nationalities entwined in its social fabric that do we. If we can find the way for people of differing ethnic backgrounds and religious viewpoints to build the relationships and structures of a new time of our national journey, it can have a healing effect in areas of the world so torn by historic memories of bygone injustice. Given our history, this especially means that Native Americans and African Americans must still be able to make further progress in fulfilling the dream expressed by Martin Luther King at the Lincoln Memorial. We still have work to do, a work that must become a personal commitment for every American.

In conclusion, I want to emphasize that each of us can play a part in creating the new era ahead. Do not heed the voices saying one person can make little difference. There is too much evidence to the contrary. Each person in your own town or neighborhood can engage immediate tasks.

I do not want to mislead you. Adapting to the changes ahead is not going to be easy. The tasks facing us require a level of care and effort usually reached by nations only in times of war. I do not exaggerate in saying we face the need for a sustained, selfless national effort. If we think we can meet the needs of this shift to a new era with a "business as usual" approach, we shall simply end up as one more powerful nation that had its day. The challenge confronting us demands a radical change in what has become our expectancy that life is an automatic cornucopia of endless entertainment and technological gadgets. It's not; life is a struggle to find meaning and relevance beyond the daily requirements of sustenance. It's natural to want a sense of meaning to be provided by someone else–by the family, the religious institution or our country. But there's only one place meaning comes from, and that's from deep within the individual inner soul. Each of us has to fight for it and find it for ourselves. Someone else cannot give it.

As it is, together we face an overriding requirement for fresh meaning–*the need to build the next phase of the American Experiment.*

The will and energy to successfully reshape America cannot be legislated by Congress. It can only be generated as each of us considers what is at stake and the price we are prepared to pay for the American future. We must be ready to give in at least equal measure to that of earlier generations of Americans, whatever that may mean for each of us individually.

We have the privilege to be living at a moment of unparalleled promise–perhaps the moment of greatest possibility the world has known. The Providence that brought America into existence and has given us such riches and power has now some new promise for America. It's a potential that can be realized only if it's linked to the efforts of the rest of humanity to realize the promise also given them by Providence.

Good night, God bless America, and as well, God bless every last person on this earth who seeks the same fulfillment in life that you and I seek.

ENDNOTES

(1) Quoted on page 514, *The Reader's Companion to American History.*

(2) The Interregnum was clearly under way.

(3) The original draft of *The Waste Land* was edited by Ezra Pound, Eliot's mentor. Pound extracted significant portions of the original, which, between 1935 and 1942, were published under the title *Four Quartets.*

(4) See *The Archetype of the Apocalypse* by Edward F. Edinger.

(5) Ibid.

(6) Edward F. Edinger was a founding member of the C.G. Jung Foundation of New York, and former chairman of the C.G. Jung Training Center in New York. He is the author of 17 books dealing with Jungian themes of archetypes, psyche, Self, and analysis.

(7) See "Unpopular Science," *American Outlook*, Summer 1999.

(8) *From Modernism to Postmodernism: An Anthology,* edited by Lawrence Cahoone, Blackwell Publishers, 1996.

(9) *New World Coming: American Security in the 21st Century*, September 1999.

(10) See *The New God-Image*, by Edward F. Edinger, Chiron Publications, 1996.

(11) Erich Neumann, *The Origins and History of Consciousness*, Princeton University Press, 1973.

(12) Jung held that the psyche is neither a psychiatric nor a physiological problem. "It is a field on its own with its own peculiar laws. Its nature cannot be deduced from the principles of other sciences

without doing violence to the idiosyncrasy of the psyche. It cannot be identified with the brain, or the hormones, or any known instinct; for better or worse it must be accepted as a phenomenon unique in kind. The phenomenology of the psyche contains more than the measurable facts of the natural sciences: it embraces the problem of the mind, the father of all sciences." C.G. Jung, *The Practice of Psychotherapy*, par. 22, Princeton University Press, 1982. Oxford mathematician Roger Penrose echoes Jung in more recent times. Says Penrose, "The notion that the human mind can ever comprehend the human mind could well be folly. It may be that scientists will eventually have to acknowledge the existence of something beyond their ken–something that might be described as the soul." *Time*, "Glimpses of the Mind," July 17, 1995. Penrose was expressing the sentiments of an earlier scientist and writer: "Let us seek to fathom those things that are fathomable," Goethe had written, "and reserve those things which are unfathomable for reverence in quietude."

(13) British neuroscientist Susan Greenfield makes the same point in another way. "I can't monitor my own consciousness objectively, because my observations would grow out of my subjective conscious state." *Science & Spirit*, Vol. 11, Issue 1, March/April 2000.

(14) Edward F. Edinger, *Ego and Archetype*, Shambhala, 1992.

(15) See *The Saturated Self* by Kenneth J. Gergen, Basic Books, 1991.

(16) See Edward F. Edinger, *Archetype of the Apocalypse*, Open Court, 1999.

(17) In his book *Archetype of the Apocalypse*, Edinger reproduces a letter on the psychology of terrorism he wrote the mass media in May 1995. The letter states:

> "Terrorism is a manifestation of the psyche. It is time we recognized the psyche as an autonomous factor in world affairs.
>
> "The psychological root of terrorism is a fanatical resentment–a quasi-psychotic hatred originating in the depths of the archetypal psyche and therefore carried by

religious (archetypal) energies. A classic literary example is Melville's *Moby Dick*. Captain Ahab, with his fanatical hatred of the White Whale, is a paradigm of the modern terrorist.

"Articulate terrorists generally express themselves in religious (archetypal) terminology. The enemy is seen as the Principle of Objective Evil (Devil) and the terrorist perceives himself as the 'heroic' agent of divine or Objective Justice (God). This is an archetypal inflation of demonic proportions which temporarily grants the individual almost superhuman energy and effectiveness. To deal with terrorism effectively we must *understand* it.

"We need a new category to understand this new phenomenon. These individuals are not criminals and are not madmen although they have some qualities of both. Let's call them zealots. Zealots are possessed by transpersonal, archetypal dynamisms deriving from the collective unconscious. Their goal is a collective, not a personal one. The criminal seeks his own personal gain; not so the zealot. In the name of a transpersonal, collective value–a religion, an ethnic or national identity, a 'patriotic' vision, etc.–they sacrifice their personal life in the service of their 'god.' Although idiosyncratic and perverse, this is fundamentally a religious phenomenon that derives from the archetypal, collective unconscious. Sadly, the much-needed knowledge of this level of the psyche is not generally available. For those interested in seeking it, I recommend a serious study of the psychology of C.G. Jung."

CHRONOLOGY
1970-2000

APPENDIX A

1 9 7 0 s

SCIENCE AND TECHNOLOGY

- First Boeing 747 "Jumbo Jet" goes into service across the Atlantic
- Direct international telephone dialing begins on a regular basis
- Soviet spacecraft Venus 8 lands on Venus
- Nuclear-powered heart pacemakers first used in Britain
- Seymour Cray builds CRAY-1 supercomputer to solve problems here-
  tofore insoluble
- U.S. Viking I and II land on Mars and send back closeup photographs
  and scientific data
- MIT scientists announce construction of a synthetic gene
- U.S. confirms testing of neutron bomb which kills people by radiation
  but leaves buildings intact
- World's first "test-tube" baby, Louise Brown, born in England

- Giant radio telescope at Aecido, Puerto Rico, sends first human message to outer space
- "Floppy disc" introduced to store computer data
- Intel introduces first microprocessor
- First pocket calculator on the market
- Pioneer 10, first human-built object to leave solar system (in 1983 personal computer), is launched
- First CAT-scan used
- First, Altair 8800, goes on the market. Sold in kit form
- A calf is produced from a frozen embryo for the first time
- National Academy of Sciences committee calls for halt genetic engineering to assess its implications
- Concorde supersonic transport begins
- Walkman cassette player introduced by Sony
- Industrial robot put into widespread use
- Compact disc developed by Sony and Philips
- First spreadsheet program for PCs developed
- Genetech established as first commercial company aimed at developing products through biotech
- Word processor begins to replace typewriters
- Space shuttle developed and proven practical
- Bar code used at supermarket check-out counters introduced
- Japanese develop artificial blood

ECONOMIC

- Dow Jones industrial average drops to 631
- U.S. devalues the dollar two times in two years
- Trans-Alaska oil pipeline opened
- North Sea oil comes on line
- Arab oil embargo and huge price rises in '73 and '78. Resulting worldwide inflation
- U.S. closes the gold window.
- Floating exchange rates replace fixed exchange rates. End of Bretton Woods era. Gold jumps from fixed rate of $35 per ounce to $800 per ounce. High water mark of U.S. global economic hegemony

- Also high water mark of the "age of Keynes"
- Inflation and unemployment both hit double-digit levels
- Rise of concern over U.S. competitiveness
- Prime rate changed 130 times, compared with 16 times in each of the '50s and '60s
- End of the post-World War II economic boom
- Nearly 30 percent of U.S. oil is imported; up from 20 percent in 1967
- Carter decontrols domestic oil prices
- Federal Express founded by 27-year-old Vietnam veteran
- Nike founded under the name of Blue Ribbon Sports
- SEC ends Wall Street's fixed commissions
- Microsoft founded by 19-year-old Harvard dropout
- Apple Computer founded
- Airline deregulation begins decade of U.S. government deregulation of economy

SOCIAL AND POLITICAL

- Richard Nixon is re-elected president
- 448 colleges and universities closed or on strike due to anti-Vietnam War protests which result in four students killed at Kent State
- Military draft ended
- Supreme Court ruling prohibits capital punishment
- Watergate break-in and subsequent Congressional hearings; President Nixon resigns. Gerald Ford becomes president
- First "Earth Day" celebrated
- Supreme Court *Roe v Wade* decision legalizes abortion
- Jimmy Carter elected president
- U.S. celebrates Bicentennial
- 26th amendment to the Constitution lowers voting age to 18
- Rise of single-interest politics
- AIDS surfaces in New York and San Francisco. Only recognized as serious national problem in 1981
- Burgeoning of neighborhood vigilante groups to maintain neighborhood security

- End of the consensus regarding what had been called "the American way of life"
- For the first time in U.S. history, more women than men admitted to institutions of higher learning
- Over 10 million people have themselves sterilized
- U.S. falls below population replacement rate
- Public opinion polls cite rise of "me-firstism"; Tom Wolfe calls '70s the "me decade"; Christopher Lasch writes of a "culture of narcissism"
- For first time in American history, a majority of Americans condone premarital sex
- Opinion polls show that a majority of people no longer expect first marriages to last a lifetime
- Americans hold fast to belief that equality means "leveling up," not "leveling down"
- High-point of the "human potential" movement
- Ivy League colleges go co-ed
- Proposition 13 in California sparks nationwide tax revolt
- Rise of the "voluntary simplicity" movement

GLOBAL

- President Nixon visits China
- Aleksandr Solzhenitsyn exiled from USSR; publishes *The Gulag Archipelago*
- "Charter 77" promulgated in Czechoslovakia. Declares adherence to human and civil rights
- U.S. evacuates Vietnam; ends 20-year involvement
- U.S. and People's Republic of China establish full diplomatic relations
- Fourth Arab-Israeli war
- London serves major economic function as center of the "Eurodollar" market
- U.S. introduces policy of detente with the Soviet Union; strategic arms limitation treaty signed
- Karol Wojtyla elected pope. Takes name of John Paul II. First non-Italian to be pope since 1523

- China begins modernization
- 35 nations sign charter of Conference on Cooperation & Security in
    Europe
- Col. Mummar Qadaffi, 27, becomes premier of Libya; raises oil prices
- Pol Pot regime slaughters nearly 2 million people in
Cambodia
- Iran establishes Islamic Republic under Ayatollah Khomeni
- Margaret Thatcher becomes prime minister of Britain
- Iranian terrorists seize U.S. embassy in Iran and hold 53 Americans as
    hostages
- "Camp David" accord signed, ending 30 years of hostilities between
    Israel and Egypt
- USSR invades Afghanistan
- Terrorism becomes major global threat
- Panama Canal Treaty signed. Gives Panama full control of the canal
    by December 31, 1999
- People's Republic of China formally seated as United Nations mem-
    ber
- Chinese open all universities, which had been shut for ten years due to
    the cultural revolution
- Three Mile Island, Love Canal, and depletions of ozone layer raise
    serious environmental concerns

1 9 8 0 s

SCIENCE AND TECHNOLOGY

- IBM personal computer introduced; soon has 75% of the PC market.
    Microsoft introduces Windows
- Introduction of compact disc players
- Challenger space shuttle disaster
- First successful surgery on a fetus before birth
- MRI machines introduced in Britain
- Compaq brings out first IBM PC "clone"
- Philips develops CD-ROM

- Successful Voyager I and II missions provide information about Saturn's moons and ring system
- First successful human embryo transfer performed. First genes from an extinct specie cloned
- $3 billion Human Genome Project launched to decipher each of the 100,000 human genes
- Human insulin produced by bacteria becomes first commercial product of genetic engineering
- Lasers used for first time to clean out clogged arteries. First Jarvik 7 artificial heart implanted
- IBM's scanning tunneling microscope makes it possible to obtain pictures at atomic resolution
- British survey detects hole in the ozone layer over Antarctica. Hole confirmed two years later
- France authorizes use of steroid drug RU486 which induces abortion in the first months of pregnancy
- Drexler's *Engines of Creation* popularizes nanotechnology
- First successful prebirth surgery on a fetus performed
- U.S. Patent and Trademark Office extends patent protection to animals. A gene from a mammal (rat) functions for the first time in another mammal (mouse)
- Patent and Trademark Office issues patent No. 4,736,866 to Harvard Medical School for a mouse developed by genetic engineering. First U.S. patent issued for a vertebrate
- Optical microprocessors are developed
- Jaron Lanier founds VPL Research to market virtual reality systems for commercial use
- First fiber optic transatlantic cable laid. Transmits 37,500 simultaneous phone conversations
- Cellular phone becomes practical and gains widespread use
- For the first time, a crime suspect is convicted on the basis of genetic fingerprinting

ECONOMIC

- AT&T breakup decree creates regional phone system and greater competition in telecommunications
- Prime rate reaches 21.5%, highest since Civil War
- Federal Reserve initiates sustained fight against inflation
- Rise in computer-driven stock trading
- Banking deregulation act removes interest rate ceilings on what institutions can pay depositors
- Average price of a new single family house tops $100,000 for the first time in nation's history
- Continued concern about U.S. competitiveness. Japan seen as No. 1 economic threat
- Japan buys heavily into U.S. bonds as well as prime commercial properties
- "Supply-side" economics in vogue. Reagan signs bill mandating deepest tax and budget cuts in history
- American corporations begin decade-long process to restructure and downsize
- U.S. becomes debtor nation for first time since 1914
- Oil prices collapse from glut on the market
- Deregulation of transportation and telecommunications industries spurs greater competition
- Computers begin to help maintain smaller inventories
- Some 36 million Americans receive monthly Social Security checks
- Japanese automobile production surpasses U.S. auto production for first time
- S&L crisis eventually expected to cost taxpayers $315 billion
- Congress votes 346 to 68 to pass Reagan increase in military spending
- Gramm-Rudman-Hollings Act mandates congressional spending limits
- Plaza Accord devalues dollar in order to spur U.S. competitiveness
- Insider trader scandals rock Wall Street. Canada and U.S. sign free-trade agreement. Reagan vetoes projectionist textile trade bill

SOCIAL AND POLITICAL

- 1980 U.S. military attempt to rescue 53 American hostages held in Iran ends in disaster and humiliation
- Ronald Reagan elected president
- "Star Wars" and major increase in U.S. military capacity
- CNN, Cable News Network, begins operation
- AIDS begins taking worldwide toll
- USA Today begins publication
- First African American governor since Reconstruction elected in Virginia
- Evolution of U.S. military doctrine as a result of new technology as well as lessons learned in Vietnam
- Widespread experiments with new modes of K-12 education
- George Bush becomes president
- Drugs and crime become primary social and political concerns
- For the first time in nation's history, women outnumber men in professional positions
- Proliferation of citizens' groups tackling local problems of crime, education, drugs, gang war, etc.
- Iran-Contra debacle and subsequent congressional hearings
- Homosexuals demonstrate in Washington demanding more federal funds to fight AIDS
- U.S. health-care spending reaches $51,926 per capita as costs skyrocket. Total 11.1% of GNP
- Drought reduces U.S. crops yields. For first time in nation's history, it's necessary to import grain
- Reagan acts to bar family planning clinics from providing abortion help if they receive federal funds

GLOBAL

- Yugoslavia's president Tito dies. Balkan nation enters post-Tito era
- Iran-Iraq war
- Creation of Solidarity union in Poland.

- Growth of the Green movement in Europe
- NASA climatologist warns of increased global warming
- Union Carbide plant in Bhopal, India leaks lethal gas, killing 2,000 and injuring 200,000
- Mikhail Gorbachev assumes power in the Soviet Union
- Gorbachev promotes *glasnost* and *perestroika* in an attempt to restructure communist system
- Soviet army withdraws from Afghanistan
- British scientists report a large hole in the ozone layer is opening over Antarctica each spring
- Chinese students demonstrate in Beijing's Tiananmen Square; army moves in killing thousands
- Opening of Berlin wall
- End of communist rule in Czechoslovakia
- Chinese economy grows at a sustained high rate
- Rise of the Asian tigers—South Korea, Taiwan, Singapore and Hong Kong
- Southern Rhodesia gains independence; renamed Zimbabwe
- Gorbachev exiles Andrei Sakharov to Gorki to silence Soviet Union's leading human rights advocate
- Terrorists blow up U.S. embassy in Bierut, killing 63 people
- Britain and China agree to return Hong Kong to China in 1997
- Iraqi forces use poison gas, killing at least 40,000 Kurdish men, women and children
- Poland ends 40 years of communist rule. Solidarity prime minister elected
- China's Deng Xiaoping, 85, architect of China's modernization, resigns last official position
- African elephant population falls by more than half in less than a decade
- Hungary's Communist party renames itself Socialist party; proclaims Hungary a democratic republic
- Lithuania, Latvia and Estonia demand autonomy; form a human chain stretching across three republics

- British Telecom shares go on sale as Britain moves to "privatize" telephone system
- Chernobyl nuclear power plant explodes, sending clouds of radioactive fallout across much of Europe
- Montreal agreement to reduce CFCs
- Corazon Aquino, widow of slain Philippine leader Benigno Aquino, elected president of Philippines
- Christian and Moslem fundamentalism both gain adherents and political power
- Congress approves $100 million in aid to those seeking to overthrow Sandinista regime in Nicaragua
- Syrian troops occupy West Beirut to end three years of anarchy

1 9 9 0 s

SCIENCE AND TECHNOLOGY

- Hubble Space Telescope put in orbit 318 miles above the Earth
- Manufacture of first superconducting ceramic chip
- Gulf War said to be first "information war." Laser-guided smart bombs achieve pinpoint accuracy
- "Expert systems"–computer programs replicating human intelligence– in widespread use in such professions as medicine and geology. Rise of virtual reality use
- Global positioning system (GPS) enables a person to identify his or her exact location on Earth
- The Internet takes off; Americans account for more than 40 percent of world's investment in computing
- "Dolly," first cloned sheep. First gene therapy operation, grafting healthy gene on to a diseased cell
- Research labs doing practical work on hydrogen power fuel cells. First fuel-cell powered car
- Pathfinder lands on Mars and sends out rover to collect and analyze soil samples
- Intel markets 64-bit processor. World Wide Web enters mainstream use

- Computerized programs used to treat mental disorders. Patients psychoanalyzed by a computer
- Oxford University researcher "clones" voice of dead vocalist Bob Marley. Samples of original electronic imprints of Marley's voice are copied, broken up, and synthesized through computers into different patterns, thus having Marley "sing" a song written after he died.
- Advances in development of synthetic skin aid burn victims
- IBM's Deep Blue victory over chess Grandmaster Garry Kasparov increases public concern about possible dominance of technology over human life.
- Bell Labs develops talking robot that can see, understand speech, touch, and talk
- Year 2000 problem, or Y2K, the most ambitious and costly technology problem in history, requires rewriting computer programs to account for the difference between the first two digits as the century changes from the 1900s to 2000. Estimates of the cost to fix the problem range as high as $600 billion, or over $1 trillion if litigation is added
- Observations made from the Keck Telescope and the Hubble Space Telescope reveal the most distant object ever seen in the universe, a galaxy some 13 billion light years from earth. Hubble Space Telescope reveals existence of a planet outside of solar system
- Neutrinos discovered to have mass
- Judge Thomas Penfield Jackson issues preliminary finding that Microsoft harmed consumers by using its monopoly power to stifle competition and innovation
- The Sanger Center in Cambridge, England, announces the virtual cracking of the genetic code of an entire human chromosome

ECONOMIC

- America's record 8-year economic boom ends in July 1990 as recession begins
- Federal Reserve Board acts to authorize J.P. Morgan & Co. to underwrite stocks, the first time a bank has had that power since the

1933 Glass-Steagall Act

- IBM posts $4.6 billion operating loss in 1992, largest operating loss of any company in history
- Sears Roebuck discontinues 97-year-old general merchandise catalogue
- General Motors' new Saturn car challenges Japanese auto makers who have 30 percent of U.S. market
- North American Free Trade Agreement (NAFTA) signed into law
- GATT, General Agreement on Tariffs and Trade, gives way to WTO, World Trade Organization
- Travel and tourism now world's largest industry. $3.5 trillion in annual sales
- U.S. economy starts to restructure
- Most sustained economic boom in America's history. 1996 GNP per capita is $10,000 greater than GNP per capita in 1967, height of the '60s economic boom, measured in constant dollars
- Dow Jones industrial average passes 3,000 in April 1991, 4,000 in February 1995, 5,000 in November 1995, 6,000 in October 1996, 7,000 in February 1997, 8,000 in July 1997, 9,000 in April 1998, 10,000 in March 1999 and 11,000 in May 1999. Dow drops record 554 points 10/27/97; bounces up and down 1,023 points in a three-day period
- *Nature* magazine carries article by scientists estimating that on a global scale, ecosystems provide services–such as regulating climate, purifying air and water, decomposing wastes, preventing erosion–worth an average of $33 trillion a year, or nearly twice the world's annual gross national product
- Multi mega-mergers in defense and telecommunications industries
- Congress repeals Glass-Steagall Act, the law that compartmentalizes America's financial system

SOCIAL AND POLITICAL

- Clean Air Act signed into law by President Bush
- Rise of awareness of sexual harassment in the workplace

- Worst violence and looting in U.S. urban history in Los Angeles resulting from a jury acquitting L.A. policemen of charges brought in connection with the beating of Rodney King
- Bill Clinton becomes president
- Smoking banned on all domestic air flights
- U.S. national debt tops $3 trillion, up from $735 billion in January 1981
- Republicans capture House of Representatives after 40 years out of leadership. The following two years they proceed to squander their mandate in an unparalleled fit of insensitivity and ineptitude
- Clinton administration seeks massive overhaul of U.S. health care system, which comprises 14 percent of GNP.– public and Congress reject administration proposals
- Terrorists bomb World Trade Center in New York
- Nation is split regarding justice of jury decision finding O.J. Simpson "not guilty" of murder
- Mall of America opens in Minnesota. With 400 stores taking in $2 million per day, it is the largest shopping mall in the world
- Mutual funds soar as Baby Boomers hit 50 and begin to look to retirement.
- Bombing of Oklahoma City federal building raises specter of home-grown terrorism
- Pro-choice and right-to-life protagonists continue legal and PR battles
- Congress places major welfare responsibility with the states
- Substantial U.S. military downsizing begins
- Branch Davidians, a fundamentalist sect, set fire to their compound in Waco, Texas, in mass suicide
- U.S. House of Representatives impeaches President Clinton

GLOBAL

- Nelson Mandela released after 27 years in prison
- East and West Germany reunite 45 years after the end of World War II. East Germans hold first free elections since 1932
- F.W. de Klerk begins dismantling South Africa's apartheid system

- Post-Tito Yugoslavia collapses into civil war
- Iraq invades Kuwait. U.S. and allies launch Desert Storm, defeating Iraqi forces in 100 hours
- President Gorbachev persuades the all-Soviet Congress to surrender power. It's the end of the Soviet Union. A new non communist political order is organized, recognizing independence of the Baltic states and the autonomy of the 15 former Soviet republics which now form the Commonwealth of Independent States (CIS)
- Boris Yeltsin becomes president of Russia
- Nelson Mandela becomes president of South Africa
- Czechoslovakia divides into the Czech and the Slovak Republics
- Israel and the PLO sign peace accord. Prime Minister Rabin murdered by Israeli fundamentalist
- Switzerland abolishes secret numbered bank accounts
- Bosnian war highlights Europe's inability to provide for its own security
- Poland holds first free elections since 1939
- Tribal animosities in Central Africa cause famine and death of Biblical proportions
- Privatization of state-run companies gains worldwide momentum
- Chinese mount history's largest experiment with democracy by having 700 million people vote in municipal elections
- European Community permits free movement of goods across national borders
- Mobutu deposed as president in the Congo
- NATO votes to admit Poland, Czech Republic and Hungary
- Cities worldwide grow to unwieldy size. Tokyo-Yokohama 27 million, Mexico City 23 million, Sao Paulo 18 million. Such cities are larger than most countries represented in the United Nations
- Europe moves to create a monetary union with a single currency
- Hong Kong returned to China after 156 years under British rule
- Diana, Princess of Wales, killed in Paris auto accident. First truly global grieving for a world figure
- Asian economic meltdown
- India and Pakistan conduct nuclear tests

- New public stock markets are established in over 50 countries
- President Milosevic launches "ethnic cleansing" of Kosovo driving hundreds of thousands of Kosovars into neighboring territories. NATO launches bombing raids of Yugoslavia
- World population reaches 6 billion in October 1999
- U.S. returns the Panama Canal to Panama
- Portugal returns Macao to China, ending European colonialism in Asia

APPENDIX B

PROJECTED TECHNOLOGY
DEVELOPMENT–2000-2020

Compiled from forecasts published by British
Telecommunications plc and Forecasting International

2000
Entire human genome mapped
Unified personal numbering for everything
3D very large scale integration with at least ten layers of devices
Common use of solar cells for residential power supply
Wall hung high-definition color displays
Hand videophone in widespread service
Artificial blood in common use
Artificial ears become routine
World industrial robot population estimated at 35 million

2001
Use of molecular computing
First UK mission to the moon
Optical inter-chip connection
Electronic notebook with contrast as good as paper
Electronic implants regularly used to stimulate muscles in disabled people

2002
Launch of space station nearly completed
Multiple channels of 100Gbits on a single fiber
Personal display tablets for TV, magazines, etc. popularized
Multi-speaker voice recognition perfected
3D optoelectronic integrated for image processing
Fire detection by gas fraction or odor
Information technology literacy essential for any employment

2003

Video download far beyond earlier speeds

Integrated logic devices with switching speed below one picosecond

Totally managed world logistics system

Engineered organisms begin to replace traditional chemicals

Personal wearable health monitor displays vital signs

Supercomputers with speeds exceeding 1 PetaFLOPS

Almost all transmissions encrypted

Movie, TV shows home entertainment on demand finally proves popular

2004

Real-time language translation for print and voice becomes common,
especially for telephones and tourists

Crime and terrorism mainly computer based become mainstream

Computers which write most of their own software

Determination of whole human DNA base sequence

Tactile sensors comparable to human sensation

2005

Folding watch computer

Global electronic currency in use

Global broadband fiber-based network

Integrated logic devices which switching speed below one picosecond

Living area use of virtual reality (scenes)

Single storage and replay devices for audio, video and data

PCs incorporating television, telephone and interactive video transmission become major consumer items

Traffic jams reach a projected 8.1 billion lost work hours

Multiple channels of 200 Terabits on a single fiber

2006

Fully automatic ships able to navigate and dock automatically

On-line voting in UK

Quantum computing obstacles overcome

Smart clothes which can alter their thermal properties

CFCs are essentially replaced by materials that do not damage the ozone layer

2007

Self-organizing adaptive integrated circuits

Hundreds of terabits per second transmissions on optical fibers over long distance

Optical neuro-computers

Totally automated factories

Systems to understand text and drawings (patent information)

Voice, handwriting and optical recognition enable human-machine interface on PCs

2008

First Mars rock sample returned to Earth

Robots for light housework

Robotic security and fire guards

Sophisticated 1 Terabit memory chip

Devices roaming within blood vessels under their own power

Multi layer solar cells with efficiency $> 50\%$

One-half of waste from households in developed countries is recycled

2009

All optic integrated logic, switching below one picosecond

Chips using one million transistors

Household access by facial recognition

Artificial "heart-in-a-box" stored for hospital use

DNA storage device becomes practical

Artificial brains with ten thousand or more cells

Holistic approaches to health care accepted by majority of medical community

Electronic banking essentially replaces checks, paper and cash in U.S. as principal means of commerce

2010

3.2 million supercomputers match computing power of human brain

Universal identity cards in UK

95% of population in advanced nations computer literate

Genetic intervention programs widely accepted for animals and plants

Genetic screening broadly used for determining/preventing most
genetic diseases

Extensive remote sensing use in environmental management

Expert systems routinely used for decision-making in management,
medicine and engineering

Significant portion (10%) of energy usage is derived from alternative
energy sources

Leisure time accounts for over 50% of lifetime activities

2011

Single electron technology devices

Effective prediction of most natural disasters

3D TV without the need for special glasses

Desktop fabrication units

Battery-powered electric cars are commonly available

Mass customization of products such as cars and appliances

2012

Cars which drive themselves a few feet apart on smart highways

Purely electronic companies exist–minimal human involvement

Robots for almost any job in home or hospital

DNA computer problems overcome

Computer systems learn by trial and error to adjust their behavior

Use of chemical fertilizers and pesticides declines by half

2013

Water decomposition by sunlight

Systems based on biochemical storage of solar energy

Highly integrated biosensors

Fine particle beam gene engineering

Intelligent materials with sensors, storage and effectors
Gene therapy routinely used to prevent/cure inherited disease
A preventive or cure for cancer and AIDS is found
Half of all automobiles are made of recyclable plastic components
Majority of books and publications are published on-line

2014
Near Earth space tours
Flying wing planes carrying 1000 passengers 6000 miles at 600 mph
Machine use of human-like memorizing, recognizing and learning
Robots for guiding blind people
Office automation systems using functions similar to brain functions
Computer-assisted vision is commercially available
Seafood grown using aquaculture provides majority of seafood consumed
Optical computers using photons rather than electrons to code information
Ceramic engines mass-produced for commercial vehicles

2015
Deep underground cities in Japan
Computer link boosts sensitivity of biological organs
Extension of average life span to over 100
Machine use of human-like creativity
Reconfigurable buildings
Human knowledge exceeded by machine knowledge
Superconducting materials commonly used for transmitting electricity
    in electronic devices
Widespread automation causes factory jobs to decline to less than 10%
    of workforce
Leisure time businesses generate over 50% of U.S. GDP

2016
Material composites replace majority of traditional metals in product
    design
Robots that have sensory input, make decisions, and learn become
    commercially available

Majority of manufactured goods use recycled materials
Neural networks using parallel processing
Microscopic machines/nanotechnology in commercial applications

2017
Superconductivity advances make maglev trains available between major cities
Bio-chips that store data in molecular bonds are commonly available

2018
Automated highway systems are commonly used to reduce highway congestion
Living organs and tissues produced genetically routinely used for replacement
Half of all goods sold in U.S. are sold through information services

2019
Genetically engineered organs and tissues are routinely used for replacement
Private corporations perform nearly all space launches
$1000 (1999 dollars) computers capable of one trillion calculations per second

2020
Parents routinely choose characteristics of their children through genetic engineering
Fission nuclear power is used for at least 50 percent of electricity generation
Hydrogen becomes routinely used in energy systems Hispanics become largest ethnic minority in U.S.
20 billion PCs computational powers equivalent to human brain

BIBLIOGRAPHY

Adams, Henry. *The Education of Henry Adams*. Houghton Mifflin Company, 1961.

Agar, Herbert. *The Land of the Free*. Houghton Mifflin Company, 1935.

Ahmed, Akbar S. "Media Mongols at the Gates of Baghdad." *New Perspectives Quarterly*. Summer 1993.

Allen, Henry. "Freudian Slippage in the Age of Prozac." *The Washington Post*. May 7, 1997.

Allen, Jane Addams. "Postmodernism and the Romantic Temper." *The World & I. December, 1998.*

Allen, Lewis Frederick. *The Big Change*. Harper & Row, 1952.

Anderson, Sherwood. *Winesburg, Ohio*. Penguin Books, 1976.

Armstrong, Karen. *A History of God*. Ballantine Books, 1993.

Arnold, Matthew. *The Portable Matthew Arnold*. Viking Press, 1949.

Attali, Jacques. *Millennium*. Random House, 1991.

Barlow, John Perry. "Unmediated Man." *New Perspectives Quarterly*. Spring 1995.

Barraclough, Geoffrey. *An Introduction to Contemporary History*. Penguin Books, 1967.

_____. *Turning Points in World History*. Thames and Hudson, 1977.

Barzun, Jacques. *The Culture We Deserve*. Wesleyan University Press, 1989.

_____. *From Dawn to Decadence*. HarperCollins Publishers, Inc., 2000.

Beatty, Jack. *The World According to Peter Drucker.* The Free Press, 1998.

Begley, Sharon. "Science Finds God." *Newsweek.* July 20, 1998.

Bell, Daniel. *The Coming of Post-Industrial Society.* Basic Books, 1973.

_____. *The Cultural Contradictions of Capitalism.* Basic Books, 1976.

_____. *The Winding Passage.* Basic Books, Inc., 1980.

_____. "American Intellectual Life, 1965-1992." *WQ*, Summer 1992.

Berle, Aldolf A. and Means, Gardner C. *The Modern Corporation and Private Property.* Macmillan Company, 1932.

Berlin, Isaiah. "Return of the Volksgeist." Interview, *New Perspectives Quarterly.* Fall 1991.

Berlinski, David. "The End of Materialist Science." *Forbes ASAP.* December 2, 1996.

Berman, Avis. "The Triumph of Abstract Expressionism." *Modern Maturity.* April-May 1985.

Berry, Thomas. *The Dream of the Earth.* Sierra Club, 1990.

Billard, Pierre. "Europe Fights 'Americanization.'" *Le Point*, Paris. Published in *World Press Review.* October 1985.

Bloom, Allan. *The Closing of the American Mind.* Simon and Schuster, 1987.

Bloom, Harold. *The Western Canon.* Riverhead Books, 1994.

Boorstin, Daniel J., *Democracy and Its Discontents.* Vintage Books, 1975.

_____. *The Republic of Technology.* Harper & Row, 1978.

_____. *The Image.* Vintage, 1992.

_____. *The Exploring Spirit.* Random House, 1975.

Boulding, Kenneth. *The Meaning of the 20th Century.* Colophon Books, 1965.

Brockman, John. *The Third Culture.* Simon & Schuster, 1995.

Bronowski, Jacob. *The Ascent of Man.* Little, Brown and Company, 1973.

Brzezinski, Zbigniew. *The Grand Chessboard.* Basic Books, 1997.

_____. *Out of Control.* Charles Scribner's Sons, 1993.

Buchan, John. *Pilgrim's Way: An Autobiography.* Carroll & Graf Publishers, Inc. 1984.

Burgess, Anthony. Interview from *L'Express* of Paris, published in *World Press Review*, December 1981.

Burnstein, Richard. "The Arts Catch Up with a Society in Disarray." *The New York Times*. September 2, 1990.

Cahoone, Lawrence, Editor. *From Modernism to Postmodernism: An Anthology*. Blackwell Publishers, 1996.

Campbell, Angus. "Now, Psychological Man." *The New York Times*. October 31, 1980.

Campbell, Joseph. *Myths to Live By*. Bantam Books, 1988.

_____. *The Inner Reaches of Outer Space*. HarperPerennial, 1986.

_____. *The Power of Myth, with Bill Moyers*. Doubleday, 1988.

_____. *The Masks of God: Creative Mythology*. Penguin Books, 1976.

Capra, Fritjof. *The Turning Point*. Bantam Books, 1988.

Chace, William M. "James Joyce: Two Sides to the Matter." *The World & I*. June, 1988.

Chandler, Alfred D., Jr. *The Visible Hand*. Harvard University Press, 1977.

Clarke, Arthur C. *Childhood's End*. Ballantine Books, 1972.

_____. *Profiles of the Future*. Bantam Books, 1967.

Clark, Kenneth. *Civilization*. Harper & Row, 1969.

_____. *What Is A Masterpiece?* Thames and Hudson, 1979.

Cochran, Thomas C. *200 Years if American Business*. Dell, 1977.

Coupland, Douglas. "Life After God: The First Generation Raised Without Religion." *New Perspectives Quarterly*. Spring 1994.

Cousteau, Jacques. "Consumer Society Is the Enemy." Interview, *New Perspectives Quarterly*. Summer 1996.

Cronin, Brian. "Finding God on the Web. *Time*. December 16, 1996.

Crowther, Hal. "In a Dying Culture, Thank God for Snobs." *The Washington Post*. August 27, 1995.

Crozier, Michel. *The Trouble with America*. University of California Press, 1984.

Crystal, David. *The Cambridge Factfinder*. Cambridge University Press, 1997.

Dante, Alighieri. *The Divine Comedy*. Penguin Books, 1977.

Dawson, Christopher. *Religion and Culture*. Sheed & Ward, 1948.

_____. *Religion and World History*. Image Books, 1975.

Dery, Mark. "The Cult of the Mind." *The New York Times Magazine*. September 28, 1998.

Dostoyevsky, Fyodor. *The Brothers Karamazov*. Signet Classic, 1980.

Drucker, Peter F. *Landmarks of Tomorrow*. Colophon Books, 1957.

_____. *The Age of Discontinuity*. Harper & Row, 1968.

_____. *Management: Tasks Responsibilities Practices*. Harper & Row, 1974.

_____. *Adventures of a Bystander*. Harper & Row, 1979.

Dube, Wolf-Dieter. *Expressionism*. Oxford University Press, 1972.

Dubos, Rene. *So Human an Animal*. Charles Scribner's Sons, 1968.

Durant, Will. *The Mansions of Philosophy*. Garden City Publishing Co., Inc., 1929.

Dyson, Freeman. Interview by Stewart Brand. *Wired*. February 1998.

_____. Infinite in all Directions. Harper & Row Publishers, 1988.

Eckermann, J.P. *Conversations with Goethe*. Frederick Unger Publishing Co., 1964.

Edinger, Edward F. *Ego and Archetype*. Shambhala, 1992.

_____. *The Bible and the Psyche*. Inner City Books, 1986.

_____. *The Creation of Consciousness*. Inner City Books, 1984.

_____. *Mellville's Moby-Dick*. Inner City Books, 1995.

_____. *The New God-Image*. Chiron Publications, 1996.

_____. *Archetype of the Apocalypse*. Open Court, 1999.

Eisner, Michael. "Planetized Entertainment." *New Perspectives Quarterly*. Fall 1995.

Eliade, Mircea. *The Myth of the Eternal Return*. Princeton University Press, 1954.

Eliot, T.S. *Collected Poems 1909-1962*. Harcourt Brace Jovanovich, 1963.

Encyclopedia Britannica CD 98.

Fitzgerald, F. Scott. *The Great Gatsby*. Charles Scribner's Sons, 1980.

Foner, Eric and Garraty, John A., Editors. *The Reader's Companion to American History*. Houghton Mifflin Company, 1996.

Frankl, Viktor E. *Man's Search for Meaning.* Washington Square Press, 1966.

Freud, Sigmund. *Civilization and Its Discontents,* W.W. Norton & Company, Inc., 1962.

_____. *On Dreams.* W.W. Norton & Company, Inc., 1952.

Friedman, Thomas L. *The Lexus and the Olive Tree.* Farrar Straus Giroux, 1999

Gablik, Suzi. "The Reenchantment of Art." *The World & I.* December 1988.

Gall, Norman. "The Ghost of 1929." *Forbes,* July 13. 1997.

Gardels, Nathan. "From Postmodernism to Postliberalism." *New Perspectives Quarterly.* Spring 1995.

_____. "Republic of Image." *New Perspectives Quarterly.* Summer 1994.

Gardner, John. *On Moral Fiction.* Basic Books, 1977.

Gates, William H., III. *The Road Ahead.* Viking, 1995.

Gergen, Kenneth J. *The Saturated Self.* Basic Books, 1991.

Gibson, Michael. "Looking Back on Symbolism." *The World & I.* December 1988. Giscard d'Estaing, Valerie-Anne and Young, Mark, Editors.

Inventions and Discoveries. Facts on File, Inc., 1993.

Gleick, James. "Addicted to Speed." *The New York Times Magazine.* September 28, 1997.

Glynn, Patrick. *God: The Evidence.* Prima Publishing, 1997.

Goldberg, Debra Ann. "Television from a Jungian Perspective." *Psychological Perspectives.* Issue 29, 1994.

Grant, Priscilla. "How Spiritual Are You?" *Self.* December 1997.

Grun, Bernard, Editor. *The Timetables of History.* Simon and Schuster, 1979.

Halberstam, David. *The Best and the Brightest.* Fawcett Crest, 1973.

_____. *The Next Century.* William Morrow and Company, Inc., 1991.

Harmon, Amy. "Escaping to Other Worlds." *The Los Angeles Times.* April 2, 1997.

Hellemans, Alexander and Bunch, Bryan. *The Timetables of Science.* Simon and Schuster, 1988.

Hesse, Hermann. *Steppenwolf.* Henry Holt and Company, 1929

_____. *Demian.* Harper & Row, 1965.

_____. *Soul of the Age: The Selected Letters of Hermann Hesse, 1891-1962.* Farrar, Straus & Giroux, 1991.

Hillis W. Daniel. "Close to the Singularity." *The Third Culture.* Simon & Schuster, 1995.

_____. "The Big Picture." *Wired.* January 1998.

_____. "In His Own Words." Interview *Upside* by John Brockman, December, 1998.

_____. "The Long Now." Interview by Pro Bronson, *Wired.* May 1998.

Hillman, James. *The Soul's Code.* Warner Books, 1996.

Homer. *The Odyssey.* Translated by Richmond Lattimore. Harper Perennial, 1991.

_____. *The Iliad.* Translated by Richmond Lattimore. University of Chicago Press, 1951.

Hughes, Robert. "Golden Oldies." *Time.* March 4, 1996.

_____. *American Visions.* Alfred A. Knopf, 1997.

Huxley, Aldous. *The Perennial Philosophy.* Harper Colophon Books, 1970.

Illich, Ivan. "From Fast to Quick." *New Perspectives Quarterly.* Winter 1997.

Jaynes, Julian. *The Origin of Consciousness in the Breakdown of the Bicameral Mind.* Houghton Mifflin, 1976.

Johnson, Paul. *A History of the American People.* HarperCollins, 1997.

Jung, C.G. *Civilization in Transition*, CW 10. Princeton University Press, 1970.

_____. *Psychology and Religion*, CW 11. Princeton University Press, 1969.

_____. *The Spirit in Man, Art and Literature*, CW 15. Princeton University Press, 1966.

_____. *C.G. Jung Letters 1906-1950.* Princeton University Press, 1973.

_____. *C.G. Jung Letters 1951-1961.* Princeton University Press, 1975.

_____. *Memories, Dreams, Reflections.* Vintage Books, 1965.

Kahn, Herman and Wiener, Anthony J. *The Year 2000.* MacMillan, 1967.

Kalb, Marvin and Kalb, Bernard. *Kissinger*. Dell, 1975.

Kandinsky, Wassily. *Concerning the Spiritual in Art*. Dover Publications, Inc., 1977.

Kane, Joseph Nathan. *Famous First Facts*. The H.W. Wilson Company, 1964.

Karl, Frederick R. "The Year of Wonders–1900." *The World & I*. December 1988.

Kaufmann, Walter, Editor. *The Portable Nietzsche*. Penguin Books, 1976.

Kelly, Kevin. *Out of Control*. Addison Wesley, 1994.

Kennedy, Eugene C. *A Time for Love*. Image Books, 1972.

Kennedy, Paul. *Preparing for the Twenty-first Century*. Vintage Books, 1994.

Kennedy, Teresa. *Welcome to the End of the World: Prophecy, Rage and the New Age*. M. Evans and Company, Inc., 1997.

Kissinger, Henry. *The White House Years, Vol 1*. Little, Brown and Company, 1979.

Knoke, William. *Bold New World*. Kodansha International, 1996.

Koolhaas, Rem. "The Generic City: Singapore or Bladerunner?" *New Perspectives Quarterly*. Summer 1996.

Kramer, Hilton. "Beyond the Avant-Garde." *The New York Times Magazine*. November 4, 1979.

_____. "Notes on Art at the End of the Eighties." *The World & I*. December 1988.

LaBier, Douglas. *Modern Madness*. Simon & Schuster, 1989.

Lang, Jack. "The Higher the Satellite, the Lower the Culture. *New Perspectives Quarterly*. Fall 1995.

Lanier, Jaron. "Our Machines, Ourselves." A Forum. *Harper's Magazine*. May 1997.

Lash, Christopher. *The Minimal Self*. W.W. Norton & Company, 1984.

Lemonick, Michael D. "Glimpses of the Mind." *Time*. July 17, 1995.

Lifton, Robert Jay. *The Protean Self*. Basic Books, 1993.

Lindsay, Hal. *The Late Great Planet Earth*. HarperPaperbacks, 1970.

Linton, Calvin D., Editor. *The American Almanac*. Thomas Nelson, Inc., 1977.

Lippmann, Walter. *A Preface to Morals*. Time-Life Books, 1964.

_____. *The Public Philosophy*. Signet Classics, 1955.

Longman, Phillip J. "The Fall of the Idea of Thrift." *The Washington Monthly.*

Lowell, James Russell. *Complete Poetical Works.* Houghton Mifflin Company, 1897.

Luce, Henry. "Will God Never Leave Us Alone?" *Fortune.* December 1955.

Lucie-Smith, Edward. *Late Modern: The Visual Arts Since 1945.* Oxford University Press, 1979.

_____. "What Romanticism Has Wrought." *The World & I.* December 1998.

Lukacs, John. *The End of the Twentieth Century.* Ticknor & Fields, 1993.

_____. *Outgrowing Democracy: A History of the United States in the Twentieth Century.* Doubleday, 1984.

MacLeish, Archibald. *Riders on the Earth.* Houghton Mifflin Company, 1978.

_____. "The Conquest of America." *The Atlantic.* 1949.

Mautner, Michael. "Will Cloning End Human Evolution?" *The Futurist.* November-December 1997.

May, Henry. *The End of American Innocence.* Oxford University Press, 1979.

May, Rollo. *Man's Search for Himself.* Dell Publishing, 1953.

_____. *The Cry for Myth.* W.W. Norton & Company, 1991.

McCaw, Craig. Interview by Mike Mills. *Washington Post Magazine.* August 3, 1997.

McCullough, Colleen. *A Creed for the Third Millennium.* Avon Books, 1985.

McHale, John. *The Future of the Future.* Ballantine Books, 1969.

Melville, Herman. *Moby Dick.* Signet Classic, 1961.

Meyrowitz, Joshua. *No Sense of Place.* Oxford University Press, 1985.

Miles, Jack. "Religion Makes a Comeback." *The New York Times Magazine.* December 7, 1997.

Minsky, Marvin. "Smart Machines." *The Third Culture.* Simon & Schuster, 1995. Molitor, Graham T.T. and Kurian, George, Editors.

Encyclopedia of the Future. Simon & Schuster Macmillan, 1996.

Mumford, Lewis. *Technics and Civilization.* Harbinger, 1963

——————. *The Pentagon of Power.* Harcourt Brace Jovanovich, 1970.

——————. *The Transformations of Man.* Harper & Row, 1956.

——————. *Interpretations and Forecasts: 1922-1972.* Harcourt Brace Jovanovich, 1979.

Murray, Peter and Linda. *Dictionary of Arts & Artists.* Penguin Books, 1985.

Myers, Bernard S. *Art and Civilization.* McGraw-Hill Book Company, 1967.

Neumann, Erich. *The Origins and History of Consciousness.* Princeton University Press, 1954.

Nisbet, Robert. *Twilight of Authority.* Oxford University Press, 1975.

——————. *The Present Age.* Harper & Row, 1988.

——————. *History of the Idea of Progress.* Basic Books, 1980.

——————. "A Conversation With Robert Nisbet." *U.S. News & World Report.*

Nixon, Richard. *The Memoirs of Richard Nixon, Vol.2.* Warner Books, 1979.

Ortega y Gasset, Jose. *The Dehumanization of Art.* Princeton University Press, 1968.

Panichas, George A. *The Reverent Discipline.* University of Tennessee Press, 1974.

——————— *The Courage of Judgment.* University of Tennessee Press, 1982.

Patterson, James T. *Grand Expectations.* Oxford University Press, 1996.

Paz, Octavio. "West Turns East at the End of History." *New Perspectives Quarterly.* Spring 1992.

Penrose, Roger. *The Emperor's New Mind.* Oxford University Press, 1989.

Perry, John Weir. *The Heart of History.* State University of New York Press, 1987.

Peters, Thomas and Waterman, Robert H., Jr. *In Search of Excellence.* Harper & Row, 1982.

Postman, Neil. *Amusing Ourselves to Death.* Penguin Books, 1986.

——————. *Technopoly.* Alfred A. Knopf, 1992.

Price, Lucien. *The Dialogues of Alfred North Whitehead.* Max Reinhardt, 1954.

Prigogine, Ilya. "Beyond Being and Becoming." Interview, *New Perspectives Quarterly.* Spring 1992.

Rees, Rowena. "This Is the Age of Strain." *The Sunday Times.* June 1, 1997.

Review & Outlook. "Reflections After Jonestown." *The Wall Street Journal,* November 30, 1978.

Richard, Paul. "When Manhattan Met Modern Art." *The New York Times,* February 14, 1988.

Robertson, James Oliver. *America's Business.* Hill and Wang, 1985.

Roberts, J.M. *The Triumph of the West.* Little, Brown and Company, 1985.

Rourke, Mary. "Redefining Religion In America." *The Los Angeles Times.* June, 21, 1998.

Rushing, Janice Hocker and Frentz, Thomas S. *Projecting the Shadow.* University of Chicago Press, 1995.

Russell, John. "The Retreat of Manhood as Mirrored in the Arts." *The New York Times.* February 1, 1981.

_____. "Modernism to Postmodernism: A New World Once Again." *The New York Times.* August 22, 1982.

Safire, William. *Before the Fall.* Belmont Tower Books, 1975.

Salinger, J.D. *The Catcher in the Rye.* Bantam Books, 1964.

Sanford, John A. *The Kingdom Within.* HarperSanFrancisco, 1987.

Sellers, Ron. "Nine Global Trends in Religion." *The Futurist.* January-February 1998.

Shorter, Edward. "How Prozac Slew Freud." *American Heritage.* September 1998.

Sobel, Dava. "Freud's Legacy." *The New York Times Magazine.* October 26, 1980.

Solzhenitsyn, Alexander. *From Under the Rubble.* Little, Brown and Company, 1974.

Sorokin, Pitirim A. *The Crisis of Our Age.* E.P. Dutton & Co., Inc. 1941.

Spengler, Oswald. *The Decline of the West.* Alfred A. Knopf, 1962.

Statistical Yearbook of the Immigration and Naturalization *Service,* 1994.

St. Augustine. *The City of God.* Image Books, 1958.

Stearns, Peter N. *Millennium III, Century XXI.* Westview Press, 1996.

Stein, Ben. "Mass Culture in the Movies." *The World & I.* December 1989.

Stevens, Anthony. *On Jung.* Penguin Books, 1991.

_____. *The Two-Million-Year-Old Self.* Texas A&M University Press, 1993.

Stock, Gregory. Interview by Roderick Simpson *Wired.* September 1997.

Stone, Alan A., M.D. "Where Will Psychoanalysis Survive?" *Harvard Magazine.* January-February 1997.

Sullivan, Mark. *Our Times: The United States 1900-1925.* Scribners, 1932.

Swimme, Brian. *The Universe Is a Green Dragon.* Bear & Company, Inc., 1984.

_____. *The Hidden Heart of the Cosmos.* Orbis Books, 1996.

_____. and Berry, Thomas. *The Universe Story.* HarperCollins, 1992.

Talbot, Michael. *Beyond the Quantum.* Bantam Books, 1988.

Tarnas, Richard. *The Passion of the Western Mind.* Ballentine Books, 1991.

Teilhard de Chardin, Pierre. *The Future of Man.* Harper Torchbooks, 1969.

Tennyson, Alfred. *The Poetical Works of Tennyson.* Houghton Mifflin Company, 1974.

Tetzeli, Rick. "Surviving Information Overload." *Fortune.* July 11, 1994.

Thompson, Damian. *The End of Time.* University Press of New England, 1996.

Toffler, Alvin. *Future Shock.* Random House, 1970.

_____. *The Third Wave.* William Morrow and Company, 1980.

Toynbee, Arnold J. *A Study of History.* Authorized abridgement by D.C. Somervell Volumes 1-10. Dell Publishing Co., Inc., 1974.

Tuchman, Barbara. "The Decline of Quality." *The New York Times Magazine.* November 2, 1980.

Turan, Kenneth. "The Art of Revolution." *Rolling Stone Yearbook 1984.*

Turkle, Sherry. *The Second Self.* Simon & Schuster, 1984.

_____. *Life on the Screen.* Simon & Schuster, 1995.

Umehara, Takeshi. "Ancient Japan Shows Postmodernism the Way." *New Perspectives Quarterly.* Spring 1992.

Urdant, Laurence, Editor. *The Timetables of American History*. Simon and Schuster, 1981.

Van der Post, Laurens. *A Walk with a White Bushman*. Penguin Books, 1988.

_____. *The Voice of the Thunder*. William Morrow and Company, 1993.

Walcott, William O. "America, The Elect Nation." *Psychological Perspectives*. Issue 31, 1995.

Wallach, Michael and Lise. "How Psychiatry Sanctions the Cult of the Self." *The Washington Monthly*, February 1985.

Wallechinsky, David. *Twentieth Century*. Little, Brown and Company, 1995.

Wall Street Journal, The. "Review & Outlook." November 30, 1978.

White, Theodore H. *The Making of the President 1960*. Mentor, 1967.

_____. *In Search of History*. Harper & Row, 1978.

Whitman, Walt. *Leaves of Grass*. Signet Classic, 1958.

Wilber, Ken. *A Brief History of Everything*. Shambhala, 1996.

Wilson, A.N. *God's Funeral*. W.W. Norton and Company, 1999.

Wolfe, Thomas. *You Can't Go Home Again*. Harper & Row, 1989.

Wright, Robert. "The Evolution of Despair." *Time*. August 28, 1995.

Yankelovich, Daniel. *New Rules*. Random House, 1981.

Zukav, Gary. *The Dancing Wu Li Masters*. Bantam Books, 1980.

INDEX

Leger, Fernard, 109
Lemaitre, Georges, 32
Lemann, Nicholas, 176
Lenin, V.I., 37, 55, 61, 63
Leo, John, 214
Leonardo da Vinci, 31, 239
Lerner, Max, 67
Les Fleurs du Mal, (Baudelaire) 120
Leslie, John, 225
Les Miserables, (Hugo) *261*
Le Vot, Andrew, 114
Lewis, C.S., 227-228
Lewis, Sinclair, 114-115
Liberal intellectualism, 67
Liberalism, 152
Liberals, 172
Life, 162, 181
Life expectancy, 213
Like a Rolling Stone, 171
L'il Abner, 116
Lincoln, Abraham, 31, 115, 245,275, 279
Lincoln Memorial, 169, 172, 175, 280
Lindbergh, Anne Morrow, 123
Lindsey, Hal, 194, 197
Lippmann, Walter, 20, 75, 121, 123, 166
Literature, 76, 102, 114-115, 117, 120, 163, 212
Little Rock, 161
Lloyd George, David, 54
Locke, John, 186
Lolita, (Nabokov) 162

London, 275
London, Jack, 40
Lord Jim, (Conrad) 40
Los Angeles, 151
Los Angeles Times, 81
Louis, Joe, 87
Louisville, University of, 207
Lovett, Robert, 176
Lowell, A. Lawrence, 138
Luce, Henry, 162, 181
Lucretius, 261
Luddite, 222
Lukacs, John, 51
Lunar Orbiter I, 182
Luther, Martin, 31, 93-94, 239

MacBeth, 115
Macks, Ernst, 36
MacLeish, Archibald, 156-160, 163, 212
Madison Avenue, 62, 168, 244
Madison, James, 60
Main Street, (Lewis) 114
Malevich, Kazimir, 107, 110
Maltese Falcon, The, (Hammett) 115
Management: Tasks, Responsibility, *Practices,* (Drucker) 81
Manchu Empire, 53
Manhattan Project, 95, 165
Man in Full, A, (Wolfe) 211
Mann, Thomas, 108
Manufacturing techniques, 56-57
Marc, Franz, 108

Monet, Claude, 105

Monetary History of the United
States, A, (Friedman,
Schwartz) 72

Montague, C.E., 52

Montgomery, 174; bus boycott,
85

Mont-Saint Michel & Chartres,
(Adams) 26

Moran, Edward, 102

Moravec, Hans, 70

Morgan, J. Pierpont, 43, 51, 60

Morrow, Lance, 203

Mount Wilson Observatory, 223

Movies, 115-116

Moynihan, Daniel Patrick, 215

Mozart, Wolfgang Amadeus, 245

Mr. Smith Goes to Washington,
116

Muir, Edwin, 117

Mumford, Lewis, 153-156, 158,
210, 237

Munich, 135

Murray, Sir Gilbert, 101

Murrow, Edward R., 166-167

Museum of Modern Art, 111

Music; classical, 245; popular,
199; reflecting change, 164;
rock, 164; sex and, 164

Muslims, 149

Mussolini, Benito, 93

Myers, Bernard, S., 108-109

Myth, definition of, 258

Mythology; ancient Greek, 216,
233, 236-237; of

humankind, 187; psyche
and, 230-231, 258;
religion and, 258; Western
tradition and, 197, 235

Nanotechnology, 225, 278

Napoleon I, 31, 54

Nash, Ogden, 115

National Association for the
Advancement of Colored
People (NAACP), 85, 88

National Banking System, 49

National Center for Human
Genome Research, 2
222

National Commission on Civic
Renewal, 207

National Commission on
Philanthropy and Civic
Renewal, 207

National Commission on Society,
Culture, and Community,
207

National Institute of Health, 69

Nationalism, 63, 152

National Laboratories, 148

National Labor Relations Board
(NLRB), 44

National Review, 67

National Security Council, 278

Nation-states, 37,170, 196, 278

Native Americans, 130, 280

Nazism, 55, 93-94, 264

Nelson, Ruben, 192

Neoconservatives, 67

Thompson, Sir George, 189
Thus Spake Zarathustra,
(Nietzsche) 120
Tibetan Book of the Dead, 123
Time, 96, 102, 107, 185, 203,
205
Times of London, 244
Titian, 105
Tobacco Road, (Caldwell) 115
Tobias, Philip, 226, 234
Tocqueville, Alexis de, 18, 80,
126, 207, 211
Toffler, Alvin, 188-190, 192, 215
Tortilla Flat, (Steinbeck) 115
Totalitarianism, 63
*Toward the Year 2000: Work in
Progress*, 186
Toynbee, Arnold, 34, 53, 62-63,
96, 108, 124, 126, 210
Traditionalism, 107
Transformations of Man,
(Mumford) 155
Transportation, 39, 46-49, 57,
161
Trans-Siberian Railway, 37
Trends, 146-151; disappearing
boundaries, 151; in Europe,
146; globalization, 153;
influence of freedom, 152;
information environment,
148; national aspirations,
146; nature of change, 147;
new geopolitical pat-
terns,146; population, 151
Trilling, Lionel, 66

Tristan and Isolde, 120
Trudeau, Garry, 204
Truman Doctrine, 166
Truman, Harry S., 167, 181
Tugwell, Rexwell, 75
Turkel, Sherry, 201
Twentieth Century Unlimited,
(Bliven) 138
Twenty-fourth Amendment, 175
Two Cultures, The, (Snow) 67
Two-Million-Year-Old Self,
(Stevens) 128

U-2 plane, 179
Ulysses, (Joyce); entrance of anti-
hero in, 117
as reflection of change, 117
Unconscious, the, 127, 129, 133;
collective and, 211, 241,
255, 257; and the conscious,
265-267; genetic engineering
and, 233; human composi-
tion and, 232; influence of,
265; Jung on the, 135;
personal, 241, 266-
267; psychic forces, 133
United Nations, 88, 167
United States; adoption of
national anthem, 115;
banking system, 49; Bill of
Rights, 279; Budget Act of
(1922), 60; budget of (1900),
40; business statistics of
(1900), 42-43;

ABOUT THE AUTHOR

W illiam Van Dusen Wishard (Van) heads WorldTrends Re
search, a Washington-based consultancy specializing in the
analysis and synthesis of global trends.

Van Wishard's book, *The American Future: What Would George and
Tom Do Now?*, was given to every member of the U.S. Congress by the
Congressional Institute. His first book, *A Perspective for the 1990s: A
World In Search of Meaning*, was a best-selling business book in Japan.
He was a major contributor to the *Encyclopedia of the Future*, published
by Simon & Schuster Macmillan.

Wishard's briefings on world trends for members of Congress and
for professional groups have been televised nationally by C-SPAN numerous times, and his Voice of America commentary has been broadcast worldwide. His speaking audiences have included such organizations as AT&T, Ernst & Young, Charles Schwab & Co., the Naval War
College, and the Young Presidents' Organization.

During the 1980s, Van Wishard was an assistant to the U.S.
Secretary of Commerce writing on global competitiveness, interna-
tional trade and U.S. economic policy. He wrote the first report on
U.S. competitiveness for the Reagan administration. He served ear-
lier as executive director of the President's Council on Minority
Business Enterprise, and as assistant to the director of the U.S.
Office of Economic Opportunity.

Wishard entered government service in 1970, following a career in international information and education programs. His initial assignment in the international arena was as part of the first civilian task force to enter Germany to re-establish contact with the German people after World War II. In the early years of the Vietnam War, he worked with a public information team providing training in democratic principles to Vietnamese students and military personnel. Other assignments took him throughout Africa, where he lived for three years. In the mid-1960s, he helped found Up With People, the international cross-cultural educational program for young people. All told, he has worked in more than 30 countries.

In 1953 Wishard was wounded in the Korean War where he served in the U.S. Army as an infantry platoon officer.

He and his wife, Anne, live in Reston, Virginia. They have a son and daughter and two grandchildren.

CPSIA information can be obtained at www.ICGtesting.com
Printed in the USA
BVOW08*1959281115

428372BV00001B/5/P

9 780738 836553